The Home Orchard

Growing Your Own Deciduous Fruit and Nut Trees

Second Edition

AUTHORS

Ted DeJong
Distinguished Professor and Pomologist Emeritus
Department of Plant Sciences, UC Davis

Louise Ferguson
UC Cooperative Extension (UCCE) Pomologist

Mary Louise Flint
UCCE Entomologist Emeritus

Pamela M. Geisel
UCCE Environmental Horticulture Advisor Emeritus

Janet S. Hartin
UCCE Horticulture Advisor Emeritus

Janine Hasey
UCCE Tree Crop and Environmental Horticulture
Advisor Emeritus

Chuck A. Ingels
UCCE Farm Advisor Emeritus

Katherine Jarvis-Shean
UCCE Orchard Systems Advisor

R. Scott Johnson
UCCE Pomologist Emeritus

Craig Kallsen
UCCE Farm Advisor Emeritus

Maxwell V. Norton
UCCE Farm Advisor Emeritus

Niamh Quinn
UCCE Human-Wildlife Interactions Advisor

Lawrence J. Schwankl
UCCE Specialist Emeritus

Beth L. Teviotdale
UCCE Plant Pathologist Emeritus

Paul M. Vossen
UCCE Farm Advisor Emeritus

The technical editors for the first edition of *The Home Orchard* were Chuck A. Ingels, Pamela M. Geisel, and Maxwell V. Norton. This second edition of *The Home Orchard* is a revision of the first. The technical editor for the second edition is John F. Karlik.

To order or obtain UC ANR publications and other products, visit the UC ANR online catalog at anrpublications.org. Direct inquiries to

UC Agriculture and Natural Resources
Publishing
2801 Second Street
Davis, CA 95618

E-mail: anrcatalog@ucanr.edu

Second edition, 2025

ISBN-13: 978-1-62711-220-8

Library of Congress Cataloging-in-Publication Data

Names: DeJong, T. M. (Theodore M.) author

Title: The home orchard : growing your own deciduous fruit and nut trees / Ted DeJong [and 14 others].

Description: Second edition. | Davis, CA : University of California Agriculture and Natural Resources, 2025. | Includes bibliographical references and index. | Summary: "The Home Orchard: Growing Your Own Deciduous Fruit and Nut Trees" provides readers with information needed to succeed at producing fruit and nuts in their yards. The topics covered include soil, varieties, irrigation, fertilization, pruning, grafting, harvesting, pest management, and more"— Provided by publisher.

Identifiers: LCCN 2025041373 | ISBN 9781627112420 paperback

Subjects: LCSH: Citrus fruits—California | Nut trees—California | Fruit-culture | Orchards

Classification: LCC SB355.5.C2 H66 2025

LC record available at https://lccn.loc.gov/2025041373

This publication has been anonymously peer reviewed for technical accuracy by University of California scientists and other qualified professionals. This review process was managed by UC ANR Associate Editor for Environmental Horticulture Janet Hartin and UC ANR Extension Advisor (Emeritus) John F. Karlik.

Illustrations not otherwise credited: Sandra Osterman, William Suckow, and Robin Walton.

Every reasonable effort has been made to obtain permissions for the use of copyrighted material in this publication. Anyone with concerns about permission issues is invited to contact us at anrcatalog@ucanr.edu.

Any questions about accessibility for ANR Publications should be directed to anrcatalog@ucanr.edu.

Printed in the United States on acid-free, partly recycled paper.

Contents

Acknowledgment

The following individuals—all of whom are current or emeritus UC Cooperative Extension Advisors—contributed editing to this book:

Kevin Day

Jim Downer

Craig Kallsen

Mohammad Yaghmour

In addition, the authors of chapter 8 received special assistance from professional grafter Art Ruble of Clovis, California and plant propagation technician Judy Lee of UC Davis.

Dedication

This book is dedicated to the late Chuck Ingels, a UC Cooperative Extension Advisor who was passionate about the home orchard.

Chapter 1

Climate and soils

Maxwell V. Norton

For the purposes of this book, we have divided California into six growing regions for deciduous fruit and nut trees (fig. 1.1). These regions are approximations—they have broad climate differences, but each contains microclimates that can be quite distinct from one another. Microclimates occur over large areas as well as within small areas, such as yards. Coastal and foothill counties tend to have the most microclimate diversity.

Your local microclimate may be affected by whether you are gardening close to water or inland, near a wooded park or an asphalt parking lot, in a sheltered area at the bottom of a hill or on an exposed hillside, or against south- versus north-facing walls. To get to know your regional climate and microclimate, you can pay attention to which fruit and nut trees grow well in your area and you can ask your neighbors and knowledgeable local nursery staff. Publications such as the Sunset Western Garden Book (Brenzel 2012) also contain useful climate maps.

Soil plays an important role in what grows well in a yard. Some soils contain mostly clay and others mostly sand. Your soil may be shallow or deep. Construction projects may have disrupted the layers, or there may be a natural barrier to the root growth of your fruit and nut trees. Knowing your soil characteristics will help you develop a suitable irrigation and fertilizing schedule.

Climate

Growing regions

What follows is a general description of the growing regions shown in figure 1.1 and the types of fruit and nut trees that are grown successfully in each. For information on varieties of these types of fruit and nuts, see chapter 3, "Varieties."

Regions 1 and 2: San Joaquin and Sacramento Valleys

The San Joaquin Valley consists of the southern portion of the Central Valley, south of Sacramento. Its cities include Bakersfield, Fresno, Merced, Modesto, and Stockton. The Sacramento Valley consists of the northern portion of the Central Valley along the Sacramento River. Its cities include Sacramento, Yuba City, Marysville, Chico, and Redding. Certain basic seasonal weather conditions apply throughout the Central Valley: The summer is hot and dry and the winter is cool and damp. Very little rain falls from May through September, and dense fog can form in

Figure 1.1. There are six primary growing regions for temperate-zone fruit and nut trees in California. The shading indicates the major commercial production areas. *Source:* Vossen and Silva 2015.

December and January. Strong, dry winds are common in spring and fall. Virtually all deciduous fruit and nuts grow well in the Central Valley.

Region 3: Central Coast

The Central Coast region extends from the Golden Gate Bridge south to Point Conception and reaches inland to include the southern portion of the Coast Ranges. Its cities include San Francisco, Oakland, San Jose, Concord, Santa Cruz, Monterey, San Luis Obispo, and Santa Maria. Right on the coast, the summer is cool and foggy and the winter is mild and damp. Strong sea breezes are common; frost, though rare, can occur. In the interior portions of the region, the summer is warmer and less foggy and the winter is cooler than on the coast, but the summer and winter extremes are generally less severe than in the neighboring San Joaquin Valley. Exceptions might be inland valley towns like King City, Paso Robles, and Cuyama, where in some years the temperature extremes may exceed those of the San Joaquin Valley. Deciduous fruit and nut trees that grow well here, particularly in the interior areas, include almond, apple, apricot, cherry, fig, nectarine, peach, pear, plum, pomegranate, prune, and walnut.

Region 4: North Coast

The North Coast region extends from the Golden Gate Bridge to the Oregon border and reaches inland to encompass the northern portion of the Coast Ranges. Its cities include Novato, Santa Rosa, Ukiah, Mendocino, and Eureka. The northern end of this region is the wettest part of California. Both summer and winter are cooler than on the Central Coast, and the area also receives more rainfall. Strong sea breezes are common on the coast, and frost can occur. The inland, higher-elevation areas of the region are similar to those of region 5 (Sierra foothills), but wetter. Deciduous fruit and nut trees that grow well in the warmer areas include apple, apricot, cherry, pear, plum, prune, and walnut.

Region 5: Sierra foothills

The Sierra foothills region corresponds roughly to what is known as the Gold Country, the lower elevations of the western slope of the Sierra. Its cities include Oakhurst, Sonora, Jackson, Placerville, Camino, Auburn, and Grass Valley. The summer is warm, with occasional rain, and the winter is cold and wet. Frost is common in winter and spring, especially at the higher elevations. Deciduous fruit and nut trees that grow well here include apple, cherry, olive, peach, pear, persimmon, pistachio, plum and plum hybrids, prune, quince, and walnut.

Region 6: Southern California

Southern California includes the coastal and inland areas from Point Conception south to the Mexican border. Its cities include Santa Barbara, Los Angeles, Riverside, San Bernardino, and San Diego. On the coast, summer is mild with some fog, and winter is mild with some rain. Strong, dry southwest winds known as Santa Anas are common in spring and fall; frost can occur, especially in the desert and at higher elevations. The climate in this region's higher-elevation areas is similar to that of the Sierra foothills. The climate in the inland desert areas is similar to that of the southern San Joaquin Valley but with a hotter, drier summer and a warmer winter. Deciduous fruit and nut trees that grow well in this zone include fig, persimmon, and low-chill varieties of apple, nectarine, peach, plum, and walnut.

Chilling hours

Deciduous fruit and nut trees need a certain number of hours with temperatures below 45°F (7°C) in winter if they are to bloom normally and grow well in spring (see chapter 2, "Growth and development"). Although just considering this temperature threshold may be adequate for home gardeners, tree response to chilling is complicated. Many commercial fruit and nut growers now use the "dynamic model" for measuring chill periods, a method developed in Israel and tested in California by UC Davis researchers. The model calculates chilling accumulation as chill portions, using a range of temperatures from about 35 to 55°F (1.7–13°C), and accounting for chill cancellation due to fluctuating warm winter temperatures.

If a fruit or nut tree does not receive enough winter chilling, flower buds may fail to develop, leaves may appear later than usual, and the bloom period may be extended. The tree may produce little or no fruit that year, and any fruit that do appear may be deformed or smaller than normal.

Different types of fruit and nut trees require different amounts of chilling (table 1.1). When selecting fruit or nut trees for your home garden, choose species and varieties that are compatible with the average number of chilling hours in your area. You can find a comprehensive tabulation of chilling hours to date for the current year for many locations in the state at the website of the UC Davis Fruit and Nut Research and Information Center, fruitsandnuts.ucdavis.edu/weather-models; there, you can also find information on the dynamic model discussed above. Table 1.2 presents historical chilling-hour data from this website for selected locations in each growing region.

Heat units and the ripening period

Once fruit and nuts reach their mature size, the time they take to become ripe enough to harvest is known as the ripening period (for more information on ripening and maturity, see chapter 10, "Harvesting fruit and nuts"). The usual length and timing of the ripening period vary for different species and varieties—and in a given year, they are influenced in part by the number of heat units that accumulate during the period. Heat units can be thought of as the number of hours at or above a designated temperature—the opposite of chilling hours. As with chilling hours, the number of heat units is different in the different California growing regions. This means, for example, that a fruit that has a long ripening period (that is, that needs a large number of heat units) may not ripen properly in a cool part of the state. Many peach varieties require prolonged heat for the fruit to develop its best flavor, and these varieties would not be appropriate for planting in some cool coastal areas.

When choosing fruit and nut varieties, look for a variety with a ripening period that is compatible with the climate in your area (for more information on the ripening and harvest period of selected varieties, see chapter 3, "Varieties"). If fall rains are common in your area, you may want to avoid late-maturing varieties. If you select varieties that ripen over a longer period of time, you may be able to harvest the fruit over a period of days or even weeks, rather than all at once.

Table 1.1. Chilling requirements of selected deciduous fruit and nut trees

Type of fruit/nut	Approximate hours at 45°F (7°C) as needed to break dormancy
Almond	250–500
Apple*	500–1,000
Apple (low-chill)	400–600
Apricot*	300–800
Cherry, sour	1,200
Cherry, sweet	700–800
Chestnut	400–500
Fig	100
Filbert (hazelnut)	800
Kiwifruit*	300–800
Olive	200–300
Peach/nectarine*	500–800
Pear*	700–800
Pear (Asian)	350–450
Pecan	250
Persimmon	100–200
Pistachio	800
Plum, American*	300–600
Plum, European*	600–800
Plum, Japanese	250–700
Plumcot	400–600
Pomegranate	100–150
Quince	300
Walnut, Persian	500–700

Source: Vossen 2002, p. 455.

*May have low-chill varieties that have been reported to require fewer than 300 hours of temperatures below 45°F (7°C) to break dormancy.

Frost

While you cannot control whether frost occurs, you can select fruit and nut-tree varieties that are hardy enough for the low temperatures in your growing region (see chapter 3, "Varieties," and also the USDA Plant Hardiness Zone Map listed in this chapter's "Further reading" section). You can also take various steps to reduce the incidence and severity of frost damage to the trees' young green tissues.

There are two types of frosts or freezes: advective and radiation. Advective freezing occurs when wind moves a cold air mass whose temperature is below freezing into an area, displacing warmer air. This type of freezing is com-

Table 1.2. Historical accumulations of chilling hours for selected locations in California, November 2019–February 2025

Location*	Accumulated chilling hours, Nov. 1–Feb. 28[†]					
	2019–2020	2020–2021	2021–2022	2022–2023	2023–2024	2024–2025
Zone 1 Fresno	1,067	1,089	1,152	1,247	777	992
Zone 2 Sacramento	786	676	940	1,127	588	746
Zone 3 San Luis Obispo	377	266	428	556	238	378
Zone 4 Santa Rosa	1,061	1,233	1,188	1,358	805	1,059
Zone 5 Camino	906	1,073	1,077	1,718	871	1,060
Zone 6 Riverside	307	313	340	502	195	228

Source: UC Davis Fruit and Nut Research and Information Center.

*For locations, see fig. 1.1.

[†]Chilling calculation method: 1 unit = 1 hour below 45°F (7°C).

mon in America's Midwest because cold fronts move quickly over the land. Radiation frosts occur on calm, clear nights as heat is lost from Earth's surface into the atmosphere, causing cold air to collect near the soil surface. In California, springtime radiation frost is the most common type of damaging frost.

Cold air, being heavier than warm air, will drain from high places to displace warmer air at lower sites. Orchards planted in valleys and at low spots are more susceptible to frost than those planted on sloping terrain. A hillside may have better air drainage and may therefore be a little warmer than the floor of the valley into which the air drains. River-bottom areas can be frost-prone because that's where the coldest air settles. At the same time, though, the temperature of air decreases with increasing altitude, so higher-elevation areas such as the upper foothills and mountains are generally colder than the surrounding lower-elevation areas. Long-time residents and the staff of local garden shops can give you good information about frost hazards in your neighborhood.

Sensitive species such as fig, even when they are dormant, can be seriously damaged by the low temperatures that occur in California's high-elevation and desert areas. Sensitive trees planted close to the south side of a house can benefit from heat that radiates from the building. Heat escaping from a household air vent may be just what a sensitive plant needs at night.

The US National Weather Service issues a frost warning whenever frost is likely. Take steps to protect your trees if frost is predicted and your trees are susceptible to damage (see chapter 11, "Integrated pest management for backyard orchards").

Soils

Soil is composed of minerals, organic matter, air, and water. Mineral particles in soil are defined by their size: Sand particles are large enough to be detected by sight and touch, silt particles are medium in size and are too small to be seen individually, and clay particles are microscopic. The organic matter in soil consists of humus (the residues of plants and animals), organisms that live in the soil, and substances such as carbon and nitrogen from decomposed living things. The air in soil is, for the most part, the same as the air in the atmosphere, although it can contain gases produced naturally or as a result of human activity. In some areas, the soil is only a few inches deep; in others, it can reach depths of 100 feet or more. Minerals and organic matter form the solid parts of soil; air and water exist in the pores, the spaces between the solid particles. A soil's texture, structure, and profile should have a significant impact on how you select, plant, irrigate, and care for deciduous fruit and nut trees. Soil texture is particularly important in developing irrigation schedules (see chapter 5, "Irrigation").

Soil texture

The relative proportions of sand, silt, and clay in a soil determine the soil's texture (fig. 1.2). Soil scientists have defined twelve soil textures and have grouped them into three categories:

- coarse: sand and loamy sand
- medium: sandy loam, loam, silt loam, silt, clay loam, sandy clay loam, and silt clay loam
- fine: clay, sandy clay, and silt clay

Coarse soils are often called light soils, and fine soils are often called heavy soils. These terms refer to how easy or difficult it is to work the soil; for example, a heavy soil is dominated by clay and is much harder to work than a sandy soil. A practical way to identify soil texture, as well as moisture, is by the "feel test" (see fig. 5.6 in chapter 5, "Irrigation"). Both the texture and the moisture level of the surface soil can be completely different from the texture and moisture level of the soil a few feet deeper. Fertilizers should be applied to sandy soils in small doses to prevent the fertilizers from being leached below the root zone and possibly polluting groundwater.

Soil structure

The arrangement of the sand, silt, and clay particles in a soil determines the soil's structure. Individual particles of silt and clay combine in soil to form aggregates—that is, clumps of various sizes and shapes that are held together by organic matter, microorganisms and their secretions, and the binding forces of clay. Soils that lack well-defined aggregates have a structure known as massive, with poor water infiltration and percolation. A common method of improving soil structure is adding some type of organic matter.

Soil profile

Whereas an annual plant has a root system only a few inches to a foot deep, trees can develop root systems several feet deep if grown in deep, well-drained soils and irrigated appropriately. Any sudden change in soil texture or any physical impediment such as a claypan, siltpan, or hardpan can restrict root growth

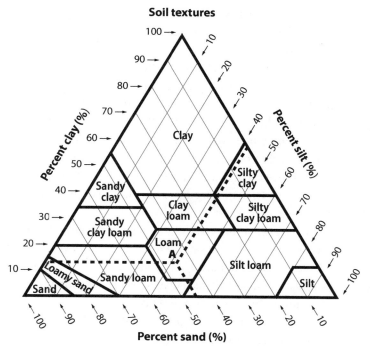

Figure 1.2. Soil textures as defined by percentages of sand, silt, and clay. The dotted lines in this soil-texture triangle indicate the percentages of clay, silt, and sand in an example loam soil, a good all-around gardening soil. *Source:* Wildman and Gowans 1975.

and prevent water from percolating deep into the soil profile. As soils age, they form layers known as horizons. The uppermost horizon, topsoil, may be only a few inches deep, or several feet. The topsoil is home to the greatest number of roots and microorganisms and usually is darker than the lower horizons. Under the topsoil is the subsoil, which has fewer roots and microorganisms. The subsoil accumulates clay particles, minerals, and salts that have leached down from the topsoil; it can also become compacted and form a barrier to water and plant roots. Distinct horizons may not be visible, depending on the soil's parent material and the climate during its development. Construction work and other digging can disturb the original soil profile by bringing subsoil or rock to the surface. Soils may be very productive, such as many soils in the San Joaquin Valley, despite not looking like rich, black prairie soils.

Soil physical problems

Physical problems include soil textures that are unsuitable for tree growth—for example, soils that are too gravelly or have too heavy a clay texture. There is little you can do to change a soil's texture. If you import sand to mix with the surface soil, you will make it easier to plant annuals but do little to help the deep root system of a tree.

The presence of a claypan, siltpan, or hardpan will impede both roots and water. If possible, penetrate the barrier pan and mix the pan soil into the soil above and below it. To correct these impervious layers, you may need to use a backhoe or trencher, but you should know what's underground before digging. If you find yourself unable to disrupt the layers, you may have to install raised beds or drain tubing to carry away excess water.

Soil stratification can impede water movement and root formation in the same way as a pan. A layer of coarse sand, for instance, can impede water percolation just as effectively as a clay layer. Try to mix up these layers before planting, if you can.

Rocky soils are challenging to cultivate. It may be impossible to grow fruit and nut trees if underlying rock substrata lie too close to the surface. To be sure, roots can successfully grow through soil containing small- to medium-size river rocks—and rocks, if not excessive in number, can be removed from the planting area.

When soil compaction occurs, it breaks down the soil structure and slows water and air infiltration. Compaction is easier to prevent than to cure. Avoid any construction and vehicular traffic near your trees; keep it at least to the edge of what will be the mature canopy line. Prevent compaction from plowing and cultivating equipment by using such equipment only when the soil is relatively dry. In the planting area, mulching, adding soil amendments (such as compost or manure), and growing fibrous-rooted cover crops (such as legumes or grasses) can improve the structure, biological activity, and water penetration of the soil.

Soil chemical problems

A soil can have any of a number of chemical problems, including high or low pH, excess total salt levels, or excessive levels of elements such as sodium, boron, or chloride. Soil analysis can be a useful tool for diagnosing these problems, although nutrient levels in the soil may not be a reliable indicator of the nutrient status of the trees planted there. UC Cooperative Extension county offices do not offer soil analysis services, but if you suspect a problem with soil chemistry, you can ask your local UC Master Gardener Program or UC Cooperative Extension county office for the names of commercial laboratories that perform soil analysis. A soil analysis should include determinations of pH, salinity (total salts, ECe), boron, nitrogen, phosphorus, and potassium. For soils from the west side of the San Joaquin Valley, a determination for excess sodium (ESP or SAR) can be requested, although excess sodium is not a common problem in home garden soils.

Soil reaction refers to the acidity or alkalinity of soil, which is expressed as pH on a scale of 0 (acidic) to 14 (basic or alkaline). Most plants grow best at a pH of 5.5 to 7.5. Soil pH has a major effect on the availability of micronutrients such as iron and zinc. For alkaline soils, which are more prevalent throughout California than acidic soils, it is wise to test the soil for both pH and micronutrients. This is especially true for iron and zinc (though these nutrient elements become insoluble and thus unavailable to plants under high pH conditions). You can raise the pH of very acidic soil (pH < 5.5) by adding lime (calcium carbonate) to the soil; the pH of alkaline soils (pH > 7.5) can be reduced through the addition of soil sulfur. With time, adding acidifying nitrogen fertilizers such as ammonium sulfate can also help reduce soil pH.

If your soil has excess levels of salts (that is, ionic forms of chemical elements, including plant nutrients), you cannot remedy the situation by adding soil chemical amendments—although, as a special case, gypsum can help displace excess sodium in the soil and thereby improve soil structure. Excess levels of salts must be reduced through leaching—that is, applying water to dissolve the salts and carry them below the plant root zone. Leaching requires adequate drainage so that water can move through the soil profile.

Mulch

A mulch is any opaque material that is spread on top of the soil surface. An organic mulch application may well be the best way to improve a soil's chemical and physical properties and create a soil environment that promotes plant growth. You can use any ground or chopped organic material, including eucalyptus leaves or pine needles. Properly applied, mulch can

- prevent light from reaching the soil surface and thus suppress weeds

- help the soil retain moisture
- enhance root growth in the topsoil
- encourage earthworms and other beneficial soil organisms
- insulate the soil from extremes of heat and cold
- prevent soil crusting and new compaction (but not reduce existing compaction)
- improve water penetration
- provide habitat for natural enemies of pests (see chapter 11, "Integrated pest management for backyard orchards")
- create attractive landscaping and good surfaces for walking
- over time, improve soil structure and add small amounts of nutrients

Although a mulch can be made of many types of material—including straw, sawdust, decomposed grass clippings, compost, shredded bark, rice hulls, and sheets of black plastic—one of the most effective and economical mulches for fruit and nut trees is wood chips. Wood chips can often be obtained for free from tree trimmers or arborists, or you can make them at home from trimmings using a mechanical chipper or shredder. If you get your chips from a tree trimmer or arborist, make sure before the product is delivered that it is well chipped, without sticks, logs, or palm fronds. Wood chips resist decomposition and are coarse enough to last through at least one growing season, and because they are not incorporated into the soil, they do not tie up soil nitrogen. Unlike black plastic, they do not eventually become a nuisance and wind up in the trash. You can use compost instead of wood chips as a mulch, but it will decompose much more rapidly and will have to be reapplied sooner. Manure-based compost can contain fairly large amounts of salt, which can cause poor growth and cause leaves to burn at the edges.

Landscape fabric can be used either alone or under wood chips. It does reduce weeds, because seed in the soil will not sprout under the fabric, but weeds may grow on top of the fabric. Also, the fabric prevents any organic mulch that covers it from contacting the soil, eliminating some of the benefits of the organic mulch. Landscape fabric also provides a hiding place for voles, increasing the potential for trunk damage.

Before you apply wood chips or other mulching materials, make sure that the garden soil is free of weeds, especially perennial weeds. Thoroughly remove or spray perennial weeds such as bermudagrass, field bindweed, and nutsedge, since these weeds will grow through mulch. You can use a pre-emergence herbicide before applying mulch to reduce weed seed germination, but this step is not necessary if the mulch layer is thick enough and coarse enough to last through the growing season.

Apply mulch in a layer 4 to 6 inches deep. It is preferable to keep the mulch several inches back from the trunks of the trees, since mulch can trap moisture in the root crown area, encouraging crown rot. If drip irrigation is used and kept away from the tree trunk, and if the climate is fairly dry, mulch can be safely placed up to the trunk.

Although the use of mulch has many benefits, it also has some disadvantages. For example, a layer of mulch on the soil can make it harder for you to tell when you need to irrigate. A load of wood chips may also contain weed seed from trees or shrubs; pull these weeds out as soon as they appear. Also, mulch does break down, so you have to reapply it.

Reference

Brenzel, K., ed. 2012. Sunset western garden book. 9th ed. Menlo Park, CA: Sunset Books.

Further reading

Faber, B., J. Walworth, D. Giraud, and D. Silva. 2015. Soil and fertilizer management. In D. Pittenger, ed., California master gardener handbook. Davis: UC Agriculture and Natural Resources Publication 3382. 37–81.

LaRue, J. H., and R. S. Johnson, eds. 1989. Peaches, plums, and nectarines: Growing and handling for fresh market. Oakland: UC Agriculture and Natural Resources Publication 3331.

O'Geen, A. T., S. B. Southard, and R. J. Southard. 2008. A revised Storie Index for use with digital soils information. Oakland: UC Agriculture and Natural Resources Publication 8335.

UC Davis Fruit & Nut Research & Information Center. Weather models. https://fruitsandnuts.ucdavis.edu/weather-models

USDA. 2012. USDA plant hardiness zone map. USDA miscellaneous publication 1475. Washington, DC: Government Printing Office. https://planthardiness.ars.usda.gov

Vossen, P., and D. Silva. 2015. Temperate tree fruit and nut crops. In D. Pittenger, ed., California master gardener handbook. 2nd ed. Davis: UC Agriculture and Natural Resources Publication 3382. 477.

Wildman, W. E., and K. D. Gowans. 1975. Soil physical environment and how it affects plant growth. Oakland: UC Agriculture and Natural Resources Publication 2280.

Chapter 2

Growth and development

Chuck A. Ingels

Growing fruit and nut trees successfully requires some understanding of how they grow and how the environment and various cultural practices influence their development. A basic understanding of the main issues involved often saves time and frustration. Because of the many differences among species and varieties available, it is difficult to generalize about all aspects of growth and development. Instead, we introduce the key aspects of tree structure and growth. This information provides a foundation for understanding the rationale for practices described in detail in this book.

Tree organs and their functions

Roots

Roots serve a crucial role in the vitality of fruit trees. Poor root health is a common cause of stunted trees. The root system performs multiple functions, including anchorage, water and nutrient absorption, nutrient and carbohydrate storage, and hormone production. For healthy growth and function, roots require water and oxygen from the soil as well as food materials produced in the aboveground shoots.

A root system consists of several types of roots. Figure 2.1 shows the parts of new fine roots, including root tips. Only the portion at the tip, beyond the root hair region, elongates through the soil. Elongating and recently matured new roots persist for varying lengths of time, but many are short-lived, surviving only a few weeks to several months. These new roots are part of the fine root system. Most are 2 millimeters or less in diameter and are often called feeder roots. A small proportion of these roots survives

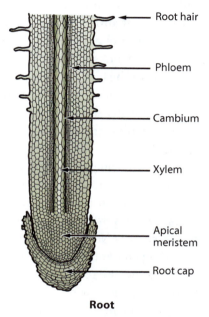

Figure 2.1. Fine roots have temporary root hairs and elongate only at the root cap. *Source:* Pittenger 2015.

and grows to become part of the large, permanent root system.

Rather than being a mirror image of a tree's aboveground growth, root growth for a fruit or nut tree is lateral and relatively shallow. Roots can extend as far as two to three times the width of the drip line of the canopy, and even farther if soil moisture is available. Taproots, if present, are shallow and branched. Branching (lateral) root formation does not follow a regular pattern, and roots are not uniformly distributed in the soil. In general, the larger the tree, the larger the root mass. Normally, 75 percent or more of the roots of fruit and nut trees may be found in the upper 2 to 3 feet of soil.

Trunk

Most fruit and nut trees purchased in the nursery have been grafted onto rootstocks. Unlike the fruiting variety that makes up the top of a grafted tree, the tree variety used as the rootstock is well adapted to a range of soil conditions and is resistant to soilborne diseases; in many cases, it also determines the mature size of the tree. The fruiting variety grafted onto the rootstock is referred to as the scion. Most fruit- and nut-tree species are difficult or impossible to propagate from cuttings, and simply planting the seed of a desirable variety almost always results in trees that produce fruit of inferior quality. Grafting provides a way to combine the qualities of the best fruit or nut varieties with those of the best roots. (See chapter 3, "Varieties," for recommended rootstock and scion varieties.) Fig, pomegranate, and olive usually are not grafted; like home-garden grape, they are usually grown from cuttings.

The graft union (also called a bud union) can usually be seen on the lower trunk of a young tree. This is the point where a bud from the desirable variety, such as Suncrest peach, was grafted in a field nursery onto a rootstock, such as Nemaguard peach (see chapter 8, "Budding and grafting"). The nursery worker then forced the bud to grow by cutting off the rootstock shoot above the new bud. A newly grafted bud usually begins growing outward before shifting upward. That is why some fruit and nut trees purchased at the nursery have a crook in the trunk—although most nurseries stake the trees grown as container stock to make the crook less obvious. After a few years' growth, the crook is almost unnoticeable, although differences in color or size above and below the union are often apparent (fig. 2.2). It is important to plant fruit trees as high as they were planted in the nursery or container to keep the graft union aboveground. If the scion is in continuous contact with soil, it becomes susceptible to the soilborne pathogens that it was grafted onto a rootstock to resist (see chapter 4, "Orchard design and planting and care of young trees"). A scion left in contact with the soil may even form its own roots, defeating the purpose of a size-controlling rootstock.

The trunk forms the structural support of a tree. It produces shoots that later form structural scaffold branches, and these in turn form lateral, fruit-bearing branches. Water and nutrients are transported

Figure 2.2. The graft union of an English walnut tree shows where it was budded to a black walnut rootstock. *Photo:* Maxwell Norton. *Source:* Wildman and Gowans 1975.

through the vascular system in the trunk, and some of the carbohydrates produced through photosynthesis move from the leaves down through the vascular system to provide nutrition to the roots. A healthy trunk is very important to a tree; any injury to the trunk, such as sunburn or string trimmer damage, can affect the health of the entire tree.

Shoots, branches, and the vascular cambium

Shoots are the new, vegetative growth that trees develop during the growing season (also called the current season's growth). After their first growing season, these shoots, and older ones, are usually referred to as branches; large branches are often referred to as limbs. Shoots generally become either upright and vigorous or lateral and less dominant. Both types serve a useful purpose: Upright shoots of young trees often become main limbs, whereas lateral shoots often become fruiting branches. A tree will usually produce more shoots and branches than it needs; these can then be pruned to establish tree structure, optimize fruit production, and control tree size. When pruning, you can head a shoot or branch (reduce its length) or thin branches (remove them entirely). Heading stimulates shoot growth below the cut and thinning opens the canopy and allows more light to penetrate to lower fruiting branches (see chapter 7, "Training and pruning," for more information on pruning).

Transport in xylem and phloem

Like the trunk, branches are made up of wood on the inside and bark on the outside. Within the wood, xylem tissue transports water and nutrients upward and outward while phloem tissue transports photosynthate downward. The xylem tissue may be further divided into that which is living and that which is no longer living. Water and dissolved mineral nutrients are conducted up the active xylem tissues of the outer portion of the wood, known as the sapwood. The inner wood, known as heartwood, consists of inactive xylem cells. These dead xylem cells no longer conduct substantial amounts of water but provide structural strength for the trunk and branches. Most starch is stored in the sapwood; heartwood is physiologically dead. Products of photosynthesis (mainly carbohydrates) are transported away from the leaves, and throughout the tree, including the roots, through the phloem. Active phloem tissues can be found on the inner bark, just outside the vascular cambium (see below). The vascular system, consisting of xylem and phloem, usually forms a continuous, multibranched system reaching from a tree's root tips to its leaf tips (fig. 2.3).

Growth by meristems

Trees grow both by elongating and by thickening. Both forms of growth occur by means of active cell division in tissues known as meristems, which are only a few cells in thickness. Cells of the meristem divide to reproduce, grow, and develop new tissues. The two most common meristems are the apical meristem, which forms terminal (lengthwise or axial) growth, and the vascular cambium, which forms lateral (widthwise) growth.

Apical meristems are found in growing tips. In buds, they may produce shoots (vegetative growth) or flowers (reproductive growth). The buds protect the meristems. Apical meristems in the roots are protected by the root cap and secretions of polymers that help lubricate the root as it pushes through soil.

The vascular cambium, often simply called the cambium, is a thin layer of actively growing cells found between the outer sapwood and the inner bark. The cambium produces the tissues for lateral growth of a tree's trunk and limbs as it gives rise to xylem (wood) on the inner side and phloem (bark) on the outer side. The seasonal additions of cambial

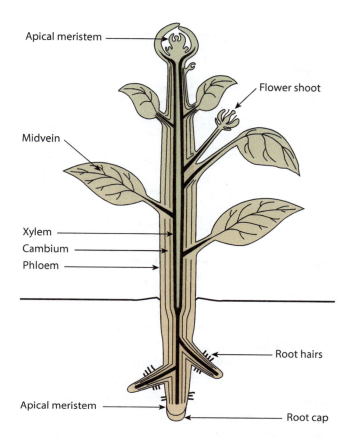

Figure 2.3. Vascular tissues are continuous from the root tips to the shoot tips. *Source:* Pittenger 2002, 10.

growth can be seen as concentric rings in a cross-section of a trunk or branch (fig. 2.4). Annual rings do not form consistently each year in all trees, and there may be false rings, particularly in subtropical species.

Trunk growth is only outward, not upward. If you were to pound a nail partway into the trunk, the nail would appear to be shorter and shorter over passing years as the cambium and resulting phloem and bark grew outward and covered it. The nail would remain at the same height; it would not move upward.

When you are budding and grafting trees, it is critically important that the cambium layer of the rootstock and the cambium layer of the bud being grafted onto it are properly matched so that the cambial cells form connective tissues between the two (see chapter 8, "Budding and grafting").

Buds

Trees produce flower buds, which form flowers, and vegetative buds, which form shoots. Both types of bud contain apical meristems. Vegetative buds are found at shoot tips (terminal buds) and laterally

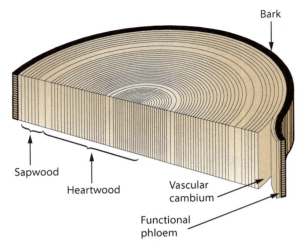

Figure 2.4. A typical tree trunk has concentric rings that show the seasonal cycle of cambial growth. *Source:* Pittenger 2002, 10.

along the sides of current-season shoots, tucked between the leaf stem (petiole) and the shoot in the leaf axil (axillary buds). Buds may also form but remain inactive (latent buds). Another type of vegetative bud is the adventitious bud, which can form on older wood where no bud previously existed. A shoot that grows from an adventitious or latent bud on the scion can usually be trained to become a major fruit-bearing branch, although its point of attachment to the limb may be weaker than that of other branches because the bud develops rapidly in the outer layers of the wood.

From late fall through early winter, buds on most deciduous trees are dormant. During the growing season, not all vegetative buds grow into shoots. Latent buds are kept from growing by a hormone known as auxin or, chemically, indoleacetic acid. Auxin is produced in shoot tips and leaves and it moves down stems through the phloem, preventing lateral bud growth and suppressing latent buds. You can temporarily suspend the inhibiting effect of auxin by cutting off a portion of a shoot or branch (heading). You can do the same in spring by simply removing (or girdling)—or in winter by filing (or notching)—a small strip of bark above a bud whose growth you wish to encourage, such as a bud grafted onto a shoot (see chapter 8, "Budding and grafting"). Because auxin is strongly influenced by gravity, the practice of bending the branches of an apically dominant tree outward is a method for producing more

lateral shoots, particularly fruiting shoots (see chapter 7, "Training and pruning").

Flowers and shoots that grow in the spring originate from buds that started forming the previous spring and summer. In a year with especially heavy fruit production, a tree may initiate far fewer flower buds. Under these conditions, the tree produces hormones that send a chemical message to the developing buds telling them not to initiate flower buds. Also, the heavy utilization of carbohydrates to produce a large crop load reduces the available carbohydrates for both shoot growth and flower bud formation in the following year. In that following year, because there are fewer flowers, and therefore fruit, the tree grows more vigorously and produces more flower buds. This is the mechanism of an alternate-bearing cycle. Some species and varieties have stronger alternate-bearing cycles than others. Appropriate pruning and early fruit thinning can bring fruit production and tree vigor into balance. Dormant pruning in the winter following a small crop season should be relatively extensive to remove more of the flower buds, whereas pruning after a large crop year should be relatively light to leave more buds on the tree and encourage flowering and fruit formation the next year.

To grow fruit and nut trees successfully, there should be balance between crop load and vegetative growth. On newly planted trees, it is a common recommendation to remove any fruit that form during the first year after planting so the tree can use its energy (carbohydrates) to create a well-developed structure of branches and roots on standard trees—although there is little research basis for this practice. Dwarf trees are precocious—that is, they produce fruit early, and so this fruit should be retained. The way to promote flower buds on young trees is by allowing lateral shoots to grow. You can accelerate tree development and flower bud formation by practicing judicious summer pruning and tipping during the first few years (in apple, plum, and apricot) (see chapter 7, "Training and pruning"). Some tree types, such as lateral-bearing walnut and some dwarf and spur-type apple varieties, need heavier dormant pruning to encourage vegetative growth.

Leaves

Leaves are the structures where the tree collects sunlight and conducts photosynthesis, a process that results in stored energy in the form of carbohydrates. The undersides of leaves have tiny openings called stomata. The stomata open in daylight to allow free movement of gases such as carbon dioxide and oxygen, and they also cool the leaf by allowing water vapor to escape in a process called transpiration.

Most fruit and nut tree leaves are simple in form, with a distinct blade and petiole (leaf stem). Some species, such as walnut and pecan, have compound leaves, in which each leaf is divided into several leaflets along a central stem.

Flowers

Flowers are the structures in which plants sexually reproduce after pollination, forming offspring that may differ genetically from the parents. The principal male structure of a flower is the stamen, at the tip of which is the pollen-bearing anther (fig. 2.5). The principal female structure is the pistil, which contains the ovary at its base, the elongated style or styles above the ovary, and the pollen-receiving stigma at its tip. In most species, it is the ovary that enlarges to form the fruit or nut.

Flowers of many deciduous fruit and nut-tree species are perfect; that is, both male and female structures are present in the same flower. Some species have separate male and female flowers, and these flowers are known as imperfect. Male flowers are termed staminate, and female flowers are known as pistillate. Walnut, pecan, chestnut, and filbert (hazelnut) are monoecious, which means that they have male and female flowers on the same tree. In contrast, pistachio and many kiwifruit varieties are dioecious, with male and female flowers on separate trees, or vines.

Pollination and fertilization

Pollination is the transfer of pollen from a flower's anther to the stigma of a compatible flower—whether that is the same flower or a different flower. Fertilization is the successful union of the pollen tube nuclei with the egg to begin fruit development. Fruit set occurs shortly after petal fall, after the egg has been fertilized. If fertilization fails to occur, the fruit usually falls off.

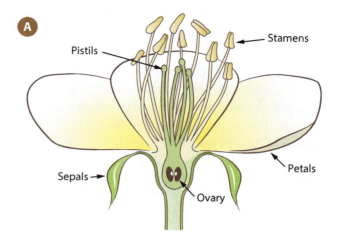

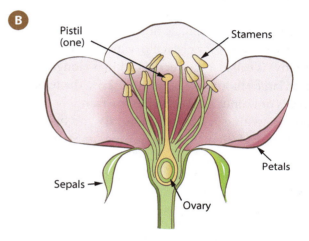

Figure 2.5. An apple (pome fruit) flower has several pistils (A); a stone fruit flower has just one (B).

Most deciduous fruit varieties, along with almond, require pollination by insect pollinators; mainly, the pollinators are honey bees, but other insects such as mason orchard bees may pollinate the flowers. Parthenocarpic fruit varieties (such as Bartlett pear) set without pollination or seed development. With self-fruitful (self-fertile) species and varieties, bees visiting flowers of a single tree can pollinate any flower on that tree and that flower will develop fruit. Although self-fruitful trees such as peach are usually pollinated by bees or other insects, pollination may occur through anther-stigma contact or with wind. With self-unfruitful types, for pollination to occur, bees must carry to the tree flowers some pollen from a tree or grafted branch of a different, compatible variety (the pollenizer). Cross-pollination occurs when the pollen of the two tree varieties pollinates the flowers of the other. Partially self-fruitful varieties will set some fruit when pollinated from other flowers on the same tree, but they set a better crop if pollinated from a different variety.

On trees that produce a lot of blossoms, only a small proportion of the blossoms need to set fruit to provide a full crop. In some years, adverse weather during bloom may greatly reduce pollination or fertilization. Proper pruning to provide an adequate number of flowers will ensure a good crop of fruit in most years because you can also use fruit thinning to regulate the number of fruit. Of course, if pruning is light, an excessive number of flowers may form, requiring a large amount of time-consuming fruit thinning after fruit set.

Walnut, pecan, chestnut, pistachio, and filbert are wind-pollinated. The male flower structure of these nut crops (except for pistachio, which is formed differently) is called a catkin; the catkin is elongated and sheds large amounts of pollen (fig. 2.6). The female flowers of walnut and pecan are small and inconspicuous, consisting primarily of an ovary and two elongated, curved stigmas. These flowers appear at the tip of current-season shoots after leaves begin to grow in the spring. In filbert, the female flowers in the winter look like small red tufts (stigmas) protruding from the bud. Female chestnut flowers are attached to the lower portion of some of the catkins. The stigmas of all these nut trees, when moist, receive whatever pollen happens to land on them. With the exception of pistachio, these species are self-fruitful, but the catkins' period of pollen shedding usually does not completely overlap with the female flowers' period of receptivity. For this reason, growers generally provide a different variety whose male flowers complete the overlap with the main variety's female flowers, and often vice versa—the male flowers of the main variety overlap the receptivity period of the pollenizer's flowers.

Fruit

Trees produce fruit to help disperse seed. Fruit are eaten by animals, roll on the ground, float in water, or blow in the wind to a new growing site. From a

Walnut

Female

Male

Leafy shoot

Filbert

Female

Male

Pecan

Female

Male

Leafy shoot

Pistachio

Female

Male

Figure 2.6. Nut crops have various flowering habits. For pistachio, male flowers and female flowers are on separate trees. After Westwood 1993, 224–225.

human perspective, fruit provide a nutritious food source. The primary nutrient content of fleshy fruit consists of sugars, vitamins, and fiber, whereas the nutrition derived from a nut is primarily fat (oil) and protein. Most nuts have high oil content and low carbohydrate content, but the edible portion of chestnuts is a high-carbohydrate, low–oil content nut.

A few basic fruit types represent most of the tree fruit and nuts that we eat. Pome fruit include apples, pears, pomegranates, and quinces. Their five stigmas arise together above the ovary and the fruit is derived from the fusion of the ovary, calyx cup (sepals), and floral tube (fig. 2.7A). The fleshy part of the pome fruit that is eaten is not the ovary, as with stone fruit, but the calyx and receptacle tissue.

Stone fruit (apricots, cherries, nectarines and peaches, and plums), almonds, and pistachios, as well as olives, are known botanically as drupe fruit (fig. 2.7B). The drupe is a one-seeded fruit derived entirely from an ovary with a stony endocarp (pit) containing the seed. Nuts, except for almonds, are hard, usually one-seeded fruit derived from the fusion of ovary, petals, and sepals (fig. 2.7C).

The flower structure of the fig is known as a syconium. The structure is cup-shaped, and the flowers develop on the interior surface of the cup, with a small opening at the tip. The fig is a multiple fruit (fig. 2.7D) derived from the fusion of ovaries and receptacles.

Beyond these general characteristics, fruit and nut-tree species have a wide variety of flowering and fruiting habits. See figures 2.8 through 2.11; also see table 7.1 in chapter 7, "Training and pruning," for more detailed information.

Biology of plant growth

Growth is a process of cell division and cell growth that results in the development of new or expanded plant tissues, organs, and other structures. Tree growth requires sunlight and a source of water and mineral nutrients. The woody framework of a tree provides the structural support for the exposure of a

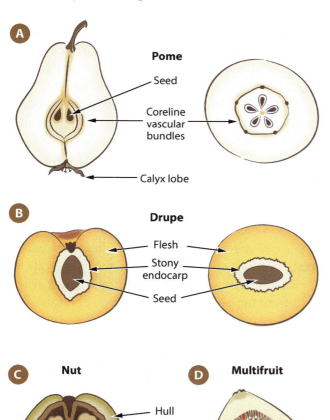

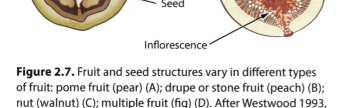

Figure 2.7. Fruit and seed structures vary in different types of fruit: pome fruit (pear) (A); drupe or stone fruit (peach) (B); nut (walnut) (C); multiple fruit (fig) (D). After Westwood 1993, 71, and Hasey et al. 1994.

Figure 2.8. Pome fruit have various flowering habits. After Westwood 1993, 220.

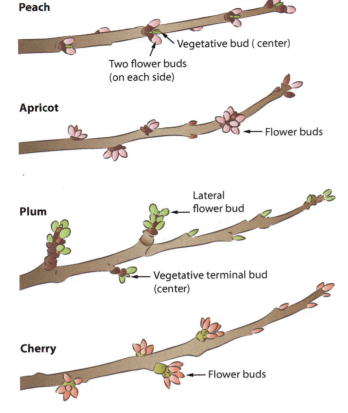

Figure 2.9. Stone fruit have various flower bud arrangements. After Westwood 1993, 220–221.

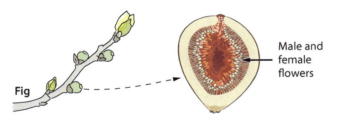

Figure 2.10. Fig has an unusual arrangement of flowers. After Westwood 1993, 222.

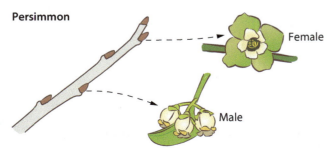

Figure 2.11. The male and female flowers are different in persimmon. After Westwood 1993, 223.

maximum number of leaves to light in order to capture the sun's energy. The tree's success as a solar energy collector depends on its ability to efficiently capture and convert light energy into chemical energy (that is, carbohydrates, mainly sugar) and then to transport, store, and utilize that chemical energy. Wood and bark provide the vascular tissue that transports water and nutrients to leaves and transports sugar and hormones away from the leaves to other parts of the tree. Woody tissues also provide a site for carbohydrate and nutrient storage through the winter.

Photosynthesis and respiration

Photosynthesis is the process by which the sun's energy is used to synthesize simple sugars from carbon dioxide (from air) and water (taken up by roots), thus converting the sun's energy into stored chemical energy. A by-product of this reaction is oxygen, which is released into the atmosphere. Photosynthesis is a complex set of reactions involving many biological compounds containing many of the nutrients required by a plant, including nitrogen, phosphorus, potassium, magnesium, iron, and manganese. These nutrients are also (1) combined with carbohydrates to synthesize the more-complex compounds needed to produce new cells for growth; (2) used in the conversion to more-complex carbohydrates (complex sugars and starch) or fats and stored in fruit, seed, stems, or roots; and (3) involved in the biological combustion that releases the chemical energy needed for cells to function (see the discussion of respiration below).

Carbon dioxide diffuses through specialized pores called stomata on the underside of leaves, which open and close based on environmental conditions. For photosynthesis to occur, the stomata must be open, adequate light must be striking the leaf, and water must be available to the plant. The opening of the stomata represents a trade-off for the plant: It allows carbon dioxide to enter the leaf for photosynthesis but allows water to escape through transpiration.

Adequate sunlight—at least 6 to 8 hours of full sunlight per day—is crucial for sufficient photosynthesis to produce flower buds and ripen fruit. If interior leaves in canopies become excessively shaded, those leaves gradually lose their capacity to carry out high rates of photosynthesis. Such leaves gradually become thin and yellow and, unless the canopy is opened up to allow more light in, they drop prematurely and the shaded branches may die. For this reason, proper pruning, which may include summer pruning, is important to the health of lower fruiting branches.

Respiration is the process in which carbohydrates are biochemically broken down (oxidized) and energy is released. In simple terms, it is photosynthesis in reverse. Respiration takes place in cells through a series of reactions in which complex carbohydrates are broken down into simple carbohydrates, carbon dioxide, and water. The energy thus released is used to carry on metabolism in various parts of the tree. Respiration occurs at all times in plants, even in harvested fruit and nuts. Respiration rates are highest in rapidly growing tissues and lowest in dormant tissues.

Uptake and movement of water and nutrients

Adequate water and mineral nutrients are crucial for the production of healthy, fruitful trees. Water and mineral nutrients are absorbed from the soil through the fine root system. Water moves into the plant both passively, through diffusion, and through an active process across root cell membranes. Soils contain large amounts of nutrients, but only a fraction of these nutrients are available to plants, since roots can only take up nutrients that are dissolved in the soil water.

The opening of stomata to allow carbon dioxide into the leaf also exposes the water within the leaf to the atmosphere, where it can evaporate. The opening of stomata is the first step in transpiration. Water evaporating inside leaves creates tension or suction in the leaf. The combined suction of the tree's many leaves is transmitted along a gradient through the tree and it pulls the water out of the soil and up through the tree. This continuously flowing column of water (which also contains minerals absorbed from the soil and organic compounds produced in the roots) exists in the xylem for as long as the stomata are open and water is available in the soil. When there is insufficient soil water, the stomata tend to close, slowing photosynthesis by reducing the movement of both carbon dioxide and water in the leaf. The fact that water and carbon dioxide concen-

trations in a leaf depend on open stomata is what ties a tree's water use so closely to tree growth. Stomatal closure reduces carbohydrate production, which is essential for shoot growth and fruit development. Trees can tolerate and be productive with some deficit in soil water, but keeping trees alive during severe drought may require limiting fruit production and reducing leaf surface area (see chapter 5, "Irrigation").

Transpiration rates depend on environmental factors, which can change the rate of evaporation and the degree to which stomata open, in addition to affecting the amount of available soil water. Day length has the greatest effect on transpiration and photosynthesis. During long days, the stomata are open for the longest time. Stomata are often fully open, and transpiration (and photosynthesis) are greatest, on warm, sunny days with low relative humidity (transpiration helps to cool trees on hot days). Transpiration virtually ceases at night because the stomata close.

Translocation is the movement of mineral nutrients, carbohydrates, plant hormones, and other dissolved compounds from one part of the plant to another. It can occur from cell to cell in the space between cells but occurs mostly in the xylem and phloem tissues (see fig. 2.3). Through translocation, essential mineral nutrients from the roots are distributed to other tissues, and carbohydrates produced in the leaves are moved to meristematic areas (shoot and root tips, cambium, and buds), storage organs (fruit, seed, stems, and roots), and other tissues.

Growth cycle in deciduous fruit trees

The general timing of root, shoot, and fruit growth in stone fruit is shown in figure 2.12. The roots of fruit trees may grow in late autumn after leaf fall and may begin growing a week or more before buds begin to swell in spring. Root growth is very active in early spring, decreases during fruit enlargement, and increases again in late summer or early fall. Shoot growth is most active in spring but slows or ceases in summer. Shoot growth may continue through the summer for young trees or headed fruit bushes (see chapter 7, "Training and pruning"). The rate of fruit growth for many species follows a sigmoid (S-shaped) curve; in some species, a lag phase occurs, forming a double-sigmoid curve.

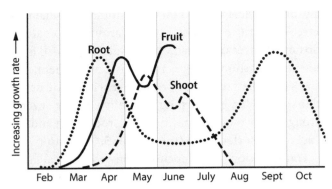

Figure 2.12. Root, shoot, and fruit growth follow a general pattern through the year. *Source:* Ingels et al. 2007.

Winter

In winter, deciduous trees go through dormant stages. Fruit-tree species require varying amounts of winter chilling to break dormancy and grow vigorously, flower, and produce quality fruit the following year (see chapter 1, "Climate and soils"). Late in the dormant period, buds begin to swell as the weather warms. Buds may begin to swell as early as January if there is a period of warm weather.

Winter is the time to do the majority of pruning for canopy management in many species, or at least to do touch-up pruning if heavy summer pruning took place. With no leaves on the trees, it is easier to see the branch structure and where to make cuts than during the growing season. However, some species (such as cherry and apricot) should not be pruned in winter in some locations, and the limbs or trunk of any species may develop canker diseases as a result of large cuts during the dormant period (see chapter 7, "Training and pruning," and chapter 11, "Integrated pest management for backyard orchards"). Exactly when to prune varies by location in California and is influenced by the severity of the winter.

Carbohydrates and nutrients, particularly nitrogen, are stored in the roots and stems for springtime flower and shoot growth. Nitrogen uptake occurs with the flow of water during the growing season, so winter is not the time to apply nitrogen fertilizers.

Depending on location, root growth nearly ceases during the early dormant period, but a very small amount of growth does occur (see fig. 2.12). A well-drained soil is especially important at this time of year because the new roots of many species can be killed by waterlogging (low soil oxygen), and this initial root growth period comes at a time when rain is frequent in many areas of California.

Spring

Although almond and many stone fruit often bloom before the official first day of spring (around March 21), pomologists usually consider spring to begin with flowering and growth. Flowering of almond, stone fruit, and pome fruit usually occurs just before or simultaneously with the beginning of vegetative growth, whereas flowering of persimmon, pomegranate, and walnut comes after growth begins. Species that flower very early, such as apricot, almond, and plum, are more susceptible to frost damage, lack of pollination, and—because rainfall is often more abundant—infectious diseases.

Spring is the time of maximum vegetative growth. Shoot elongation is most rapid then, and the leaves quickly develop and mature for maximum photosynthesis. When leaves mature, they develop a waxy or leathery texture, which inhibits the inward and outward movement of water. For this reason, foliar nutrient applications are often made by midspring. Typically, a mature tree's shoot growth will cease or greatly slow by late spring or early summer, at which time a terminal bud will set at the shoot tip; this cessation of growth occurs earliest on stressed trees. For most species, some further growth may occur during the summer, but overall growth at that time is far less than in the spring.

Spring is the time to begin summer pruning to shape young trees or to remove or tip unwanted vigorous shoots on mature trees. You can identify these unwanted shoots at a fairly early stage because they usually grow straight up and are more vigorous than lateral shoots. Left unchecked, these shoots will often branch out and shade lower fruiting wood by summer.

For most species, spring is also the period of maximum fruit growth. In the early stages, fruit growth is caused mainly by cell division, whereas in the later stages most fruit growth occurs by cell expansion. Some varieties of apricot, cherry, and peach ripen in late spring, especially in warmer regions. During late spring and summer, flower buds begin to form for the next spring's flowers. Excess fruit set in the spring may cause hormonal signals telling the tree to produce more vegetative buds and fewer flower buds.

For this reason, it is necessary in many species to thin fruit in early spring to prevent an alternate-bearing pattern (see chapter 9, "Fruit thinning").

Root growth is reduced during mid-to-late spring because most of the tree's chemical energy is directed toward shoot and fruit growth. One or more flushes of root growth can occur in late summer as shoot growth diminishes and fruit is harvested.

Summer

For almond and most fruit species, summer is the time of reduced vegetative growth and of fruit ripening. Prune unwanted vigorous upright shoots on fruit trees and train young tree shoots at least once in early summer or midsummer. Summer pruning allows more sunlight to reach the leaves of lower fruiting wood, which improves flower bud development there and productivity in the next year. Summer pruning can also help reduce tree vigor in trees with excessive shoot growth.

Much of a tree's carbohydrate energy is directed into fruit growth and ripening during the summer. Flower bud formation for the next year's flowers occurs mainly during summer. Overproduction of fruit leads to formation of fewer flower buds for the next year, while low fruit production leads to formation of more flower buds. Roots usually grow less in early summer but growth increases again in late summer.

Fall

Fall is harvest time for late apple varieties, walnut, pecan, chestnut, and most fig, persimmon, and pomegranate varieties. The late-summer flush of root growth in many species may continue into early fall. By late fall, shoot growth ceases and terminal buds appear at the tip of virtually all shoots, signaling the onset of dormancy. Nitrogen, other mineral nutrients, and carbohydrates are translocated into woody tissues for overwinter storage before the leaves fall, which triggers the cessation of chlorophyll production in the leaves. With the disappearance of chlorophyll, yellow and orange pigments already in the leaves become visible.

Further reading

Hasey, J. K., R. S. Johnson, J. A. Grant, and W. O. Reil, eds. 1994. Kiwifruit growing and handling. Oakland: UC Division of Agriculture and Natural Resources Publication 3344.

Ingels, C. A., P. M. Geisel, and M. V. Norton, tech. eds. 2007. The home orchard. Oakland: UC Agriculture and Natural Resources Publication 3485.

LaRue, J. H., and R. S. Johnson, eds. 1989. Peaches, plums, and nectarines: Growing and handling for fresh market. Oakland: UC Agriculture and Natural Resources Publication 3331.

Micke, W. C., ed. 1996. Almond production manual. Oakland: UC Agriculture and Natural Resources Publication 3364.

Pittenger, D. 2015. Introduction to horticulture. In D. Pittenger, ed., California master gardener handbook. 2nd ed. Davis: UC Agriculture and Natural Resources Publication 3382. 9–36.

Ramos, D. D., ed. 1997. Walnut production manual. Oakland: UC Agriculture and Natural Resources Publication 3373.

Vossen, P., and D. Silva. 2015. Temperate tree fruit and nut crops. In D. Pittenger, ed., California master gardener handbook. 2nd ed. Davis: UC Agriculture and Natural Resources Publication 3382.

Westwood, M. N. 1993. Temperate-zone pomology: Physiology and culture. Portland, OR: Timber Press.

Westwood, M. N. 2009. Temperate zone pomology: Physiology and culture. 3rd ed. Portland, OR: Timber Press.

Wildman, W. E., and K. D. Gowans. 1975. Soil physical environment and how it affects plant growth. Oakland: UC Agriculture and Natural Resources Publication 2280.

Chapter 3

Varieties

Paul M. Vossen

California is the most important state in the United States for production of temperate tree-fruit and -nut crops. It leads the nation in the production of apricots, peaches, nectarines, plums, prunes, pears, almonds, walnuts, pistachios, figs, persimmons, and pomegranates. Many of these fruit and nuts can also be enjoyed from backyard trees throughout the state. They can make beautiful, practical additions to the home garden and landscape due to their striking flowers, edible harvest, and provision of shade.

Temperate tree-fruit and tree-nut crops

This chapter introduces selected deciduous fruit and nuts that can be grown in the home garden in California; many of them can be grown in other parts of the United States too. California has very diverse climates, as does the rest of the country, so some species perform better in some regions than others. For example, in California, almond and pistachio trees produce best in hot, inland valleys, whereas apple trees often produce the best fruit in colder regions; diseases such as bacterial canker and brown rot may rule out growing some stone fruit in wet areas of the North Coast; the early spring frosts in cold locations in the Sierra may preclude successful stone fruit production in many years; and sunburn may be a serious problem in hot desert regions. In many of the interior parts of the United States, winter temperatures are too cold to grow many fruit and nut species, but pome fruit, some stone fruit, and some nuts grow and produce well. Also, many U.S. regions have substantial summer rainfall and humidity, which can lead to serious foliar diseases. Check with your local Cooperative Extension office to learn which species and varieties are most successful in your region.

All fruit crops have associated pest problems. Some pests, like gophers, are common to many fruit species. Others are specific to fruit families or genera. A full discussion of pest problems of fruit is outside the scope of this publication, but we offer general guidance in the calendar notes in the appendix.

Types of deciduous fruit and nut trees

Pomology is the technical term for the science and art of fruit culture. Scientists who study fruit and nut crops are known as pomologists. Scientists who study citrus and avocados, two subtropical evergreen tree-fruit crops, are also pomologists, but they are said to specialize in subtropical horticulture.

The diverse fruit and nut crops featured in this chapter are temperate-zone trees native to climates with distinct summer-winter patterns. The fruit, nut, and miscellaneous fruit crops grown in California featured in this chapter include the fruit types discussed below.

Pome fruit

Apple (*Malus domestica*), pear (*Pyrus communis*), Asian pear (*P. serotina, P. pyrifolia*), and quince (*Cydonia oblonga*) are grouped together by botanists because their fruit type is a pome (see fig. 2.7). The flowers of pome fruit arise conjointly above the ovary, and the fruit are derived from the fusion of the ovaries, calyx cup (sepals), and floral tube. The fleshy part of the pome fruit that is consumed is nonovarian calyx (sepal) and receptacle tissue. Pome fruit and stone fruit (listed below) are members of the Rosaceae family.

Stone fruit

Apricot (*Prunus armeniaca*), sweet and sour cherry (*Prunus avium* and *P. cerasus*, respectively), nectarine and peach (*P. persica*), European plum (*P. domestica*) and prune (dried European plum), and Japanese plum (*P. salicina*) are stone fruit belonging to the genus *Prunus*. Their fruit is botanically known as a drupe (see fig. 2.7), a one-seeded fruit derived entirely from an ovary with a stony endocarp containing the seed. Plumcot, pluot, and aprium are complex interspecific hybrids between various plum and apricot species.

Nut crops

Almond also belongs to the genus *Prunus*. Almond (*Prunus dulcis*), chestnut (*Castanaea* spp.), filbert (*Corylus* spp., also known as hazelnut), pecan (*Carya illinoinensis*), pistachio (*Pistacia vera*), English or Persian walnut (*Juglans regia*), and black walnut (*J. hindsii*) are, with the exception of almond, hard, woody, usually one-seeded fruit derived from the fusion of ovary and perianth (petals and sepals) (see fig. 2.7).

Other tree fruit

Fig (*Ficus carica*), oriental persimmon (*Diospyros kaki*), and pomegranate (*Punica granatum*) do not fit into the above categories, yet they are important trees in the home garden in California. The fruit of fig, a multiple fruit (see fig. 2.7), is derived from the fusion of the ovaries and receptacles (the part of the flower stalk that bears the floral organs) of many flowers. Pomegranate is a small tree or shrub with large, apple-sized fruit that are covered in a leathery skin. The seed has a fleshy seed coat called an aril, which can be eaten. Persimmon is neither a pome fruit, a stone fruit, nor a nut crop.

Dormancy and winter chill

The growth of deciduous fruit and nut trees follows an annual pattern. Typically, these trees grow rapidly during the spring and first half of summer. Later in the season, the growth rate declines. In the fall, growth stops as day length and temperature decrease, the trees drop their leaves, and growth inhibitors (hormones) are produced that prevent the tree from growing. In the winter, the tree's internal processes are in a state of rest, known as dormancy, due to the presence of these growth inhibitors. Dormancy prevents the trees from beginning to grow during winter; if the trees grew at such times, the new growth could be damaged by freezing temperatures later in the winter or early spring.

Dormancy is broken when sufficient cold temperature breaks down the growth inhibitors. This cold period is called chilling, winter chill, or sometimes vernalization. A specific number of cumulative hours of chilling (temperatures lower than 45°F [7°C] or so, depending on the mathematical model used) is required to break dormancy; the number of hours differs from cultivar to cultivar. Once the required number of chilling hours is reached, active growth resumes in the spring, but only after temperatures are warm enough for growth processes to begin. Most of Northern California receives between 800 and 1,500 hours of chilling each winter. Southern California and the coastal areas in Northern California may receive only 100 to 400 hours. It is primarily the lower elevations in Southern California that have very few hours of winter chilling and that require special care in cultivar selection; most higher-elevation areas of Southern California receive adequate chilling hours.

Deciduous fruit and nut trees grow best in climates in which the winters are warm enough that dormant plant tissue is not killed from extreme low temperatures but cool enough that buds receive adequate chilling to break dormancy. Flower and shoot buds of deciduous fruit and nut trees normally grow in the spring only after exposure to sufficient winter cold. After winters with inadequate chilling, the trees leaf out late in the season (delayed foliation), blossoming is prolonged, buds may deteriorate or drop, and fruit set is typically reduced.

Low-chill cultivars

Over the years, plant scientists and breeders around the world have selected and developed fruit and nut cultivars that require less chilling: Many require 300 hours or less at temperatures below 45°F (7°C). The development of these low-chill cultivars has extended the range of climates and latitudes that allow for production of temperate tree fruit and nuts. Certain cultivars of apple, pear, apricot, nectarine, peach, and Japanese and hybrid plums are reported to have low chilling requirements (see the "Cultivars" section, below). In general terms, the relatively low chilling requirements of quince, fig, persimmon, almond, chestnut, and pecan have enabled many cultivars to thrive in areas with low winter chill. Filbert (hazelnut) and pistachio are not suitable for the low elevations of Southern and coastal California because of the current lack of low-chill cultivars. Some low-chill sweet cherry varieties are in development.

Cultivars

The remainder of this chapter describes selected cultivars of the major and minor temperate fruit and nut crops that are suitable for home gardeners in California. The tables are intended as a starting point and could easily be doubled or tripled in size if all heirloom cultivars and newer cultivars available at nurseries or through mail order were included. Climate zones—discussed in chapter 1, "Climate and soils"—determine which cultivars of temperate tree-fruit and tree-nut crops perform best in the home garden; when fruit and nuts are harvested; and which pest and disease problems are most common.

Certain cultivars are primarily eaten fresh, while other cultivars tend to be used more often for cooking, canning, and freezing. Because individual tastes differ, there is considerable disagreement among experts about which cultivars are best suited for which uses. Most cultivars produce fruit of excellent quality if they are pruned, thinned, irrigated, and harvested at the proper maturity and eaten right away. The comments in this section regarding these issues are offered as points of interest only, not as official advice endorsed by the University of California.

Pome fruit

Apple

Apples (*Malus domestica*) are adapted to many areas of California. A cool climate is needed for coloration in most red cultivars. Winter chilling requirements for most cultivars are 500 to 1,000 hours below 45°F; low-chill cultivars need about 200 to 500 hours below 45°F. Foggy days and dews can cause heavy cosmetic russetting on fruit. There are hundreds of apple cultivars (fig. 3.1), and some cultivars have several strains, each with their own characteristics. Several root-

Figure 3.1. Numerous apple cultivars on display. *Photo:* P. M. Vossen.

stocks are available that impart dwarfing and pest resistance. Spur-type cultivars have short shoot growth and abundant spur production and may do poorly on the most-dwarfing rootstocks. Apple cultivars exhibit considerable genetic diversity. Some require as few as 70 days to mature; others take 180 days or more. Some cultivars are very cold-hardy; others are tender. Apples generally require cross-pollination from another cultivar that blooms at the same time and produces abundant, viable pollen. Many cultivars are self-unfruitful and have sterile pollen; others are partially self-fruitful (not all of their pollen is viable); a few are self-fruitful. As with all fruit trees, it is best to plant apple trees from January to March, although potted trees can be planted at any time.

Apple rootstocks

Apple rootstocks	Comments
M7a	Semidwarf rootstock. Usually produces a tree about 60% the size of the same tree on seedling rootstock. Performs well in irrigated replant situations but suckers and can struggle in very coarse soils
M9	Dwarfing rootstock. Usually produces a very small tree, about 30–40% the size of the same tree on seedling rootstock. Commercially, the most frequently planted rootstock worldwide. However, a poor performer if not adequately managed. Poorly anchored, very few suckers, with a brittle root system. Must be trellised or supported by staking. Susceptible to fire blight and wooly apple aphid
M26	Semidwarf to dwarfing rootstock. Usually produces a tree 30–50% the size of the same tree on seedling rootstock. Performs poorly in most California locations. Usually needs a support system and is susceptible to fire blight disease
M111	Semidwarf rootstock. Usually produces a tree about 70–80% the size of the same tree on seedling rootstock; very little suckering. Tolerates many soil conditions, including light, sandy soils. Has some resistance to both fire blight and woolly apple aphid. Imparts earlier bearing than seedling but not as early as more-dwarfing stocks. Requires irrigation. Vigor can be difficult to control
Mark	Dwarfing rootstock. Relatively new. Similar in size to M9. Very precocious. Questionable performer in all apple-growing regions of California
Seedling	Used for nonirrigated sites, low-vigor sites, and weaker cultivars. Very vigorous; produces large, full-size trees that come into bearing late (7–10 yr). Susceptible to woolly apple aphid. Trees can fill a 30 × 30 ft. space and grow 20 ft. tall

Standard apple scion cultivars

Apple scions	Comments	Harvest					
		San Joaquin Valley	Sacramento Valley	Central Coast	North Coast	Sierra foothills	Southern California
Fuji	Round to flat apple with very sweet yellow-orange flesh. Skin is red if given enough sunlight and cool temperatures. One of the best sweet eating apples. Stores well	Oct–Nov	late Oct–Nov	Nov	Nov	late Oct–Nov	—
Gala	Small to medium-size, conic red apple with excellent flavor and keeping qualities. The best cultivar for the early season. Will not cross-pollinate Golden Delicious	late Jun	late Jun	early Jul	late Jul	early Jul	late Jun
Gravenstein	Medium-large fruit with short, fat stem. Skin is greenish yellow, overlaid with red stripes. Excellent flavor when fully ripe. Crisp, subacid, and aromatic. A good sauce and pie apple. Stores and ships poorly. High percentage of windfalls. Sterile pollen	late Jun	late Jun	early Jul	late Jul	early Jul	—

Standard apple scion cultivars, continued

Apple scions	Comments	Harvest					
		San Joaquin Valley	Sacramento Valley	Central Coast	North Coast	Sierra foothills	Southern California
Golden Delicious	Conic apple with a long stem, yellow to green skin, yellow flesh, and russet dots. Sweet, juicy, fine-textured. Number one on the California North Coast for fresh eating quality and processing. Stores well but susceptible to bitter pit, bruising, russetting. Partially self-fruitful and is a good general pollinator for other cultivars that require cross-pollination	late Aug	late Aug	Sep	late Aug–Sep	Sep	—
Granny Smith	Round, green- to yellow-skinned apple that is quite firm. Keeps very well. Crisp flesh. If harvested early, it is green and tart. Late-harvested fruit are yellow and sweet	Oct–Nov	late Oct–Nov	Nov	Nov	late Oct–Nov	—
Jonathan	Round, red apple with pure white flesh. Crisp, juicy, and slightly subacid. Excellent for eating fresh, sauce, and juice. Highly susceptible to mildew, fire blight, and Jonathan spot	Aug	Aug	late Aug–Sep	mid-Aug–Sep	mid-Aug	—
Pink Lady	Very attractive color, excellent flavor. Very susceptible to fire blight. Ripens 1–2 wk after Granny Smith. High chilling requirement, use Fuji as pollinizer	Oct–Nov	late Oct–Nov	Nov	Nov	late Oct–Nov	—
Red Delicious	Conic apple with tapered base and five distinct lobes. Skin color varies from solid red to a mixture of red and green stripes. Crisp, sweet, mild-flavored yellow flesh. Many strains. Best used fresh. Stores well	late Aug	late Aug	Sep	late Aug–Sep	Sep	—
Rome Beauty	Round fruit with a deep cavity, no lobes, and little russet. Several strains, including the old standard and several new strains with solid red skin, such as Taylor and Law. Stores moderately well. Tree leafs out late, flowers late, and produces flowers and fruit on long spur growth that requires modification in pruning. Good for baking	Oct–Nov	late Oct–Nov	Nov	Nov	late Oct–Nov	—

Other apple cultivars

Apple scions	Comments	Cultivars
Spur type	Strains (mutations) of the original cultivars that have shorter internodes and are naturally dwarfing. Best on seedling rootstock	Golden Delicious Spur (Nugget Spur, Goldspur, Yelo Spur, and Starkspur), Red Delicious Spur (Silverspur, Crimson Spur, and Skyspur), Bisbee Spur, Spurred Royal, Oregon Spur, Wellspur, Scarletspur, Cascade Spur, Starkspur, Spur McIntosh, Granny Smith Spur, Greenspur, Granspur, Rome Beauty Spur, Law Spur, Spuree, Winesap Spur, Arkansas Black Spur
Low-chill	These cultivars are adapted to areas of California with limited winter dormancy because they have low winter chilling requirements (<300 hr)	Anna, Beverly Hills, Dorsett Golden, Einshemer, Gordon, Tropical Beauty
Antique	These cultivars do well in much of California if there is adequate chilling and summer heat is not too intense. They are hard to find because they have limited commercial value. Many have excellent flavor and perform well in home gardens	Arkansas Black, Baldwin, Black Twig, Cox's Orange Pippin, E. Spitzenburg, McIntosh, Newtown Pippin, Northern Spy, Red Golden, Rhode Island Greening, Sierra Beauty, Smith Cider, Staymen Winesap, Wagner, Winesap, Winter Banana
Early summer	These cultivars do not have the high-quality characteristics of standard cultivars but ripen early when no other fresh apples are available. They are suitable for eating fresh and cooking	Akane: Similar to Jonathan but earlier, good solid red color, white flesh, good for juice and eating fresh Jerseymac: Large, good red color, excellent flavor, firmer than McIntosh, stores 4 to 8 wk Jonamac: Similar to McIntosh but has better color, firmness, and storage life Paulared: High-quality, white flesh, stores fairly well, tree requires thinning Vista Bell: Terminal bearing habit, white-fleshed fruit, stores well
Disease resistant	Several scab-resistant apple cultivars have been developed in breeding programs for the eastern United States, where this disease is quite severe due to summer humidity and rain. Some have received limited testing under California growing conditions. In growing districts with extended spring rains, organic growers should experiment with these cultivars to see how they perform in their orchards	Enterprise: A large-fruited, late-maturing, dense, crisp cultivar that has good keeping qualities. The skin is dark red over a yellow-green background. One of the best of the scab-resistant cultivars Florina: A promising scab-resistant selection from France, with large, round-oblong, purple-red fruit; ripens late and has a mixed sweet tart flavor Freedom: A late-season cultivar with large fruit and mild flavor; not completely immune to scab Goldrush: A scab-immune selection with Golden Delicious parentage; late-maturing, large, firm-textured, and tart, with an excellent flavor; stores well Jonafree: A midseason apple that compares with Jonathan, with soft flesh and uneven coloring Liberty: One of the best-quality apples of the disease-resistant cultivars; is very productive and requires heavy early thinning to achieve good size; ripens in midseason, has an attractive red color with some striping, and a good, sweet flavor Prima: An early-season, uneven-ripening, moderate-quality cultivar Priscilla: A late-season cultivar with small fruit, soft flesh, and mild flavor Pristine: Moderate to large, tart, yellow apple immune to scab and resistant to fire blight and mildew Red Free: Matures in early July, heat-sensitive, small-fruited; susceptible to water core, sunburn, and russet Williams Pride: Early maturing, scab immune; also resistant to fire blight and mildew; medium to large fruit with a round-oblique shape; attractive red striped color on a green-yellow background

Note: "—" indicates that information is not available.

Pear

Of all the deciduous fruit-tree species, pears (*Pyrus* spp.) are the most tolerant of wet soil conditions, but they perform best on deep, well-drained sites. Pears are the most pest-ridden of all fruit trees, and they require the most sprays to produce quality fruit. Without dwarfing rootstock or summer pruning, pear trees get very large, requiring a spacing of 18 by 18 feet. Pear trees have a tendency to grow very upright and must be trained to develop a spreading growth habit. Most pear cultivars are self-sterile and require cross-pollination by another cultivar to get a good crop set. One exception is in the Sacramento River Delta region, where Bartlett is self-fruitful, setting crops of parthenocarpic fruit. Fire blight (a bacterial disease) is a serious problem in pears. Bartlett, which makes up 75 percent of the world's production and acreage, has a chilling requirement of about 800 hours (fig. 3.2). Days from full bloom to harvest range from about 115 to 165 for European and Asian pears.

Figure 3.2. Bartlett pears. *Photo:* P. M. Vossen.

Pear rootstocks

Pear rootstocks	Comments
Betulaefolia	Best rootstock for most Asian pears. An Asian seedling. The most vigorous, producing the largest tree on the poorest site. Best tolerance of wet and drought conditions. Resistant to root aphid and root rot, and imparts some resistance to fire blight. Poor rootstock for D'Anjou
Calleryana	Moderately vigorous rootstock. Resistant to wet feet (Phytophthora), fire blight, root aphid, and most nematodes. Not the best rootstock for Asian cultivars. Produces a tree a bit larger than French Seedling
French Seedling	Seed from Bartlett or Winter Nelis are used for this rootstock, which withstands both wet feet and dry conditions. Resistant to oak root fungus but is very susceptible to fire blight. Good for general use
Old Home × Farmingdale	A *Pyrus communis* rootstock propagated by cuttings or layering. Somewhat dwarfing. Compatible with most cultivars. Imparts some resistance to fire blight
Quince (several strains)	Semidwarfing rootstock. Resistant to root aphid, root rot, and most nematodes. Trees are 50% of standard size and are very productive. Compatible with Anjou, Comice, Flemish Beauty, and Swiss Bartlett. Graft incompatible with Bartlett, Bosc, Clapp, and Seckel; requires an interstem of Old Home. On poor sites, trees tend to be runty. Fruit quality is lower than on other rootstocks. Several strains are used for pear rootstocks, but they vary only slightly in their tolerance to wet feet and size control. Quince is the only dwarfing stock available

European pear scion cultivars (*Pyrus communis L.*)
Most of these cultivars have the traditional pear shape and are harvested green, before they begin to drop off the tree. They are then stored at 33 to 45°F for several weeks. As the fruit is brought up to room temperature, it softens and turns buttery. If allowed to ripen on the tree, "stone" cells develop within the flesh that make the fruit gritty

Pear scions	Comments	Harvest					
		San Joaquin Valley	Sacramento Valley	Central Coast	North Coast	Sierra foothills	Southern California
Bartlett	The best-quality pear fruit. Bell-shaped, with white flesh and excellent flavor. Tree is susceptible to fire blight. Fruit keep relatively well, up to 2 mo after maturing. Ripens well without refrigeration	Jul	Jul	late Aug	late Aug	Aug	NA
Bosc	Midseason cultivar that bears heavy crops regularly. Fruit are long and tapering, with a long neck and stem. Skin is golden russet brown	Oct	Oct	Oct	Oct	Oct	NA
Comice	Inconsistent bearer. Excellent fruit, green with red blush. Delicate skin, chubby shape. Very vigorous tree, does best on Quince rootstock. Late-maturing	Oct	Oct	Oct	Oct	Oct	NA
D'Anjou	Good winter pear with excellent keeping qualities. A large, vigorous tree. Egg-shaped fruit with a small shoulder. Light green to yellow-green color with a white flesh. French origin. There is a red strain called Red Anjou	Sep	Sep	Sep	Sep	Sep	NA
Seckel	The small fruit are reddish green, with very dense, sweet, flavorful flesh. Excellent quality for the home orchard. Resistant to fire blight and pear scab	Sep	Sep	late Sep	late Sep	Sep	NA
Warren	Excellent-quality dessert pear grown on many small-scale farms, the tree is highly resistant to fire blight. Medium to large fruit with pale green skin, sometimes blushed red. Smooth flesh is juicy and buttery, with excellent flavor. Self-fertile	Aug	Aug	late Aug	late Aug	Aug	NA
Winter Nelis	Medium-small, almost round fruit with light russetting over a green skin. Resistant to blight. Large tree. Regular producer, but late	Oct	Oct	Oct	Oct	Oct	NA
Low-chill	These pear cultivars are adapted to the low latitudes of Southern California because they have low winter chilling requirements (<300 hr)	Baldwin, Carnes, Fan Stil, Florida Home, Garber, Hengsan, Hood, Kieffer, Orient, Pineapple, Seleta, Spadona					

Asian pear scion cultivars (*Pyrus serotina* L.)

Asian pears are round fruit that remain very firm, crisp, and juicy when eaten ripe. They are also known as salad pears or pear apples. The best rootstock for these cultivars is Betulaefolia. Generally require cross-pollination. To size properly, spurs should be thinned in dormant season and fruit should be heavily thinned in early spring. Harvest by taste and pick exposed fruit first. Unlike European pears, Asian pears ripen on the tree

Asian pear scions	Comments	Harvest					
		San Joaquin Valley	Sacramento Valley	Central Coast	North Coast	Sierra foothills	Southern California
Chojuro	Greenish-brown to brown russet skin. Coarse, tasty flesh	late Jul	late Jul	Aug	early Aug	early Aug	Aug
Hosui	Brown skin, juicy white flesh with a sweet aromatic flavor	late Aug	late Aug	Sep	early Sep	late Sep	early Sep
Kikusui	Yellow-green skin. White flesh, excellent flavor. Fruit drop from tree when ripe	Aug	Aug	late Aug	mid-Sep	late Aug	NA
Niitaka	Very large, juicy fruit with an aromatic flavor	late Sep	late Sep	mid-Oct	Oct	Oct	late Sep
Nijisseiki	Also known as Twentieth Century. Excellent quality. Very popular cultivar, yellow-green skin	Aug	Aug	late Aug	mid-Sep	late Aug	NA
Shinko	Brown russet skin; large fruit; firm, crisp flesh; very aromatic flavor. Has the most resistance to fire blight of any Asian Pear cultivar commonly grown	late Sep	late Sep	mid-Oct	Oct	Oct	late Sep
Shinseiki	Amber yellow skin. White flesh is crisp but softens rapidly; less flavor than other cultivars	Aug	Aug	late Aug	mid-Sep	late Aug	NA
Tsu Li	Blooms early. Use Ya Li (see below) as pollinizer. Chinese type (pear shape). Light green color, crisp, tasty flesh	late Sep	late Sep	mid-Oct	Oct	Oct	late Sep
Ya Li	Blooms early. Use Tsu Li (see above) as pollinizer. Chinese type (pear shape). Light, shiny yellow color; crisp, tasty flesh	late Sep	late Sep	mid-Oct	Oct	Oct	late Sep

Pomegranate

Pomegranates (*Punica granatum* L.) (fig. 3.3) are fruit that grow on a shrub-like tree that has shiny foliage and a long flowering season. The tree suckers profusely, is very long-lived, and can reach 15 to 20 feet tall if unpruned, although some smaller varieties can be found. It thrives in hot, dry areas and is sensitive to frost in fall and spring. Fruit crack with first fall rains and do not mature well in cool climates. The tree tolerates wet, heavy soil but performs better in deep, well-drained loams. Pomegranates are propagated from cuttings and require only a short chilling period. Trees are drought-tolerant and, if you are not interested in high yields, require very little nitrogen fertilizer. They are resistant to oak root fungus (*Armillaria mellea*) and are not attacked by codling moth or twig borers, but are highly attractive to aphids and leaffooted bugs. Unharvested ripe fruit attract ants and fruit flies.

Figure 3.3. Small pomegranate fruit and flowers. *Photo:* P. M. Vossen.

Pomegranate cultivars

		Harvest					
Pomegranates	Comments	San Joaquin Valley	Sacramento Valley	Central Coast	North Coast	Sierra foothills	Southern California
Ambrosia	Huge fruit, pale pink skin; similar to Wonderful	Sep	Sep	Oct	Oct	Sep	Sep
Eversweeet	Very sweet, almost seedless fruit. Red skin, clear juice. Good for coastal areas	late Aug	early Sep	Oct	Oct	early Sep	early Sep
Foothill Early	Early ripening, high-color fruit, pale kernels, mild flavor	mid-to-late Aug	mid-to-late Aug	Sep	Sep	Sep	Sep
Granada	Deep crimson fruit color. Matures early but needs heat	Aug	early Sep	Oct	Oct	early Sep	early Sep
Ruby Red	Matures late (with Wonderful) but not as sweet or colorful as Wonderful. All fruit mature at once	Sep	Sep	Oct	Oct	Sep	Sep
Wonderful	Large, deep-red fruit. Large, juicy, red kernels. Small seed. Matures late. Juice is made into grenadine syrup. Most common cultivar sold in California	mid-to-late Sep	mid-to-late Sep	Oct	Oct	Sep	Sep

Quince

Quince (*Cydonia oblonga* Mill.) fruit grow on a small tree or shrub (8–12 ft. tall) with twisted, bumpy branches (fig. 3.4). Quince trees are grown as flowering ornamentals or for fruit processing. They are adapted to many climates and tolerate poor drainage better than most other deciduous fruit trees. Quince trees bloom late, which means that they avoid spring frosts. Quince has many of the same pest problems as apple and pear and requires multiple in-season sprays to be pest-free. Cultivars are self-fruitful. Quince is used as a dwarfing rootstock for pear.

Figure 3.4. Quince fruit and leaves. *Photo:* P. M. Vossen.

Quince cultivars

Quinces	Comments	Harvest					
		San Joaquin Valley	Sacramento Valley	Central Coast	North Coast	Sierra foothills	Southern California
Champion	Green-yellow flesh. Pear-shaped fruit	early Oct	early Oct	Oct	Oct	Oct	early Oct
Orange	Orange-yellow flesh. Golden skin. Rich flavor. Low-chill cultivar	early Sep	early Sep	Sep	Sep	Sep	early Sep
Pineapple	The preferred cultivar. Pineapple flavor. White flesh. Golden skin. Low-chill fruit	early Oct	early Oct	Oct	Oct	Oct	early Oct
Smyrna	Large fruit with brown pubescence. Light, tender flesh. Yellow skin. Low-chill fruit	early Oct	early Oct	Oct	Oct	Oct	early Oct
Van Deman	Pale yellow, coarse flesh. Orange skin turns red when cooked	early Sep	early Sep	Sep	Sep	Sep	early Sep

Stone fruit

Almond

Almonds (*Prunus dulcis*) are stone fruit but are consumed as nuts. Please see "Nut crops," below.

Apricot

Apricots (*Prunus armeniaca* L.) (fig. 3.5) bloom in February and early March. In some areas of the state, such as the North Coast counties, this usually coincides with cold and rain; consistent crops are unlikely in these areas. Apricots perform best in climates with dry spring weather. They are susceptible to late-spring frosts. Bacterial canker is a

Figure 3.5. Apricots. *Photo:* Milan Krstic, iStockphoto.com.

common disease of young trees in California. Plant trees at a spacing of about 10 to 20 feet. Apricots are mostly self-fruitful and ripen in May to July (100–120 days from full bloom). The hot weather in areas of the Central Valley can cause the fruit of susceptible varieties to "pit burn" (soften and turn brown around the pit), which lowers quality. Trees are susceptible to Eutypa canker and are commonly pruned in the summer or when the potential for rain is otherwise low.

Apricot rootstocks

Apricot rootstocks	Comments
Citation	One of the best rootstocks for apricots. Slightly dwarfing. Less susceptible to bacterial canker; tolerant of wet feet
Lovell Peach	Imparts some resistance to bacterial canker. Susceptible to oak root fungus. Not as tolerant of wet soil as other apricot rootstocks
Marianna 2624	Somewhat resistant to oak root fungus. Tolerates wet feet much better than apricot or peach rootstock. Space trees 20 feet apart
Prunus besseyi	Semidwarfing rootstock. Short-lived. Suckers profusely. Produces inferior fruit in the scion cultivar

Apricot scion cultivars

		Harvest					
Apricot scions	Comments	San Joaquin Valley	Sacramento Valley	Central Coast	North Coast	Sierra foothills	Southern California
Autumn Royal	Blenheim sport (mutation). Ripens in late summer to fall	Jun	Jun	early Jul	late Jun	late Jun	Jun
Moorpark	Excellent flavor, ripens unevenly, highly colored	Jun	Jun	early Jul	late Jun	late Jun	Jun
Patterson	Excellent flavor; versatile—useful for canning and freezing as well as fresh consumption	early June	mid-Jun	mid-Jun	mid-Jun	mid-Jun	June
Royal (Blenheim)	Large, very flavorful, used for eating fresh and drying. Can have pit burn symptoms in the Central Valley	Jun	Jun	early Jul	late Jun	late Jun	Jun
Tilton	Large fruit, heavy producer. Mild flavor. Used for canning	early Jul	Jul	late Jul	late Jul	Jul	Jul
Low-chill	These apricot cultivars are adapted to the low latitudes of Southern California because they have low winter chilling requirements (<300 hr)	Early Gold, Goldkist, Newcastle					
Other cultivars	These cultivars should be evaluated for your climate zone and site before being selected	Earl Golden, Gold Cot, Golden Amber, Goldrich, Honey Cot, King, Pomo, Riland, Rosa, Royalty, Sun Glo, Tom Cot					

Cherry

Two types of cherries (*Prunus avium* L., *Prunus cerasus* L.) can be planted: sweet, for fresh eating (fig. 3.6), and sour, for pies and preserves. Generally, cherries are the most difficult fruit trees to keep alive. They do not tolerate poor drainage, and management of water and irrigation is critical. They are very susceptible to brown rot, bacterial canker, canker diseases, root and crown rots, several viruses, and gophers. Trees should be planted 14 to 20 feet apart in well-drained soil and up on a small mound or berm. Most sweet cherry varieties require cross-pollination (many cultivars are self-sterile and intra-sterile, as noted below). Sour cherries are self-fertile and do not require pollenizers, but perform poorly and are short-lived in the hotter areas of California. The fruit of both types require less than 100 days to mature.

Figure 3.6. Sweet cherries. *Photo:* P. M. Vossen.

Cherry rootstocks

Cherry rootstocks	Comments
Colt	Somewhat dwarfing rootstock, with slight resistance to Phytophthora. The leading rootstock in California
Gisela series	In most cases, these dwarfing rootstocks produce smaller trees (8–10 ft.) and may impart increased susceptibility to bacterial canker. They also tend to impart early bearing. The smaller trees are easier to cover with netting to discourage birds. Most lose production potential after 8 to 10 years
Mahaleb	Very susceptible to root and crown rots. Some resistance to buckskin virus, bacterial canker, and root lesion nematode. Better salt tolerance than Colt
Mazzard	Good rootstock for cherries in coastal California. Produces a large, vigorous tree that is delayed in coming into bearing. Less susceptible to root rots and gophers than Mahaleb but more susceptible to bacterial canker than Mahaleb
Stockton Morello	Somewhat dwarfing rootstock. Not readily available. Makes an overgrowth at the bud union. Propagated from a cutting. As tolerant as Mazzard to wet feet. Somewhat resistant to gophers; less susceptible to bacterial canker. Generally a very good rootstock

Sweet cherry scion cultivars

Sweet cherry scions	Comments	Harvest					
		San Joaquin Valley	Sacramento Valley	Central Coast	North Coast	Sierra foothills	Southern California
Benton	Newer variety, similar to Bing in appearance and ripening. Self-fruitful	early Jun	early Jun	mid-Jun	mid-Jun	mid-Jun	NA
Bing	Industry standard. Deep mahogany red fruit. Produces very heavily. Very susceptible to bacterial canker. Pollenized by Van, Black Tartarian, or Sam. Bing, Lambert, and Royal-Ann will not pollinate each other (they are intrasterile)	early Jun	early Jun	mid-Jun	mid-Jun	mid-Jun	NA

Sweet cherry scion cultivars, continued

Sweet cherry scions	Comments	Harvest					
		San Joaquin Valley	Sacramento Valley	Central Coast	North Coast	Sierra foothills	Southern California
Black Tartarian	Small, black fruit. A good pollenizer for Bing and most other cultivars	Jun	Jun	late Jun	late Jun	late Jun	NA
Brooks	A large red fruit with excellent mild flavor. Produces few doubles even in hot climates	mid-May	mid-May	Jun	Jun	Jun	NA
Early Burlat	Moderate-size fruit. Ripens 2 wk before Bing. Soft flesh. Pollenized by Bing and Tartarian	mid-May	mid-May	Jun	Jun	Jun	NA
Early Ruby	Early season. Large, dark red fruit. Prolific. Fruit hold on tree	early Jun	early Jun	Jun	Jun	Jun	NA
Lambert	Dark, large, firm fruit. Pollenized by Van. Late season. Lambert, Bing, and Royal-Ann do not pollinate each other	late Jun	late Jun	Jul	Jul	Jul	NA
Lapins	Large size, good flavor. Ripens 1 to 2 wk after Bing. Self-fruitful	mid-Jun	mid-Jun	late Jun	late Jun	late Jun	NA
Rainier	Yellow-red blush. Large, crack-resistant fruit	Jun	Jun	late Jun	late Jun	Jun	NA
Royal-Ann	Yellow fruit with a red blush. Pollenized by Van. Late season. Royal-Ann, Lambert, and Bing will not pollinate each other	early Jun	early Jun	Jun	Jun	Jun	NA
Stella	Dark-fleshed fruit. Matures just after Bing. Self-fruitful but often sets better with pollinizer	late Jun	late Jun	Jul	Jul	Jul	NA
Tulare	Dark red, dense flesh with very good flavor, average size. Little doubling and somewhat resistant to rain cracking. Excellent pollinizer for Brooks	mid-May	mid-May	Jun	Jun	Jun	NA
Van	Large, dark fruit. Pollenized by Bing or Lambert	Jun	Jun	late Jun	late Jun	Jun	NA
Low-chill	None available						

Sour cherry scion cultivars

Sour cherry scions	Comments	Harvest					
		San Joaquin Valley	Sacramento Valley	Central Coast	North Coast	Sierra foothills	Southern California
Early Richmond	Very early in season. Bright red fruit	early Jun	early Jun	Jun	Jun	Jun	NA
Meteor	Semidwarf	early Jun	early Jun	Jun	Jun	Jun	NA
Montmorency	The leading sour cultivar. Medium-sized, dark red fruit	early Jun	early Jun	Jun	Jun	Jun	NA
North Star	Semidwarf. Self-fruitful	early Jun	early Jun	Jun	Jun	Jun	NA
Low-chill	None available						

Nectarine

Nectarines *(Prunus persica)* are fuzzless peaches (fig. 3.7). They do well in most of California if given the proper growing conditions. Nectarines require very well-drained soil, abundant nitrogen fertility, plenty of summer water, fruit thinning, and sprays to prevent peach leaf curl and brown rot. Nectarines are very susceptible to thrips damage (fruit scarring or russetting). New cultivar developments have greatly improved this fruit as a tree for backyard and commercial use. Trees can bear the second year. Nectarines (like peaches) are self-fruitful and do not require a pollenizer tree. Tree spacing should be about 8 to 12 feet.

Figure 3.7. Nectarines, with smooth skin. *Photo:* P. M. Vossen.

Nectarine rootstocks

Nectarine rootstocks	Comments
Citation	A peach-plum hybrid that provides some dwarfing and usually results in short-lived trees. Not recommended for nectarine or peach
Lovell Peach	The best choice for coastal California. A seedling that tolerates wet winter soil better than any other peach rootstock. Produces a full-sized tree that is managed easily. Plant 8 to 14 feet apart
Nemaguard Peach	The best choice for the Central Valley. A nematode-resistant rootstock best adapted to sandy, dry sites
Prunus besseyi	Semidwarfing rootstock. Suckers profusely. Produces inferior fruwit on the scion cultivar. Has not performed well. Somewhat incompatible with all nectarine cultivars

Nectarine scion cultivars

Nectarine scions	Comments	Harvest					
		San Joaquin Valley	Sacramento Valley	Central Coast	North Coast	Sierra foothills	Southern California
Arctic Glo	Small. Fantastic flavor. White flesh. Early	mid-Jun	mid-Jun	early Jul	Jun	Jun	Jun
Fairlane	Outstanding-quality late nectarine, moderate size	early Sep	early Sep	mid-Sep	mid-Sep	mid-Sep	Sep
Fantasia	Large, brightly colored yellow freestone. Late	late Jul	Aug	late Aug	mid-Aug	Aug	Aug
Flamekist	Excellent quality. Large, firm, yellow, clingstone	late Aug	early Sep	Sep	Sep	Sep	Sep
Flavortop	Large, excellent flavor. Yellow, freestone. Midseason	mid-Jul	late Jul	Aug	Aug	Aug	late Jul
Goldmine	Large, great flavor. White flesh. Freestone	Aug	late Aug	Sep	Sep	Sep	Sep

Nectarine scion cultivars, continued

Nectarine scions	Comments	San Joaquin Valley	Sacramento Valley	Central Coast	North Coast	Sierra foothills	Southern California
		Harvest					
Heavenly White	Large, excellent flavor. White flesh	late Jul	late Jul	mid-Aug	early Aug	early Aug	NA
May Grand	Large, yellow-fruited, freestone. Early and with high quality. High chilling requirement	early Jun	mid-Jun	late Jun	late Jun	Jun	Jun
Panamint	Medium-size fruit. Red skin, golden flesh. Freestone, low-chill cultivar	late Jul	early Aug	Aug	Aug	Aug	Aug
Red Gold	Large, excellent flavor. Stores well. Late	late Aug	early Sep	Sep	Sep	Sep	Sep
Rose	Old favorite white freestone with excellent flavor and low-chilling requirement	mid-Jul	late Jul	Aug	Aug	Aug	late Jul
Royal Giant	Large fruit with excellent flavor and quality	early August	early August	mid-Aug	mid-Aug	mid-Aug	Aug
Ruby Grand	Moderate-sized fruit with outstanding classic nectarine flavor	mid-Jul	mid-Jul	late Jul	late Jul	late Jul	Jul
Snow Queen	Earl-season white freestone, juicy and tasty	late Jun	Jul	late Jul	late Jul	late Jul	Jul
Summer Grand	One of the best. Large, yellow, freestone	mid-Jul	late Jul	Aug	Aug	Aug	late Jul
Low-chill	These nectarine cultivars are adapted to the low latitudes of Southern California because they have low winter chilling requirements	Desert Dawn, Desert Delight, Panamint, Pioneer, Rose, Silver Lode					

Peach

Peaches *(Prunus persica)* are very popular fruit trees that can be grown successfully in many parts of California (fig. 3.8). They require adequate summer watering, deep and well-drained soil, high nitrogen fertility, fruit thinning, and sprays to prevent peach leaf curl and brown rot. Peach trees are short-lived (15–20 yr). Peaches (like nectarines) are self-fruitful (self-compatible), which means that they do not require a pollenizer tree. Plant trees 12 by 16 feet to 18 by 18 feet apart.

Figure 3.8. Peaches, with fuzzy skin. *Photo:* P. M. Vossen.

Peach rootstocks

Peach rootstocks	Comments
Citation	A peach-plum hybrid that provides some dwarfing and usually results in short-lived trees. Not recommended for nectarine or peach
Lovell Peach	The best choice for coastal California. A seedling that tolerates wet winter soil better than any other peach rootstock, but still requires good drainage. Produces a full-sized, small tree that is managed easily. Plant 8 to 14 feet apart
Nemaguard Peach	The best choice for the Central Valley. A nematode-resistant rootstock best adapted to sandy, dry sites. Full-size tree
Prunus besseyi	Semidwarfing rootstock. Suckers profusely. Produces inferior fruit on the scion cultivar. Has not performed well. Somewhat incompatible with all peach cultivars

Peach scion cultivars

Thousands of peach cultivars have been developed worldwide. Some perform better in warmer areas; others have better fruit quality when grown in cooler climates along the coast of California. Three listed below (La Feliciana, Loring, and Veteran) are somewhat more disease resistant than the others

Peach scions	Comments	Harvest					
		San Joaquin Valley	Sacramento Valley	Central Coast	North Coast	Sierra foothills	Southern California
Autumn Gold	Medium-large fruit. Yellow flesh. Keeps well	Sep	Sep	Oct	Oct	Oct	NA
Babcock	Medium-size. White flesh. Freestone, low-chill cultivar	late Jun	Jul	Jul	late Jul	Jul	late Jun
Earligrande	Excellent flavor. Yellow-red blush. Semi-freestone, low-chill cultivar	May	late May	Jun	Jun	Jun	May
Early Elberta	Very similar to Fay Elberta but ripens 10–15 d earlier	mid-Jul	mid-Jul	late Jul	late Jul	late Jul	NA
Fairtime	Large fruit. Yellow, firm flesh. Excellent flavor	Sep	Sep	Oct	Oct	Oct	NA
Fay Elberta	Large fruit. Yellow flesh. Freestone	late Jul	late Jul	mid-Aug	early Aug	Aug	NA
Forty-Niner	Large fruit. Yellow flesh. Freestone	late Jul	late Jul	mid-Aug	early Aug	Aug	NA
Indian Blood	Cling. Red skin and flesh. Tart. Prolific	late Aug	late Aug	Sep	Sep	Sep	NA
Loring	Very large fruit. Red skin. Yellow flesh. Freestone	late Jul	Aug	late Aug	late Aug	Aug	NA
Nectar	White flesh. Pink skin. Excellent flavor	late Jul	late Jul	mid-Aug	early Aug	Aug	NA
O'Henry	One of the best. Large fruit. Yellow flesh. Freestone. Useful for freezing and drying	late Jul	late Jul	mid-Aug	early Aug	Aug	NA
Redhaven	Yellow. Semi-freestone. Needs heavy thinning	early Jul	Jul	late Jul	late Jul	Jul	NA
Rio Oso Gem	Very large fruit. Yellow flesh. Freestone	Aug	late Aug	Sep	Sep	Sep	Sep

Peach scion cultivar, continued

Peach scions	Comments	San Joaquin Valley	Sacramento Valley	Central Coast	North Coast	Sierra foothills	Southern California
		Harvest					
Springcrest	Medium-sized. Yellow flesh. Semi-freestone	early Jun	mid-Jun	late Jun	late Jun	late Jun	NA
Suncrest	Large fruit. Yellow flesh. Freestone. Midseason	early Jul	Jul	late Jul	late Jul	Jul	NA
Veteran	Red blush. Elberta type. Freestone. Dependable, heavy producer, excellent flavor	late Jul	Aug	late Aug	late Aug	Aug	NA
Low-chill	These peach cultivars are adapted to the low latitudes of Southern California because they have low winter chilling requirements	August Pride, Babcock, Bonita, Desertgold, Early Amber, Earligrande, Florida Grand, FlordaPrince, Midpride, Tropic-Berta, Topic Sweet					

Plum and prune

Plum (*Prunus domestica, Prunus salicina*) trees are among the best-adapted fruit trees for almost any location in California. They are easy to grow. Available rootstocks are very tolerant of wet winter soil. Plum and prune bloom late enough to avoid most spring frosts and experience few pest problems. Plum trees get relatively large and require spacing of 12 to 18 feet. Most plums, but not all, require cross-pollination to set adequate crops; plan to plant two different cultivars. There are two different kinds of plums: Japanese (*Prunus salicina*) and European (*Prunus domestica*). European types are either very sweet fresh plums or plums used for drying (prunes) (fig. 3.9). Most Japanese plums bloom earlier and mature earlier than European plums, and they typically require less chilling (fig. 3.10). Both types of plums require about 140 to 170 days to mature.

Figure 3.9. European plums (can be dried as prunes). *Photo:* P. M. Vossen.

Figure 3.10. Japanese plums. *Photo:* P. M. Vossen.

Plum and prune rootstocks

Plum and prune rootstocks	Comments
Citation	A peach-plum hybrid that produces a tree about 80% the size of standard. Tolerates wet soil. One of the best rootstocks for Japanese plums, but of questionable value for prunes
Lovell Peach	Less susceptible to bacterial canker, but the most intolerant of heavy soil, wet feet, oak root fungus, and root rots. Produces a moderately large tree that fruits earlier and sets more consistent crops. Compatible with most plum or prune cultivars
Marianna 2624	The overall best choice. Resistant to oak root fungus, root rots, root knot nematodes, and crown gall, but susceptible to bacterial canker and root lesion nematode. A cutting that is shallow-rooted and produces a smaller tree. It is the best adapted to poor, wet soil conditions, but suckers heavily
Myrobalan 29C	A cutting selection immune to root knot nematodes. Susceptible to oak root fungus, root rot, and root lesion nematode. Produces a tree with just a little less vigor than the Myrobalan seedling
Myrobalan Seedling	The largest and most vigorous of the plum or prune rootstocks. Hardy, long-lived, and adapted to most soil. Tolerates wet winter soil conditions. Susceptible to oak root fungus and nematodes, but somewhat resistant to root and crown rots
Nemaguard Peach	Nematode-resistant rootstock best adapted to sandy, dry sites. Full-sized tree that is suitable for Japanese plum
Prunus besseyi	Semidwarfing rootstock. Suckers profusely. Produces inferior fruit quality on the scion cultivar. Partially incompatible with all plum cultivars

Plum scion cultivars

Plum scions	Comments	Harvest					
		San Joaquin Valley	Sacramento Valley	Central Coast	North Coast	Sierra foothills	Southern California
Autumn Rosa	Large. Purple skin. Self-fertile. Japanese plum	late Aug	late Aug	Sep	Sep	Sep	NA
Beauty	Green skin, amber flesh, heart-shaped. Poor keeper. Japanese plum	Jun	Jun	Jul	Jul	Jun	Jun
Burgundy	Red skin and flesh. Self-fertile. Holds well. About 250–350 hr chilling	late Jul	early Aug	mid-Aug	mid-Aug	mid-Aug	Aug
Casselman	Moderate-size, dark purple plum with orange flesh and excellent flavor and very long storage life. Self-fertile and a good pollinizer	early Sep	early Sep	Sep	Sep	Sep	NA
El Dorado	Purple skin. Amber flesh. Large, oblong	early Jul	mid-Jul	Aug	Jul	Jul	Jul
Elephant Heart	Purple skin with red flesh. Large, heart-shaped. Japanese plum. Tart flavor. High chilling requirement.	Aug	Aug	late Aug	late Aug	Aug	NA
Friar	Black skin. Amber flesh. Average taste, old cultivar. Japanese plum	mid-Jul	mid-Jul	late Jul	late Jul	Jul	NA

Plum scion cultivars, continued

Plum scions	Comments	Harvest					
		San Joaquin Valley	Sacramento Valley	Central Coast	North Coast	Sierra foothills	Southern California
Golden Nectar	Large. Yellow flesh. Tender skin. Great flavor. Japanese plum	late Aug	late Aug	Sep	Sep	Sep	NA
Howard Wonder	Large, pink skin. Yellow flesh. Japanese plum	early Aug	early Aug	late Aug	late Aug	Aug	NA
Kelsey	Green-yellow skin and flesh. Japanese plum	early Aug	early Aug	late Aug	late Aug	Aug	Aug
Laroda	Red-purple skin. Yellow flesh. Excellent flavor	mid-Jul	mid-Jul	late Jul	late Jul	late July	Jul
Late Santa Rosa	Very similar to Santa Rosa but ripens about 3–4 wk later	mid-Jul	mid-Jul	late Jul	late Jul	late Jul	late Jul
Mariposa	Green-yellow skin. Red flesh. Large, heart-shaped. Japanese plum. 250–300 hours chilling. Use Santa Rosa, Nubiana, or Laroda as pollinizer	Aug	Aug	late Aug	late Aug	Aug	Aug
Nubiana	Reddish-purple skin. Yellow flesh. Flat shape, compact upright tree. Japanese plum. Self-fertile	early Aug	early Aug	late Aug	late Aug	Aug	NA
President	Large. Blue skin. Yellow flesh. European plum	late Aug	late Aug	Sep	Sep	Sep	NA
Roysum	Light purple skin. Yellow flesh	Sep	Sep	Oct	Oct	Oct	NA
Santa Rosa	Purple skin. Amber flesh. Excellent flavor. Japanese plum	mid-Jun	mid-Jun	late Jun	mid-Jun	late Jun	late Jun
Satsuma	Red skin and flesh. Small, round. Japanese plum	early Aug	early Aug	late Aug	late Aug	Aug	Jul
Shiro	Light golden-yellow skin. Yellow flesh. Delicate flavor	early Jul	early Jul	late Jul	mid-Jul	Jul	NA
Simka	Dark black skin. Yellow flesh. Oblong. Self-fertile	early Aug	early Aug	late Aug	late Aug	Aug	NA
Sprite Cherry Plum	Black, sweet skin. Exotic flavor. Small	early Aug	early Aug	late Aug	late Aug	Aug	NA
Wickson	Green-yellow skin. Yellow flesh. Large, heart-shaped. Japanese plum	Aug	Aug	Aug	late Aug	late Aug	NA
Low-chill	These plum cultivars are adapted to the low latitudes of Southern California because they have lower winter chilling requirements	Beauty Burgundy, Delight, Howard Wonder, Kelsey, Mariposa, Meredith, Methley, Santa Rosa, Satsuma, Sprite					

Prune scion cultivars

Prune scions	Comments	Harvest					
		San Joaquin Valley	Sacramento Valley	Central Coast	North Coast	Sierra foothills	Southern California
French	Medium-size fruit. Self-fertile. Late-maturing. European plum	Aug	Aug	late Aug	late Aug	Aug	NA
Green Gage	Greenish-yellow skin. Amber flesh. Old, European plum	Aug	Aug	late Aug	late Aug	Aug	NA
Imperial	Large fruit. Requires cross pollination. Late-maturing. European plum	Aug	Aug	late Aug	late Aug	Aug	NA
Italian	Large fruit. Purple skin. Yellow flesh. European plum	Aug	Aug	late Aug	late Aug	Aug	NA
Tulare Giant	Large fruit with excellent flavor. Suitable for fresh consumption. Pollinize with 'Muir Beauty.' European plum	early Aug	early Aug	late Aug	late Aug	Aug	NA

Plum-apricot hybrids

Plum-apricot hybrids (*Prunus salicina* × *Prunus armeniaca*), which include pluot, plumcot, and aprium, are relatively new tree fruit that are unique in that they are a cross between two similar species that normally do not cross. Pluot fruit resemble plums with smooth skin and narrower leaves while aprium fruit resemble apricots with fuzzy skin and wider leaves. Plumcots are variable and intermediate between these two. These hybrids are grown commercially and some are offered to home gardeners for production. Their primary attraction is their novel fruit quality. They require cross-pollination in most cases, so more than one cultivar of each type is needed. Their exact pollination requirements are not known, so it would be best to have one or more different plumcots, plums, pluots, apriums, or apricots in the vicinity as a pollen source. These hybrids also tend to take longer than nonhybrids to set fruit—usually 5 to 7 years. They tend to grow quite vigorously and may require summer pruning to maintain size within limited spaces.

Plum-apricot hybrid rootstocks

Plum-apricot hybrid rootstocks	Comments
Citation	A peach-plum hybrid that produces a tree about 80% the size of standard. Tolerates wet soil. One of the best rootstocks for Japanese plums and plum-apricot hybrids
Marianna 2624	Resistant to oak root fungus, root rots, root knot nematodes, and crown gall, but susceptible to bacterial canker and root lesion nematode. A cutting that is shallow-rooted and produces a smaller tree. It is the best for poor, wet soil conditions but tends to sucker
Myrobalan 29C	A cutting selection that is immune to root knot nematodes. Susceptible to oak root fungus, root rot, and root lesion nematode. Produces a tree with just a little less vigor than trees on Myrobalan seedling
Myrobalan Seedling	The largest and most vigorous of the plum or prune rootstocks. Hardy, long-lived, adapted to most soil. Tolerates wet winter soil conditions. Susceptible to oak root fungus and nematodes but somewhat resistant to root and crown rots
Nemaguard Peach	Nematode-resistant rootstock best adapted to sandy, dry sites. Full-sized tree that is suitable for Japanese plum and some plum-apricot hybrids

Plum-apricot hybrid scion cultivars

Plum-apricot hybrid scions	Comments	Harvest					
		San Joaquin Valley	Sacramento Valley	Central Coast	North Coast	Sierra foothills	Southern California
Dapple Dandy	Pluot. Pale green to yellow-red skin with pink flesh. Very large with small pit and excellent flavor. Requires pollinizer: Santa Rosa, Flavor Queen, or Flavor Supreme	early Aug	early Aug	mid-Aug	mid-Aug	mid-Aug	NA
Flavor Supreme	Pluot. Green to brown skin. Red, juicy flesh. Excellent size and flavor. Requires cross pollination—Santa Rosa and Late Santa Rosa suggested	early Jun	mid-Jun	Jul	Jul	Jul	NA
Flavor King	Pluot. Red-purple skin. Good size, irregular ripening, sweet flavor. Cross-pollinated with Flavor Grenade, Beauty Plum, or Burgundy Plum	early Aug	mid-Aug	late Aug	late Aug	NA	NA
Flavor Queen	Pluot. Green-golden skin. Yellow, firm flesh. Good size. Excellent, very sweet flavor	late Jul	mid-Jul	Aug	Aug	Aug	NA
Flavor Grenade	Pluot. Green skin with red blush. Elongated shape, excellent flavor. Best pollinated with Burgundy plum	early Aug	mid-Aug	late Aug	late Aug	late Aug	NA
Flavorella	Plumcot. Golden-yellow skin. Very sweet, excellent flavor	early Jun	mid-Jun	Jul	Jul	Jul	NA
Flavor Ann	Aprium. Golden skin and flesh. Strong, sweet apricot flavor	mid-May	late May	Jun	Jun	Jun	NA
Flavor Delight	Aprium. Golden skin and flesh. Strong, sweet apricot flavor. Reliable production. Sets best with cross-pollination from an apricot	mid-May	late May	Jun	Jun	Jun	NA
Low-chill	These cultivars are adapted to the low elevations of Southern California	Flavor King, Flavor Grenade, Flavor Rosa, and Flavor Delight					

Nuts

Almond

Almonds (*Prunus dulcis*, formerly *Prunus amygdalus*) (fig. 3.11) are stone fruit that are consumed as nuts. Most almonds produced commercially in the United States are grown in California. The earliest to bloom of stone fruit (February), almonds generally do poorly in North Coast counties, where the weather is cold and rainy when they bloom. Almonds are very susceptible to spring frosts and do not tolerate wet soil. The Central Valley and the drier regions of the South Coast are very favorable for almonds. Almonds are very susceptible to bacterial canker. Many varieties require cross-pollination. Some new, commercially available varieties are self-compatible; however, they have not been not tested by the University of California for their performance in home gardens. Some are cross-unfruitful due to incompatibilities. Almonds are harvested by shaking trees when hulls begin to split. Almonds need 180 to 240 days for nuts to mature. After harvest, the nuts (embryo and shell) are dried to a minimum moisture content.

Figure 3.11. Healthy almond fruit. *Photo:* Jack Kelly Clark.

Almond rootstocks

Almond rootstocks	Comments
Almond Seedling	Long-lived, deep-rooted; needs well-drained soil. Not used much due to disease susceptibility
Lovell Peach	Produces a smaller tree than almond rootstock; susceptible to many diseases and root knot nematodes
Mariana 2624 Plum	Marginally compatible with most almond cultivars. Resistant to oak root fungus, root rots, root knot nematodes, and crown gall, but susceptible to bacterial canker and root lesion nematode. A cutting that is shallow-rooted and produces a smaller tree. It is the best for poor, wet soil conditions but tends to sucker
Almond-peach hybrids	Newer stocks that are nematode-resistant and vigorous. Provide good anchorage compared to Nemaguard
Nemaguard Peach	Nematode-resistant; good for sandy soil

Almond scion cultivars

Almond scions	Comments	Harvest					
		San Joaquin Valley	Sacramento Valley	Central Coast	North Coast	Sierra foothills	Southern California
Carmel	Excellent quality. Nut well sealed in the shell. Excellent pollenizer	Aug	Aug	Sep	Sep	Aug	Aug
Mission	Late-blooming, productive tree. Hard shell, short kernel	Aug	Aug	Sep	Sep	Aug	Aug
Neplus Ultra	Large, soft-shelled nut. Long, flat kernel. Good pollenizer	Aug	Aug	Sep	Sep	Aug	Aug
Nonpareil	The most popular paper-shelled cultivar. Interfruitful with Price, Mission, and Carmel	Aug	Aug	Sep	Sep	Aug	Aug
Price	Very similar to Nonpareil. A good pollenizer	Aug	Aug	Sep	Sep	Aug	Aug

Chestnut

Little research has been done on the chestnut (*Castanaea* spp.) in California (fig. 3.12). Thus, we know little about its specific adaptability or productive capacity. Chestnuts are monoecious (separate female and male flowers are borne on one plant, like walnuts) and some cultivars are self-unfruitful; therefore, two different cultivars should be grown for cross-pollination to produce consistent crops. Trees reach a height of 80 feet and spread to 60 feet under ideal conditions. Chestnuts are excellent and fruitful shade trees if grown in very well drained soil. Chestnuts are almost pest-free in California. Seedling is the only known rootstock. Edible chestnuts should not be confused with the poisonous California buckeye (*Aesculus californica*). Fresh chestnuts contain about 50 percent moisture. Unlike other nuts, chestnuts have low oil content (8%).

Figure 3.12. Chestnuts without the burr: with the hull, without the hull but with the pellicle, and nut meat without the pellicle.

Chestnut cultivars

		Harvest					
Chestnuts	Comments	San Joaquin Valley	Sacramento Valley	Central Coast	North Coast	Sierra foothills	Southern California
Colossal	The industry standard and the overall best choice. Large-fruited. Excellent quality. Parentage unknown	early Oct	early Oct	late Oct	late Oct	mid-Oct	early Oct
Dunstan	A cross of American and Chinese cultivars. Medium-small nuts. Sweet and blight-resistant. Late-flowering	early Oct	early Oct	late Oct	late Oct	mid-Oct	early Oct
Eurobella	Large nut. Good pollenizer for Colossal	early Oct	early Oct	late Oct	late Oct	mid-Oct	early Oct
Seedling	Not a "named" cultivar. Each tree is genetically different. Unknown fruit quality. Unknown tree shape and fruit size. Only known rootstock	early Oct	early Oct	late Oct	late Oct	mid-Oct	early Oct
Silverleaf	Medium-sized nut. Good pollenizer for Colossal, but shell splits are a problem	early Oct	early Oct	late Oct	late Oct	mid-Oct	early Oct
Others	These cultivars are available for trial	Castel del Rio, Fowler, Marrone di Maradi, Montesol					

Filbert (hazelnut)

The nut-bearing filbert (*Corylus* spp.) plants grow naturally as suckering shrubs but can be trained as trees by continually removing the suckers. They reach a height of 15 to 20 feet, with an even greater spread. Filberts are monoecious (with separate male and female flowers on the same plant, like walnuts) but are self-unfruitful; cross-pollination is required to set fruit, so two different cultivars must be planted. Filberts are grown commercially in Oregon. Crop production is not consistent in California, which may be due to summer heat that causes catkins (male flowers) to fall off prematurely. Filberts are grown on their own roots. They need a 180-day growing season. Filbert fruit (fig. 3.13) are contained in a spiny burr that turns brown and splits into sections.

Figure 3.13. Filberts, or hazelnuts, in the shell. *Photo:* P. M. Vossen.

Filbert cultivars

Filberts	Comments	San Joaquin Valley	Sacramento Valley	Central Coast	North Coast	Sierra foothills	Southern California
		Harvest					
Barcelona	The old industry standard. Use Davianna or Du Chilly as pollenizer	Sep	Sep	Oct	late Sep	late Sep	NA
Brixnut	A secondary main production nut. Use Davianna or Du Chilly as a pollenizer	Sep	Sep	Oct	late Sep	late Sep	NA
Butler	Pollenizer for Ennis	Sep	Sep	Oct	late Sep	late Sep	NA
Davianna	Use Barcelona or Du Chilly as a pollenizer	Sep	Sep	Oct	late Sep	late Sep	NA
Du Chilly	Use Barcelona or Davianna as a pollenizer	Sep	Sep	Oct	late Sep	late Sep	NA
Ennis	A new cultivar that has better quality than Barcelona. Use Butler as a pollenizer	Sep	Sep	Oct	late Sep	late Sep	NA
White Aveline	General pollenizer	Sep	Sep	Oct	late Sep	late Sep	NA

Pecan

Pecans *(Carya illoensis)* are grown on seedling rootstocks. Pecans are not a good choice for Northern California. They require a deep, well-drained soil, a hot climate to mature the nuts properly, and adequate soil moisture. Most varieties are attractive to aphids that drip honeydew, creating sticky surfaces. At least two different cultivars must be planted for good pollination, because even though pecans are largely self-fertile, the flowers are dichogamous, which means that there is little overlap between pollen shedding and stigma receptivity. Most cultivars require at least 180 days for nuts to mature. Commercial production in California is limited to the southern San Joaquin Valley. Pecans are native to the United States and grow well in the south-central states. Their native range extends into the Midwest; cultivars grown there tolerate cold winters and short growing seasons. The cultivars listed here require a very long growing season and freedom from frost. They can be tried in the warmest regions of the state. The trees get as large as walnut trees and should be trained as central leader or modified central leader.

Pecan scion cultivars

		Harvest					
Pecans	Comments	San Joaquin Valley	Sacramento Valley	Central Coast	North Coast	Sierra foothills	Southern California
Apache	Late pollen shed. Early receptivity	Oct	late Oct	NA	NA	late Oct	late Oct
Barton	Early pollen shed and receptivity	Oct	late Oct	NA	NA	late Oct	late Oct
Bradley	Excellent pollenizer for Western Schley	Oct	late Oct	NA	NA	late Oct	late Oct
Choctaw	Late pollen shed. Early receptivity	Oct	late Oct	NA	NA	late Oct	late Oct
Comanche	Late pollen shed. Early receptivity	Oct	late Oct	NA	NA	late Oct	late Oct
Shawnee	Early pollen shed. Midseason receptivity	Oct	late Oct	NA	NA	late Oct	late Oct
Sioux	Early pollen shed and receptivity	Oct	late Oct	NA	NA	late Oct	late Oct
Western Schley	Early pollen shed and receptivity	Oct	late Oct	NA	NA	late Oct	late Oct
Wichita	Late pollen shed. Early receptivity	Oct	late Oct	NA	NA	late Oct	late Oct

Pistachio

Pistachio (*Pistacia vera)* trees require long, hot, dry summers and mild winters. April frosts kill flowers, and cool summers do not promote good kernel development. Adequate winter chilling and good weather (pistachio is wind pollinated) are required. Pistachios are a poor choice for coastal California and will not produce fruit in low elevations of Southern California. Most other warm regions in the state are well suited to backyard pistachio production. Pistachio trees are dioecious (male and female flowers on different trees); a male tree must be planted near or grafted onto a female tree to get a good crop set. Trees become large and should be planted about 20 feet apart. The nuts must be harvested before falling to the ground and the hulls must be removed by hand or they will dry onto the shell. Unless eaten green, pistachios must be roasted immediately after harvesting to prevent them from becoming moldy.

Pistachio rootstocks

Pistachio rootstocks	Comments
Pistacia atlantica	Resistant to many nematodes, but susceptible to cold (below 15–20°F) and Verticillium wilt. Not commercially available
Pistacia integerrima	Resistant to *Verticillium*. Very susceptible to cold damage
Pistacia terebinthus	The best rootstock. Most tolerant of cold. Resistant to nematodes. Susceptible to Verticillium wilt. Not commercially available
UCB-1	A hybrid of a *P. atlantica* female with a *P. integerrima* male. Clones and seedling rootstocks available. Cold- and salt-tolerant. Most commonly used rootstock, currently
Plaltinum	A hybrid of a *P. integerrima* female and *P. atlantica* male. Only available as a clone

Pistachio scion cultivars

Pistachios	Comments	Harvest					
		San Joaquin Valley	Sacramento Valley	Central Coast	North Coast	Sierra foothills	Southern California
Kerman	Female. Late nut maturity. High blank nut %	Sep–Oct	late Oct	NA	NA	late Oct	late Oct
Peters*	Male. Pollenizer for Kerman. High chill requirement	—	—	—	—	—	—
Famoso†	Male. Pollenizer for Kerman	—	—	—	—	—	—
Golden Hills	Female. High splits. Few blanks	Sep	Sep	NA	NA	NA	NA
Lost Hills	Female. Large nuts. High splits, fewer blanks	Sep	Sep	NA	NA	NA	NA
Randy	Male. Pollenizer for Golden Hills and Lost Hills						
Gumdrop	Female. Early bloom and maturity. High splits	Aug–Sept	Sep	NA	NA	NA	NA
Tejon	Male. Pollenizer for Gumdrop						
Joley	Female. Smaller nuts. Few blanks. High splits. Not commercially available	Sept	late Oct	NA	NA	late Oct	late Oct
Sfax	Smaller, good-quality nuts. Not commercially available	Oct	late Oct	NA	NA	late Oct	late Oct

Note: "—" indicates that information is not available.

*Peters produces no crop.

†Famoso produces no crop.

Walnut

Walnuts (*Juglans regia*) need a deep, well-drained soil (at least 5 ft.). Shoots, particularly blossoms, do not tolerate frosts. (*Juglans hindsii* is the Northern California black walnut and is not usually planted for nuts. It is usually used as a rootstock.) Once growth begins in the spring, rainy weather can cause severe losses due to walnut blight. Trees range in size from very large (80 ft. tall) to medium height (40–50 ft. tall). They require a spacing of 30 to 60 feet. Walnut culture has changed drastically in the last few years due to the introduction of new cultivars. Production in coastal climates should be limited to the late-leafing cultivars. Walnuts are monoecious (with separate male and female flowers on one tree) and dichogamous (pollen is shed when female flowers are not receptive); two different cultivars must be planted to ensure overlapping bloom periods, fertilization, and fruit set. The fruit exhibit various colorations (fig. 3.14). Black cultivars are difficult to crack and to process.

Figure 3.14. Walnuts, showing different nut meat coloration. *Photo:* P. M. Vossen.

Black walnut scion cultivars

Black walnut scions	Comments	Harvest					
		San Joaquin Valley	Sacramento Valley	Central Coast	North Coast	Sierra foothills	Southern California
Seedling	Not a true cultivar. Seedlings of Northern California Black Walnut trees	Oct	late Oct	late Oct	late Oct	late Oct	NA

Eastern black walnut scion cultivars

Eastern black walnut scions	Comments	Harvest					
		San Joaquin Valley	Sacramento Valley	Central Coast	North Coast	Sierra foothills	Southern California
Thomas, Ohio, and Meyers	Cultivars that may be worthy of consideration	Oct	late Oct	late Oct	late Oct	late Oct	NA

Standard walnut scion cultivars

Standard walnut scions	Comments	Harvest					
		San Joaquin Valley	Sacramento Valley	Central Coast	North Coast	Sierra foothills	Southern California
Chandler	Best choice for coastal California. New cultivar. 80% fruitful lateral buds. Produces a smaller tree that requires careful pruning and training. Blooms late. Leafs out late	Oct	late Oct	late Oct	late Oct	late Oct	NA
Hartley	The main cultivar grown in California. Excellent-quality nuts. Huge tree but requires little pruning. 5% fruitful lateral buds. Leafs out late, blooms late. Good choice	Oct	late Oct	late Oct	late Oct	late Oct	NA
Howard	New cultivar. 80% fruitful lateral buds. Produces a smaller tree that requires careful pruning and training. Blooms late. Leafs out late	Oct	late Oct	late Oct	late Oct	late Oct	NA
Mayette	Old-time cultivar. Plant as a pollenizer for late-blooming cultivars. Poor producer. Leafs out late. Blooms late. Large tree	Oct	late Oct	late Oct	late Oct	late Oct	NA
S. Franquette	Old-time cultivar. Should be planted as a pollenizer for the late-blooming cultivars. Poor producer. Leafs out late. Blooms late. Large tree, but requires little pruning	Oct	late Oct	late Oct	late Oct	late Oct	NA
Tehama	Good choice. New cultivar. 80% fruitful lateral buds. Produces a smaller tree that requires careful pruning and training. Blooms late. Leafs out late	Oct	late Oct	late Oct	late Oct	late Oct	NA

Miscellaneous deciduous fruit

Fig

Figs (*Ficus carica* L.) can be grown easily, but they require a protected location in the cooler parts of the state because they require heat for the fruit to mature properly. Fig trees do best in well-drained soil but tolerate wet soil better than most other fruit trees. Gophers must be controlled. Figs are grown on their own roots from cuttings. Trees reach a height of 20 to 30 feet, with an equal spread, but can be pruned to a smaller size. Most cultivars do not require cross-pollination. Several cultivars set fruit (fig. 3.15) parthenocarpically, and several cultivars have two crops per year (shown below as "Jun/Sep"). The "breba" crop (first crop) matures in midsummer in 100 to 120 days, and the second (main) crop matures in late summer or fall. Figs require very little winter chilling and are considered a "borderline" temperate-zone species by many pomologists. The Smyrna types require caprification (pollination by Capri figs nearby).

Figure 3.15. Fig fruit. *Photo:* P. M. Vossen.

Fig scion cultivars

Fig scions	Comments	Harvest					
		San Joaquin Valley	Sacramento Valley	Central Coast	North Coast	Sierra foothills	Southern California
Adriatic	Good fresh but especially good for drying. Yellow skin and amber flesh	Jun/Sep	Jun/Sep	Oct	Oct	Jun/Sep	Jun/Sep
Black Mission	The most dependable cultivar for the home orchard. Purple-black skin with red flesh	Jun/Sep	Jun/Sep	Nov	Nov	Jun/Sep	Jun/Sep
Brown Turkey	Large fruit. Excellent quality. Purple-green skin. Red flesh	Jun/Sep	Jun/Sep	Nov	Nov	Jun/Sep	Jun/Sep
Italian Everbearing	Brown. Turkey type. Very prolific	Jun/Sep	Jun/Sep	Nov	Nov	Jun/Sep	Jun/Sep
Kadota	Requires high temperatures and a long growing season to perform well. Yellow-green fruit with amber flesh. Produces both breba and a second crop with moderate pruning	Jun/Sep	Jun/Sep	Nov	Nov	Jun/Sep	Jun/Sep
Osborn	Performs well only in cool coastal areas. Purple-bronze fruit with amber flesh. Very prolific	Jun/Sep	Jun/Sep	Oct	Oct	Jun/Sep	Jun/Sep
Sierra	Light colored skin with a fresh, sweet fruit flavor and a soft, almost creamy interior. Introduced by University of California breeders in 2005 to be used by growers in the Central Valley. Excellent fresh or dried	—	—	—	—	—	—
Panache Tiger Stripe	Light yellow–colored fig with green stripes. Red-purple interior with sweet raspberry-citrus flavors. Extended harvest to early November	—	—	—	—	—	—
White Genoa	Good for coastal locations. Large fruit. Yellow-green, thin skin. Strawberry flesh. Ripens when others won't	Jun/Sep	Jun/Sep	Oct	Oct	Jun/Sep	Jun/Sep

Note: "—" indicates that information is not available.

Persimmon

Oriental persimmon (*Diospyros kaki*) is a very good
fruit tree for home gardens (fig. 3.16). It blooms late,
avoiding spring frosts, and does not require much
winter chilling. It performs well throughout the state.
It does not need ideal soil, and it tolerates poor drainage in winter and dry conditions in summer. The
fruit are almost pest free. Oriental persimmons do
not need cross-pollination, but if cross-pollinated,
seeds will develop.

Figure 3.16. Persimmon. *Photo:* P. M. Vossen.

Persimmon rootstocks

Persimmon rootstocks	Comments
Diospyros kaki	An adequate rootstock. Produces a long taproot and small, branching, fibrous roots
Diospyros lotus	Most widely used seedling rootstock. Best choice. Compatible with most cultivars. Tolerates wet soil
Diospyros virginiana	This native species produces a very good, fibrous root system and tolerates drought and excess moisture fairly well, but may sucker profusely and may produce trees of variable size

Persimmon scions

Persimmon scions	Comments	Harvest					
		San Joaquin Valley	Sacramento Valley	Central Coast	North Coast	Sierra foothills	Southern California
Baru	Round, orange skin. Sweet brown flesh	Oct	late Oct	Nov	Nov	late Oct	late Oct
Diospyros virginiana	Native species, not a cultivar. Very small, very flavorful fruit. Must be eaten when soft	Oct	late Oct	Nov	Nov	late Oct	late Oct
Fuyu	Large, flat, orange-red color. Flesh is firm like an apple and nonastringent when ripe. Cross-pollination is not required, but when present, fruit will have seeds. Trees are smaller, requiring 14 to 16 ft. Fruit loses astringency at maturity while still firm and crunchy	Oct	late Oct	Nov	Nov	late Oct	late Oct
Hachiya	Large, deep orange-red, acorn-shaped fruit. Flesh turns brown around the seeds and must be very soft to eat. Does not need cross-pollination. Trees get large and require 20 ft. Fruit is astringent until very ripe and soft	Oct	late Oct	Nov	Nov	late Oct	late Oct
Hyakume	Cinnamon chocolate–colored flesh	Oct	late Oct	Nov	Nov	late Oct	late Oct

Further reading

Hasey, J. K., R. S. Johnson, J. A. Grant, and W. O. Reil, eds. 1994. Kiwifruit growing and handling. Oakland: UC Division of Agriculture and Natural Resources Publication 3344.

Larue, J. H., and R. S. Johnson, eds. 1989. Peaches, plums, and nectarines: Growing and handling for fresh market. Oakland: UC Agriculture and Natural Resources Publication 3331.

Micke, W. C., ed. 1996. Almond production manual. Oakland: UC Agriculture and Natural Resources Publication 3364.

Ramos, D. E., ed. 1997. Walnut production manual. Oakland: UC Division of Agriculture and Natural Resources Publication 3373.

Vossen, P. 2000. Chestnut culture in California. Oakland: UC Agriculture and Natural Resources Publication 8010. http://anrcatalog.ucdavis.edu

Vossen, P., and D. Silva. 2015. Temperate tree fruit and nut crops. In D. Pittenger, ed., California master gardener handbook, 2nd ed. Oakland: UC Agriculture and Natural Resources Publication 3382. 459–536.

Westwood, M. N. 2009. Temperate zone pomology: Physiology and culture. 3rd ed. Portland, OR: Timber Press.

Chapter 4

Orchard design and planting and care of young trees

Chuck A. Ingels

It can be exciting to think of a new orchard and the fruit it will produce. However, it's easy to rush too far ahead and end up having to fix problems that could have been anticipated. It's easier to move a tree with a pencil and eraser while making a plan than to move a tree that is already in the ground.

Planning and preparation

Fruit and nut trees are a long-term investment, so it is important that orchards or landscapes that include fruit trees be carefully designed and prepared. Factors to include in your planning include:

- source amount of irrigation water available
- water delivery method
- soil quality and adequate drainage
- sufficient sunlight (6 to 8 hours per day)
- species, varieties, and pollenizer requirements
- training method(s) to be used
- spacing and space requirements, including space to maneuver between trees or groups of trees
- location of any belowground wires or pipes, including septic systems

Site selection

Plant your new fruit trees where they will receive full sun for 6 to 8 or more hours per day during the growing season. A location with too much shade will reduce the amount and quality of fruit the tree can produce. Sunny exposures also encourage the best tree growth and development. Trees that are susceptible to wind or frost damage should be planted in locations that are sheltered from wind and where the trees may benefit from heat retained by buildings or trees.

Fruit and nut trees grow and produce best in soil that is at least 2 to 3 feet (1 m) deep and preferably 3 to 5 feet deep. The soil should be uniform, with no compacted or stratified soil layers, and well drained (without high clay content). If the soil in your garden is not deep enough, or you have removed or compacted some topsoil during construction, your trees' growth may be stunted and the fruit may be small. Special attention to watering and fertilization, however, may make it possible for you to grow fruit trees successfully in as little as 1 to 2 feet of good topsoil. Methods of improving poor soils are described below.

Select a site that has a ready supply of water from a hose or from drip or sprinkler irrigation. Bear in mind how large the tree will be when mature: An unpruned standard-sized fruit tree can reach 20 to 25 feet (7.5 m) or taller, so avoid planting trees under power lines or other overhead obstructions—unless the height will be controlled by pruning. Plant far enough away from fences, walls, buildings, and other trees for the future growth of the tree. In very unusual cases, the roots of fruit and nut trees can damage building foundations. Allow enough space around the tree for current and future pruning, spraying, harvesting, leaf raking, and other maintenance operations. Good air circulation around trees can help prevent disease. Take advantage of the fact that fruit trees can be quite beautiful when in bloom: Plant them where you can see and enjoy them. If you plant a tree near a sidewalk or lawn, be prepared to harvest fruit regularly in order to keep it from dropping to the ground and creating a nuisance. A backyard or side yard may be preferable to a front yard if fruit theft is a concern.

Preparing the planting site

Many home gardens have soil that is loose and well drained. Many others, however, have less-than-ideal soil conditions for drainage and root growth, including heavy clay soil, soil that has been compacted by heavy equipment, or layers of dense soil (hardpan) beneath the soil surface. Ideally, a compacted soil should be cultivated or excavated to a depth and width that will allow adequate root exploration and movement of water through the soil. Some commercial growers use tractor-mounted, deep-ripping shanks or backhoes before planting to break through compacted zones or to mix stratified soils. For the home gardener, it may be possible to break through compacted soil or hardpan with tools that are available at equipment rental outlets, such as pickaxes, powered soil augers, trenchers, or jackhammers with clay spade attachments (fig. 4.1). Such work is best done with soil that is neither too dry nor too wet, but that has the consistency of a wrung-out sponge. Other alternatives are simply to create large mounds, or berms, for tree planting (fig. 4.2)—or to build raised beds at the planting site about 1 to 2 feet tall and fill them with a mix of native soil and good-quality topsoil (fig. 4.3).

If you have deep, well-drained loam soil with good tilth, you will not have to add soil amendments or fertilizer to the soil at planting. You may, however, want to add compost, well-rotted manure, gypsum, fertilizer, or other amendments to your soil if it is less than ideal for planting. Use a rotary tiller or a spade when working the amendment in to make sure it is mixed thoroughly into the soil. In heavy clay soils, undecomposed and poorly mixed organic amendments may rot and become toxic to new roots. It is best to wait until new top growth is several inches long before you apply nitrogen fertilizer—young trees do not need nitrogen immediately, and nitrogen can readily leach through soil. Also, excessive nitrogen can burn young roots. If your soil requires added phosphorus or potassium, it is best to work it into the soil before you plant because these nutrients are not very mobile in soil.

Figure 4.2. Planting on berms is an excellent way to improve drainage around the root crown and to increase the loose soil for roots to explore. *Photo:* Paul Vossen.

Figure 4.3. This raised planter bed with sandy loam topsoil has been planted with dwarf citrus trees. The soil underneath is heavy clay with fractured hardpan. *Photo:* Chuck Ingels.

Figure 4.1. A jackhammer with a clay spade can be used to break up soil that has been compacted by heavy equipment. *Photo:* Chuck Ingels.

Soil sampling for nutrient analysis

To determine if soil nutrients and pH are appropriate or if toxic salts are present, it is wise to send a soil sample to a soil analytical laboratory, which can be found through an internet search. Contact a laboratory to ask about its pricing and its recommended sampling protocol. A soil analysis may not be necessary if trees and other plants are growing well in your area, or if you have just a few trees in a healthy landscape. But if tree problems occur in future years, another soil analysis can determine if nutrient levels have changed and if some nutrients have become deficient. If a soil nutrition problem is suspected at the planting site, the soil should be analyzed for pH and for levels of phosphorus, potassium, calcium, magnesium, sodium, and boron, as well as for salinity (total salts). Other micronutrients can also be sampled for an additional cost. Soil nitrogen levels are often included in a soil analysis, but this value is often not critical, since nitrogen is eventually required in most cases and is easy to add. (See chapter 6, "Fertilization," for more information.)

Since the majority of tree roots are in the top 2 feet of soil, it is ideal to take two soil samples—one from between 0 and 12 inches and another from between 12 and 24 inches. If different sections of your planting area are notably different from each other—sloping versus flat, for example—consider sampling these areas separately. A shovel works fine for sampling, but a soil sampling tube is useful for both soil sampling and later for determining soil moisture content (fig. 4.4). Remove mulch or other organic matter from the soil surface. Place soil from six or more spots in each area and at each depth in a clean paper bag and mix the soil thoroughly, crushing clods and removing roots and rocks. Place about a pint of this mixture in a sealable plastic bag and send it to the laboratory.

Orchard layout and spacing

Besides aesthetic design considerations, the main factors that determine spacing and layout are the intended training method and mature tree size. Genetic dwarf trees and trees on highly dwarfing rootstocks can be planted closer together than trees of standard size.

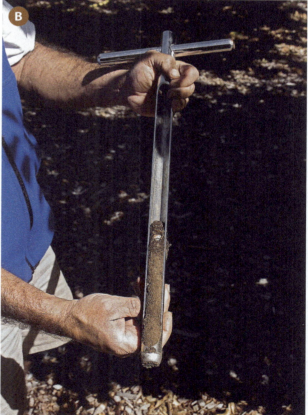

Figure 4.4. A soil sampling tube can help you determine soil condition and soil moisture content (A); a removed soil core (B). *Photos:* Chuck Ingels.

As you will see in chapter 7 ("Training and pruning"), there are many ways to train fruit trees. If you have a large planting area and your goal is maximum fruit production, you may want to consider using standard-size trees—with open-center training for stone fruit and almonds or central-leader training for pome fruit—with spacing of 20 feet between trees. With a large area you could also consider planting larger trees, such as walnuts or pecans, but be sure you have the ability to spray tall trees if needed. For best sunlight access, plan for the biggest trees to be planted north of smaller trees.

In a home orchard you can use planting patterns in aesthetically pleasing ways, but for maximum fruit production, you should plant trees in a square or triangular orientation (fig. 4.5). If you need to drive a tractor through the orchard, be sure the rows are far enough apart. Be sure to allow enough room to maneuver with an orchard ladder when the trees are mature. Orchards with wide spacing take much longer to come into full bearing than those with closer spacing. Ultimately, production is usually greatest with large open-center or central-leader trees.

If your main goal is maintenance without a ladder, consider planting genetic dwarf trees or using fruit-bush training. Genetic dwarf trees can be planted about 8 to 10 feet apart, or even closer.

A tree that will be trained as a fruit bush can also be planted about 8 to 10 feet apart, or as close as 4 to 6 feet in hedgerows. Spacing of 3 feet has been found by some to be too dense for vigorous trees because growth is unmanageable and production is reduced. You can also plant two, three, or four trees in a "hole," with the trees about 18 to 24 inches apart from each other. Ideally, different varieties of the same species should be used in a multi-tree cluster for similar growth habits and spray schedules. The varieties could be early-, mid-, and late- maturing for successive ripening, and pollinizer varieties can be included in the cluster if needed. Label each tree variety. Clusters of multiple trees should be spaced about 10 to 12 feet apart on center. Alternatively, to save money on tree costs, you could graft multiple varieties onto young fruit-bush trees (see chapter 8, "Budding and grafting").

Espalier training can be ideal for both long, narrow spaces and for open areas. Espalier-trained tress are also easy to cover with bird netting for pest manage-

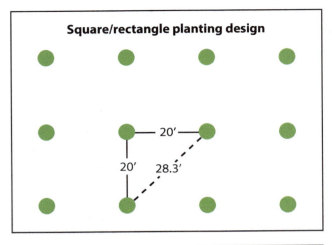

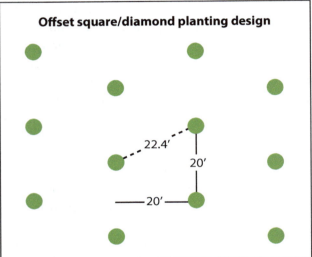

Figure 4.5. Examples of orchard planting plans.

ment purposes (see chapter 7, "Training and pruning"); using row cover is likewise straightforward. In-row spacing of espalier trees depends on trellis height and expected tree vigor. Trellis height is typically 6 to 8 feet; the higher the trellis, the closer the in-row planting distance can be. A full-size tree on a deep, fertile soil can quickly fill a trellis and then can become difficult to control, especially with most stone fruit and figs. For such trees, a spacing of 12 to 15 feet (3.7–4.6 m) is advisable. Trees on moderately dwarfing rootstocks, as well as most apples and pears, can be planted 8 to 10 feet apart, depending on the expected vigor. Genetic dwarf trees and trees on very dwarfing rootstocks can be planted as close as 3 to 5 feet apart; trees in modern high-density apple orchards are often planted 2 to 3 feet apart. Spacing of trellis rows depends on tree height. A good rule of thumb for ensuring adequate exposure to sunlight is to space trellis rows no closer together than the ultimate height of the trees.

If you're planting fruit trees in a lawn, it is advisable to grow them in groups and keep them separate from the lawn. This approach allows you to water the trees separately from the lawn—tree roots require less frequent but deeper irrigation than is usually given to turf. Furthermore, grouping trees and mulching around them reduces the danger of injuring trunks with a string trimmer.

Replant disease

When a mature tree is removed and a new tree is planted in its place or even nearby, growth and fruit production on the replacement tree may be permanently lower than on a tree planted in soil where no tree previously existed. This phenomenon is known generally as replant disease (or "sick soil syndrome"), which affects both commercial and backyard orchards—especially stone fruit, almonds, and apples, but also other tree species, and even grapevines and roses. Effects on a replanted tree can range from slight to severe, and the ability to grow a new healthy tree may be compromised for up to 15 years after it is replanted. Pathogens survive in dead roots and organic matter until they are exposed to attack when roots decompose. Removal of as much of the root system as possible can shorten this time frame.

Replant disease can result from interacting physical, chemical, and biological factors, but the biological aspects usually dominate. Many factors can contribute to this condition, including tree species, rootstock, and soil type and drainage, and specific causes may vary in different regions. The disease is often worst when the same or related species (such as stone fruit and almonds) are involved, but there may be effects even if a completely unrelated tree species is replanted. The use of a dwarfing rootstock as the replant tree may exacerbate the condition, compared to a standard rootstock, because dwarfing rootstock is genetically less vigorous.

Replant disease is caused by a complex of various fungal pathogens in the soil, including *Pythium*, *Rhizoctonia*, and *Phytophthora*, and it often involves plant parasitic nematodes. The malady is separate from common pathogens that may have caused the previous tree to decline or die, such as oak root fungus (*Armillaria mellea*), Verticillium wilt (*Verticillium dahliae*), and crown gall (*Agrobacterium tumefaciens*).

To prevent replant disease, commercial growers often treat the soil with chemical fumigants, although limitations on their use are increasing. Home orchardists must rely on nonchemical methods, some of which can be effective. You may find that replant trees grow and produce just fine, especially if they are not planted in exactly the same spot as the previous tree and if any nearby tree roots are removed. But if the replant trees struggle, consider taking steps to prevent the problem.

One option is to simply plant fruit trees in other areas of the garden, but in a designated orchard, such a strategy may be limited. One method that home orchardists (though not commercial growers) can pursue is to replace soil in the planting area with soil in which fruit trees have not grown and tree roots are not present. Remove soil from an area about 5 to 6 feet in diameter and at least a foot deep, with the hole deeper in the center, where the new tree will be planted. Add slightly more replacement soil and mound it slightly to prevent a basin from forming after soil settles. Ideally the soil will come from the same property so that irrigation management will be similar—avoid soil of a far different texture. Don't mix the replacement soil with the existing soil because doing so will distribute pathogens. Instead, simply fill the hole with the replacement soil. Replacing the soil may enable the replant tree to get off to a good start. Remove as many roots as possible within a diameter of 5 to 6 feet around the replant tree.

A unique method for reducing the effects of replant disease has been studied in commercial apple orchards in Washington. This method involves incorporating into the soil, several months before replanting trees, a 50:50 mix of seed meal of two species of mustard (*Brassica juncea* and *Sinapis alba*). After incorporation, the soil is tarped for a week. The technique has been shown to improve both the vegetative growth and the yield of trees planted after the removal of old orchards.

Choosing and planting trees

Tree selection

Although you can plant containerized fruit and nut trees at any time of year, there are advantages to purchasing and planting (dormant) bare-root trees, which are available January through March (depending on location in California). The best bare-root trees have a trunk diameter between ½ and ⅝ inch; a tree of that trunk diameter will usually have a better survival rate and be quicker to establish than a smaller or larger bare-root tree. If you are unable to plant bare-root trees soon after purchase, you should temporarily heel them in by covering the roots with soil, sawdust, or compost, and then keep them moist to prevent the roots from drying out.

At the nursery, select trees that are healthy and do not show signs of disease. The roots of a bare-root tree should be strong, healthy, and mostly unbroken (fig. 4.6). They should also be relatively straight, preferably with no sharp kinks or twists of large roots. Branch development may be a selling point in a bare-root tree in the nursery, but it is not essential since much of the trunk and most or all branches will be cut off at planting time.

For a containerized tree, the leaves and shoots should have vigorous growth and a dark green color (fig. 4.7). Ideally, the branches should be spaced evenly along the trunk. Because low branching is often desirable for tree management and later harvest, at least some of the branches should originate within about 2 feet of soil level. If possible, inspect the roots and avoid trees that are severely root-bound. Also avoid trees that were potted recently (early in the same spring) from a bare root and have not yet established enough of a root system to hold the container soil in place upon transplanting.

Planting the tree

Once the surrounding soil is loosened and compacted layers are broken up, dig the planting hole just bigger than the width of the roots. This excavated soil will be used to backfill the hole; do not add amendments or fertilizers to the planting hole. Strive for straight sides rather than a cone-shaped hole, and for a flat bottom that will facilitate tree placement and backfilling. Check hole depth with a tape measure. Unless the soil was already severely compacted beneath the hole, it is best to leave the soil directly below the root system undisturbed to help prevent the tree from settling. If deeper soil layers were dug or augured, be sure to form a base firm enough to prevent the tree from settling and a basin from being

created—which could lead to poor drainage and soil saturation, resulting in root death. If the sides of the planting hole are slickened by digging or augering (as can happen in clay soils), loosen the sides with a

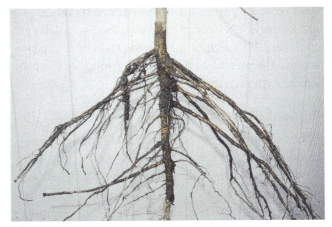

Figure 4.6. Roots of a healthy bare-root peach tree. *Photo:* Chuck Ingels.

Figure 4.7. A healthy containerized peach tree in midspring shows vigorous growth and dark green foliage. *Photo:* Chuck Ingels.

shovel to help roots grow out of the planting hole and into the native soil. Avoid planting trees in very wet soil.

In high-rainfall areas or where soil does not drain well, fruit trees can be planted slightly "high" to facilitate surface drainage and thereby help avoid crown rot disease (fig. 4.8), especially in finer-textured soils. When properly planted, the soil line on the trunk (visible as a change in color where the soil surface met the trunk in the field) should be at or slightly above the level of the surrounding ground, and the bud union should be at least 4 inches above the soil surface. Placing a shovel handle or other straightedge across the hole can be a helpful way to check planting height during the filling process. As a general rule, after the soil has settled, the uppermost large root should be no more than an inch or two below the soil surface. Tree anchorage is not improved from deep planting, but from subsequent root growth. Gently pull the tree up if it was planted too deep. After planting, settle the soil by inserting a hose and filling the planting hole rather than tamping soil. The soil should slope slightly downward from the tree to prevent water from accumulating near the trunk. Apply

a layer of mulch or wood chips a few inches thick in a radius 2 to 3 feet around the tree. Keep the mulch a few inches away from the trunk to minimize the likelihood of crown rot and to eliminate hiding places for insect pests. Consider the following additional strategies when planting trees.

Bare-root trees. Before you put a bare-root tree into the ground, examine its roots. Cut off any that are broken or kinked. Avoid shortening very long roots. Instead, dig a bigger hole to accommodate the roots and straighten them to prevent kinking. Begin backfilling loose soil and settle the soil with water (fig. 4.9). Add the remaining soil, and again settle with water.

Container-grown trees. Container-grown trees may have circling or girdling roots, which should be gently pulled away from the root ball before the tree is planted (fig. 4.10). A tree that has been in a pot for several months to a year may be unsuitable for planting without cutting circling roots. Fill the hole with soil and settle it with water. Be sure to keep the top of the root ball free of backfill soil (fig. 4.11). A cap of soil on top of a root ball often creates an interface between the field soil on top and the container mix below and also limits percolation of water due to the disparity in texture of the root ball (nursery) soil and the backfill soil.

Holeless planting. In poorly drained soils, you can plant the tree on a mound or berm to prevent crown rot. A simple method of planting on a mound is to loosen soil under and around the planting site, set the tree in the middle of this cultivated soil, and pile

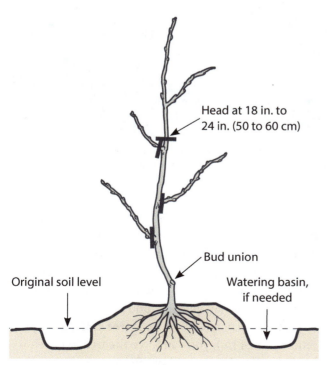

Figure 4.8. How to plant and prune a deciduous fruit or nut tree. In higher-rainfall areas, plant the tree on a slight mound, especially if drainage is poor. *Source:* Adapted from Vossen and Silva 2015, 502.

Head at 18 in. to 24 in. (50 to 60 cm)

Bud union

Original soil level

Watering basin, if needed

Figure 4.9. Avoid shortening roots. Instead, dig the hole larger to accommodate the roots as they are. Fill the soil around the roots of a bare-root tree. Place tree in the hole and backfill. Settle the soil with water. *Photo:* Chuck Ingels.

Figure 4.10. For container stock, pull any wound roots away to straighten them before planting. *Photo:* Chuck Ingels.

Figure 4.11. This containerized tree, shown after planting, has had no soil backfilled over the soil in the pot. *Photo:* Chuck Ingels.

Figure 4.12. A simple method of planting a tree on a mound in higher-rainfall areas involves loosening the soil in a large circle (A), setting the tree in the middle of the circle (B), and placing soil over the roots (C). Be sure to allow for some soil settling and make sure the mound can be watered. *Photos:* Muchtar Salzman.

soil over the roots (fig. 4.12). Be sure to make the mound wide enough to allow for a way to irrigate after planting.

Post-planting care

Pruning the newly planted tree

We prune young trees to develop structure and prune older trees for fruit production. In this section, we discuss pruning of newly planted trees that will be trained to a vase shape, typical for most fruit trees.

The taller nut trees, such as walnuts and pecans, are grown as single-leader trees, and so should not be headed (shortened) low to the ground.

An important goal of many home orchardists is to maintain relatively small trees to facilitate pruning, thinning, pest management, and harvesting. By heading the newly planted bare-root tree at knee height (about 18–24 in.), you can force the tree to develop low branches. We want about five main scaffold branches to develop. However, if it's important to you to have access to the area under the tree—for equipment passage, for example—the trunk can be headed higher up, as high as 36 inches from the ground. Make sure, though, to cut the new tree back by at least one-third of its original length. Otherwise, shoot growth may be inadequate.

Many bare-root trees either have no lateral branches below the trunk heading cut—or have only spindly or broken lateral branches that should be removed (see fig. 4.8). Still, some bare-root trees may have undamaged lateral branches with wide branch angles that are large enough to retain. Branches that are about ³⁄₁₆ to ¼ inch (4.8 to 6.4 mm) in diameter at the base can be shortened to stubs of two or three buds (figs. 4.13 and 4.14). You can retain well-placed, well-attached branches that are larger than about ½ inch in diameter where they join the trunk and then cut them back by about one-third to one-half their original length (fig. 4.15). Any retained stubs or branches should be spaced vertically and radially around the trunk, if possible. Even if only one healthy branch is present, you can stub or shorten it. By retaining one or more lateral branches you can get better vertical spacing between scaffold branches; otherwise, nearly all the branches will arise from just below the heading cut on the trunk. Just make sure

Figure 4.14. Healthy branches of this bare-root peach tree were cut back to short stubs. New shoots that grow from them or from the trunk will be selected as scaffold branches. *Photo:* Chuck Ingels.

Figure 4.15. This bare-root apple tree has well-placed branches in terms of filling a circle around the trunk (A). The branches were cut back to about one-third their original length to begin developing the first tier of branches (B). The trunk was headed to begin to form the second tier and a new leader. *Photos:* Chuck Ingels.

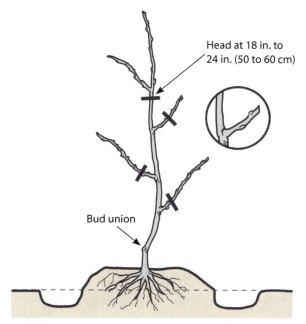

Head at 18 in. to 24 in. (50 to 60 cm)

Bud union

Figure 4.13. Retain several branches spaced vertically and radially around the tree. Thinner branches should be shortened to three to five buds (see inset) and thicker branches can be cut back to one-third to one-half their original lengths. *Source:* Adapted from Vossen and Silva 2002, 486.

that any shoots that grow from these retained lower shoots do not get shaded out by the new top growth. Later, you should thin the shoots that grow from buds on stubs to only one shoot per stub, or as many as two shoots for retained branches that are longer. These shoots will later become the tree's main scaffold branches.

When purchasing containerized fruit trees, carefully consider each tree's branch height and placement. Branches at 2 feet at the time of planting will be at 2 feet at maturity. Because the tree in a container may be older, with some already established structure, there may be fewer options for developing low branching. If you would like a lower-branching tree, though, you may be able to head it back the following winter.

Sunburn protection at planting

The bark of your newly planted tree needs protection from sunburn, which can heat and dehydrate the bark and lead to bark cracking, infestation with borer insects, and wood decay (fig. 4.16). To prevent this, apply to the trunk a 1:1 mixture of white latex paint and water (the exact proportions of paint and water are not critical—dilution simply makes the paint easier to apply). You can also use tree trunk whitewash products sold at nurseries. Organically acceptable whitewashes are also available. In the warm interior areas of California, extend the paint application area from the soil surface (after soil settling) and up the entire trunk, including over the dormant buds, or at least up to the new tree's first main branch.

Irrigation

Newly planted trees should be watered thoroughly to settle the soil around the roots. Insert a garden hose to settle soil. Form a doughnut-shaped ring around the outer edge of the root ball of a container-grown tree, or just beyond the spread of the roots of a bare-root tree, and fill the ring with water (fig. 4.17). If using drip irrigation, place the drip line near the tree and use two emitters per tree, about 1 foot from either side of the trunk (fig. 4.18), and water thoroughly.

After the initial irrigation, newly planted trees generally do not require much irrigation until the weather turns warm and new growth is several inches to 1 foot long. Container-grown trees that are transplanted in the summer, however, often have a relatively large canopy and require frequent watering on top of the root ball until their roots become established in the surrounding soil, usually 4 to 6 weeks.

A healthy first-year tree may require about 5 to 15 gallons (19–57 l) of water per week in the summer in hot areas of California, depending on the extent of canopy growth—or less than that if you use mulch (see table 5.1 in chapter 5, "Irrigation"). The frequency and amount of irrigation both depend on the soil type, the irrigation method, weather conditions, ground cover, and tree size (see chapter 5, "Irrigation"). For best growth, the soil in the root zone

Figure 4.16. A 50:50 mix of interior white latex paint and water is painted onto the newly planted bare-root tree. You can substitute an organic-based or other whitewash material for the paint. Paint from the top of the tree to 2 inches below the soil level. *Photo:* Chuck Ingels.

Figure 4.17. To irrigate, form a doughnut-shaped ring around the root ball and flood this basin. Within a few months, construct a wider, doughnut-shaped ring. If using drip or sprinkler irrigation, simply flatten the soil on the mound. *Photo:* Chuck Ingels.

Figure 4.18. Drip irrigation has been added after planting of a bare-root tree, with emitters (indicated by arrows) placed on either side of the tree. *Photo:* Chuck Ingels.

should be moist at all times yet never saturated, although the soil surface may be allowed to dry. To determine whether you have adequate soil moisture, periodically dig a small test hole about 8 to 10 inches deep with a soil sampling tube, shovel, or trowel and examine the soil in the root zone (see fig. 4.4). Use the soil moisture feel test to determine how wet the soil is (see fig. 5.4 in chapter 5, "Irrigation").

Training young trees— additional choices

You can train a deciduous fruit or nut tree into any of a number of basic structures: open center, central leader, modified central leader, espalier, or fruit bush. The structure you choose depends on the species of tree, the height at which you wish to maintain the tree, your growing conditions, and your personal taste. If you want a tree to grow to its full size, you can simply let the tree grow without any pruning during the first growing season and then prune during the dormant season when the leaves are gone and the branches are clearly visible. You can accelerate the tree's training, though, by using summer pruning to modify its structural development during the first growing season and then fine-tuning the training during the first dormant season. If you want to create a fruit bush, you will have to prune about twice during the summer. To grow espalier trees, you will have to apply training and pruning during the first season (for more information on training and pruning, see chapter 7, "Training and pruning").

Weeds

Weeds compete with young trees for water and nutrients. If left uncontrolled, they can slow a tree's growth. Keep the ground within at least 3 feet (1 m) of the tree trunk free of grass, weeds, and other vegetation. A layer of mulch, together with hand weeding, can provide good weed control. Avoid hoeing or using string-type weed trimmers because they may injure roots, or nick or even girdle the trunk, allowing introduction of crown gall disease.

Further reading

Carson, J., G. Shimizu, C. Ingels, P. Geisel, and C. Unruh. 2002. Fruit trees: Planting and care of young trees. Oakland: UC Agriculture and Natural Resources Publication 8048. https://doi.org/10.3733/ucanr.8048

Hickman, G. W., and P. Svihra. 2002. Planting landscape trees. Oakland: UC Agriculture and Natural Resources Publication 8046. https://doi.org/10.3733/ucanr.8046

Hodel, D., and D. Pittenger. 2015. Woody landscape plants. In D. Pittenger, ed., California master gardener handbook. Oakland: UC Agriculture and Natural Resources Publication 3382. 303–335.

LaRue, J. H., and R. S. Johnson, eds. 1989. Peaches, plums, and nectarines: Growing and handling for the fresh market. Oakland: UC Agriculture and Natural Resources Publication 3331.

Mazzola, M., S. S. Hewavitharana, and S. L. Strauss. 2015. Brassica seed meal soil amendments transform the rhizosphere microbiome and improve apple production through resistance to pathogen reinfestation. Phytopathology 105(4):460–469. https://doi.org/10.1094/PHYTO-09-14-0247-R

Vossen, P., and D. Silva. 2015. Woody landscape plants. In D. Pittenger, ed., California master gardener handbook. Oakland: UC Agriculture and Natural Resources Publication 3382. 459–536.

Chapter 5

Irrigation

Janet S. Hartin, Lawrence J. Schwankl, R. Scott Johnson, and Chuck A. Ingels

The use of recommended irrigation practices is crucial to growing productive, healthy trees and to conserving water. This chapter will help you develop an effective irrigation schedule based on your climate and microclimate, as well as on the age and size of your trees and the characteristics of your soil. The chapter includes information on various irrigation systems, from simple garden hoses and soaker hoses to sophisticated drip systems and smart controllers. It also includes an expanded section on managing irrigation under drought and water restrictions.

Importance of proper irrigation

Applying the right amount of water at the right time is important to maximizing fruit production and optimizing tree health. Applying too much or too little water can result in poor production and unhealthy trees, sometimes leading to death. Young and newly planted trees are especially susceptible to damage due to poor irrigation practices. Underirrigating trees during their first 1 to 3 years can affect fruit production and health throughout the trees' lifespan. Under-watering also results in stress for older trees, increasing their susceptibility to pests such as mites and wood-boring insects. Applying too much water, on the other hand, can be equally damaging to trees, or even more so. Roots subject to continuously wet, poorly drained soil are susceptible to several fungal diseases that, over time, can be debilitating or fatal.

Proper water management helps conserve water, an important issue amid recurring droughts, climate change, and the existence of urban heat islands that increase the water needs of our plants. Proper water management also helps reduce the waterway pollution caused when pesticides and fertilizers are transported during runoff or when water drains below the root zone.

Estimating tree water requirements

The amount of water needed by your trees depends largely on climate and local conditions (microclimate), as well as their age, size, and stage of development. For optimal yield and health, water returned to the atmosphere through evapotranspiration (ET), which is the combined loss of water due to soil evaporation and plant transpiration, should be replaced during each irrigation. During the hot summer months, trees require more water than in other seasons because the evapotranspiration rate is higher at that time of year. In general, trees do not require irrigation during their dormant seasons. During an average year, watering should begin 1 month after budbreak; during a dry winter, one or more deep irrigations may be necessary 1 month before budbreak. Recently planted trees need more frequent, but shorter, irrigations than do mature trees due to their smaller, shallower root systems.

Irrigating trees based on climate

Temperature, solar radiation, wind speed, and relative humidity drive plant evapotranspiration. We think of evapotranspiration in units of length (depth) as we do rainfall (for example, inches of rain). The rate of evapotranspiration involves units of depth per time—for example, inches per day. Detailed computer models have been developed to estimate daily (and even hourly) evapotranspiration rates for healthy, actively growing cool-season grass with access to an unlimited water supply. This rate is referred to as reference evapotranspiration (ETo). The California Irrigation Management Information System (CIMIS), managed by the California Department of Water Resources, reports both real-time and historical reference evapotranspiration (https://cimis.water.ca.gov/).

Figure 5.1 lists historical daily reference evapotranspiration for eighteen major climate zones in California, shown on the accompanying map. (Note that the climate zone numbers used in figure 5.1 are not the same as the U.S. Department of Agriculture or Sunset climate zone numbers.) Information contained in the figure's table is useful for refining the required water needs of your specific trees. Remember, however, that these numbers represent the water use of cool-season grass, which is 20 to 25 percent higher than the water use of mature mulched orchards and about 50 percent more than younger trees.

Figure 5.2 summarizes differences in monthly reference evapotranspiration in three distinct CIMIS climate zones. Note the lower reference evapotranspiration rates along the coast (zone 1) compared with reference evapotranspiration rates in hotter, drier inland areas (zones 12 and 18).

For further information on using climate-based methods for scheduling irrigations, whether based on real-time or historical data, visit the CIMIS website, which provides water use data for different areas of California and guidance on using the data. Many water districts also provide local reference evapotranspiration values.

Irrigate trees based on tree age and size

Trees' water use is related to their sun-exposed leaf area. Those with greater leaf areas (for example, older and more mature trees) use the most water. To estimate canopy area on a planar (looking down) basis, measure the tree canopy diameter and divide it in half to determine its radius. Then use the following formula:

$$\text{area} = \pi \times \text{radius}^2 \text{ (or, area} = 3.14 \times r^2).$$

This works well for most temperate fruit trees because their canopies develop in a roughly spherical shape. Adjustments are required for espalier trees, which use far less water than rounder, broader trees.

You can readily customize table 5.1 to the irrigation needs of your own orchard by using the following formula to convert inches for your climate zone, as found in figure 5.1, into gallons (thus converting units of depth to volume):

tree water use (gal./day) = tree water use (in./day) × tree canopy area × 0.623.

Example: If the water use of the tree is 0.25 inch per day (which is the average in zones 13, 14, and 15 in August) and the tree canopy is 314 square feet (tree radius of 10 ft.):

tree water use (gal./day) = 0.25 × 314 × 0.623 = 48.9 (round to 49) gallons/day.

Remember to factor in irrigation system efficiency. Sprinkler systems average about 75 percent efficiency and drip systems about 90 percent.

Example: Adding to the example above, the actual amount of water that would need to be applied by a sprinkler system to ensure that a tree receives its necessary 49 gallons is 63 gallons, per the following equation:

49 gal. (net water need)/0.75 (which is 75% sprinkler irrigation efficiency) = 65.3 gal.

You can determine the sprinkler distribution uniformity of your sprinkler system by conducting a catch can test, which is an effective and relatively simple way to determine a sprinkler system's application (flow) rate and the evenness of its water application (distribution uniformity). Run the can test at the same time of day that you irrigate (preferably early morning) to match the water pressure. You may need to conduct more than one catch can test to measure all water applied by different sprinklers that irrigate the same trees. The procedure is as follows:

1. Set six to ten straight-sided cans uniformly along the radius beneath sprinklers. (Tuna or cat food cans work well.) Run the sprinklers for 30 minutes.

2. Turn off the sprinklers and, with a ruler, measure the inches of water collected in each can. Record on a piece of paper the approximate location of each can and the amount of water collected.

3. Determine the average depth of water collected in each can by adding the depth of water collected from all the containers and dividing that sum by the number of containers.

Note that if the amounts of water collected in the cans differ by more than 20 to 25 percent, the system is not operating optimally and the evenness of water application (distribution uniformity) is lower than it should be. In that case, correct problems—for example, straighten heads and remove vegetation from around heads if it blocks spray—that result in low spots. Repeat the catch can test. The distribution uniformity should greatly improve.

4. Determine the flow (application) rate of your system

Example:

Irrigation time = 30 min (0.5 hr)

Water collected in each container:

Sum of depths (in.) in containers =

(8⁄16 + 6⁄16 + 7⁄16 + 9⁄16 + 11⁄16 + 10⁄16 + 2⁄16 + 8⁄16 + 6⁄16 + 9⁄16) = 76⁄16 in. = 4.75 in.

Container	Amount of water collected (in.)
1	1⁄2 (= 8⁄16)
2	3⁄8 (= 6⁄16)
3	7⁄16
4	9⁄16
5	11⁄16
6	5⁄8 (= 10⁄16)
7	1⁄8 (= 2⁄16)
8	1⁄2 (= 8⁄16)
9	3⁄8 (= 6⁄16)
10	9⁄16

Average depth of water applied = sum of container depths ÷ number of containers = 4.75 in. ÷ 10 containers = 0.475 in.

Application (flow) rate (in./hr) = average depth of water applied (in.) ÷ sprinkler test operation time (hr) = 0.475 in. ÷ 0.5 hr = 0.95 in./hr

To convert a sprinkler application rate given in inches per hr to the number of gallons per minute for a given area of tree canopy, use the following formula:

(application rate (in./hr)) × (tree canopy diameter (ft.))^2 × 0.0083 = (application rate (gal./min))

For example:

Sprinkler application rate = 0.95 in./hr

Tree canopy diameter = 10 ft.

0.95 in./hr × (10 ft.)^2 × 0.0083 = 0.79 gal./min of water applied to this tree canopy area

Compare the water application rate (in./hr) from the example above to the water use of the tree (gal./hr) to determine how long you need to irrigate (see example below). Remember, it's better to give trees deep, infrequent irrigations than to irrigate them often and shallowly.

Example: An inland deciduous tree 10 feet in diameter uses 20.7 gallons of water per day during midsummer. Using the sprinkler system described above (application rate = 0.79 gal/min), how long should each irrigation be?

If water were to be applied daily, the operation time of the sprinklers should be

20.7 gal/day ÷ 0.79 gal./min = 26.2 min/day (round to 26 min/day).

Instead of irrigating each day, it would be better to irrigate every few days to provide deeper watering and encourage deeper rooting. If irrigations were scheduled every 3 days, the irrigation time would be

26 min/day × 3 days = 78 min.

As the irrigation times get longer, runoff may become a problem and water cycling may be necessary.

Adjust irrigation based on microclimates

While figure 5.1 and table 5.1 provide good starting points for irrigating your trees, you will likely need to make some modifications to fit your local conditions (microclimates).

Below are examples:

- Trees shaded by buildings or other trees use less water than trees in full sun. As a general rule, shaded trees use about one-third as much water as those growing in full sun.

- Trees growing in or near asphalt or concrete have greater water needs than mulched trees growing in orchard settings away from these hotter surfaces. Their water needs can be 40 percent higher than trees growing in mulched conditions with only living plants in the vicinity.

Figure 5.1. Average daily reference evapotranspiration (ETo) in CIMIS climate zones (computed from CIMIS monthly reference evapotranspiration climate zone data). *Source:* Jones et al. 1999.

Reference EvapoTranspiration (ETo) Zones

1 COASTAL PLAINS HEAVY FOG BELT lowest ETo in California, characterized by dense fog

2 COASTAL MIXED FOG AREA less fog and higher ETo than zone 1

3 COASTAL VALLEYS & PLAINS & NORTH COAST MOUNTAINS more sunlight than zone 2

4 SOUTH COAST INLAND PLAINS & MOUNTAINS NORTH OF SAN FRANCISCO more sunlight and higher summer ETo than zone 3

5 NORTHERN INLAND VALLEYS valleys north of San Francisco

6 UPLAND CENTRAL COAST & LOS ANGELES BASIN higher elevation coastal areas

7 NORTHEASTERN PLAINS

8 INLAND SAN FRANCISCO BAY AREA inland area near San Francisco with some marine influence

9 SOUTH COAST MARINE TO DESERT TRANSITION inland area between marine & desert climates

10 NORTH CENTRAL PLATEAU & CENTRAL COAST RANGE cool, high elevation areas with strong summer sunlight; zone has limited climate data & the zones selection is somewhat subjective

11 CENTRAL SIERRA NEVADA mountain valleys east of Sacramento with some influence from delta breeze in summer

12 EAST SIDE SACRAMENTO-SAN JOAQUIN VALLEY low winter & high summer ETo with slightly lower ETo than zone 14

13 NORTHERN SIERRA NEVADA northern Sierra Nevada mountain valleys with less marine influence than zone 11

14 MID-CENTRAL VALLEY, SOUTHERN SIERRA NEVADA, TEHACHAPI & HIGH DESERT MOUNTAINS high summer sunshine and wind in some locations

15 NORTHERN & SOUTHERN SAN JOAQUIN VALLEY slightly lower winter ETo due to fog and slightly higher summer ETo than zones 12 & 14

16 WESTSIDE SAN JOAQUIN VALLEY & MOUNTAINS EAST & WEST OF IMPERIAL VALLEY

17 HIGH DESERT VALLEYS valleys in the high desert near Nevada and Arizona

18 IMPERIAL VALLEY, DEATH VALLEY & PALO VERDE low desert areas with high sunlight & considerable heat advection

Monthly Average Reference Evapotranspiration by ETo Zone (in./mo)

Zone	Jan	Feb	Mar	Apr	May	Jun	Jul	Aug	Sep	Oct	Nov	Dec	Total
1	0.93	1.40	2.48	3.30	4.03	4.50	4.65	4.03	3.30	2.48	1.20	0.62	32.9
2	1.24	1.68	3.10	3.90	4.65	5.10	4.96	4.65	3.90	2.79	1.80	1.24	39.0
3	1.86	2.24	3.72	4.80	5.27	5.70	5.58	5.27	4.20	3.41	2.40	1.86	46.3
4	1.86	2.24	3.41	4.50	5.27	5.70	5.89	5.58	4.50	3.41	2.40	1.86	46.6
5	0.93	1.68	2.79	4.20	5.58	6.30	6.51	5.89	4.50	3.10	1.50	0.93	43.9
6	1.86	2.24	3.41	4.80	5.58	6.30	6.51	6.20	4.80	3.72	2.40	1.86	49.7
7	0.62	1.40	2.48	3.90	5.27	6.30	7.44	6.51	4.80	2.79	1.20	0.62	43.3
8	1.24	1.68	3.41	4.80	6.20	6.90	7.44	6.51	5.10	3.41	1.80	0.93	49.4
9	2.17	2.80	4.03	5.10	5.89	6.60	7.44	6.82	5.70	4.03	2.70	1.86	55.1
10	0.93	1.68	3.10	4.50	5.89	7.20	8.06	7.13	5.10	3.10	1.50	0.93	49.1
11	1.55	2.24	3.10	4.50	5.89	7.20	8.06	7.44	5.70	3.72	2.10	1.55	53.1
12	1.24	1.96	3.41	5.10	6.82	7.80	8.06	7.13	5.40	3.72	1.80	0.93	53.4
13	1.24	1.96	3.10	4.80	6.51	7.80	8.99	7.75	5.70	3.72	1.80	0.93	54.3
14	1.55	2.24	3.72	5.10	6.82	7.80	8.68	7.75	5.70	4.03	2.10	1.55	57.0
15	1.24	2.24	3.72	5.70	7.44	8.10	8.68	7.75	5.70	4.03	2.10	1.24	57.9
16	1.55	2.52	4.03	5.70	7.75	8.70	9.30	8.37	6.30	4.34	2.40	1.55	62.5
17	1.86	2.80	4.65	6.00	8.06	9.00	9.92	8.68	6.60	4.34	2.70	1.86	66.5
18	2.48	3.36	5.27	6.90	8.68	9.60	9.61	8.68	6.90	4.96	3.00	2.17	71.6

Variability between stations within single zones is as high as 0.02 inches per day for zone 1 and during winter months in zone 13. The average standard deviation of the ETo between estimation sites wihtin a zone for all months is about 0.01 inches per day for the 200 sites used to develop the map.

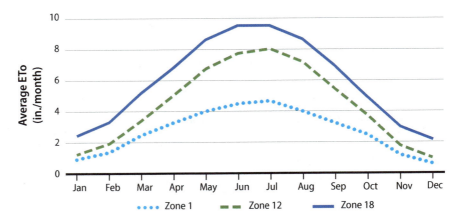

Figure 5.2. Monthly ETo in CIMIS zones 1, 12, and 18. After Jones et al. 1999.

Table 5.1. Daily water use (gal./day) based on tree evapotranspiration, age, and size

Tree size, or area plant covers in ft², to the drip line	Evapotranspiration			
	0.10 in./day (cool day, early spring, or late fall, foggy)	0.20 in./day (warm day in spring or fall, some fog)	0.25 in./day (hot day, midsummer, no fog)	0.30 in./day (very hot [100°F], windy, midsummer)
	Daily water use in gal/day			
New tree (1 ft²)	0.062	0.12	0.16	0.19
1 yr old (4 ft²)	0.25	0.50	0.62	0.75
2 yr old (10 ft²)	0.62	1.2	1.6	1.9
3 yr old (36 ft²)	2.2	4.5	5.6	6.7
4 yr old (100 ft²); mature semidwarf	6.2	12	16	19
Large standard mature tree (300 ft²)	19	38	47	56
1 acre solid cover (43,560 ft²)	2,700	5,400	6,800	8,100

- Trees subjected to poor-quality water (from a well, a recycled water source, or even a nearby swimming pool) need to be regularly leached to remove built-up salts. Not removing them can impair tree health as well as crop production.

- Poorly drained soils prone to runoff (usually heavier, higher in clay), and compacted soils) need to be on a different irrigation schedule from sandier soils, which lose water beneath the root zone if water is applied too quickly (see the next section for more detail).

- Trees will need more water if surrounded by other living plants that use water (cover crops, turf too close to trees, and so on)—as compared to mulched trees not surrounded by vegetation that competes for moisture.

Schedule irrigations based on soil texture

Irrigation scheduling involves applying the right amount of water at the right time. Expressed another way, irrigation scheduling is about frequency and duration. The frequency of irrigation depends largely on soil texture, or particle size distribution (table 5.2).

While loamy soils that hold adequate water but also drain well are favorable for plant growth, most soil textures, when irrigated correctly, also support productive, healthy orchards. Soils higher in clay percentage hold much more water than soils higher in sand percentage (see the soil texture triangle in fig. 1.2) and should be watered less frequently but for longer durations. Since they absorb water more slowly, they are more prone to runoff than sandy

Table 5.2. Soil water-holding capacity of various soil textures (in./ft.)

Sand	1.0–1.5 in. of water
Loam	1.5–2.0 in. of water
Clay	2.0–2.5 in. of water

soils, especially when sprinkler systems with high precipitation rates (flow rates) are used. Sandier soils drain much faster and need more frequent irrigation but for shorter periods of time—which prevents deep percolation and, in turn, water loss below the root zone.

In figure 5.3, note the broader wetting area of the clay soil and the additional time water needs to reach the same depth that it reaches in sandy soil.

There are several methods of determining the texture (particle size composition) of your soil, from a simple "feel test" (fig. 5.4)—which estimates particle size distribution—to submitting soil samples to soil-testing laboratories for more thorough evaluation. (Sometimes these evaluations involve other needed analyses, such as pH, electrical conductivity, and so on.)

As a first step in learning to determine soil moisture by the feel method, get an idea of how a handful of the soil feels at its extremes of soil moisture: wet and dry. The soil's field capacity is the soil moisture held in soil after the area has been allowed to drain following an irrigation. This is usually 2 to 3 days after a thorough irrigation.

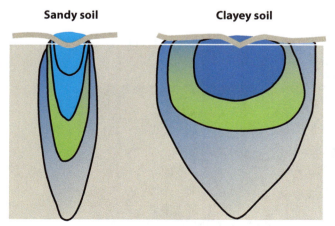

Figure 5.3. Comparative movement of water downward and outward in sandy and clayey soils. *Source*: Colorado State University.

Determine the soil's dry limit by sampling and feeling soil away from the planted area that has gone a long time (weeks) since it was last irrigated. This soil will be at what is termed the "permanent wilting point." For healthy trees, you want your soil moisture to be somewhere between these wet and dry limits. See figure 5.4 for help in determining soil texture and soil moisture content.

Irrigation system

Garden hose (used alone or to supplement another irrigation system)

A simple, effective method for watering a backyard tree is to use a garden hose—whether you attach a sprinkler to the hose or allow the water to seep into the ground and irrigate outward from the trunk until it covers an area equal to the entire canopy of the tree. Watering in quadrants for a certain length of time helps ensure even water application throughout the root zone. Keep the trunk dry to conserve water and prevent disease.

A good way to determine how much water the hose applies is to see how long it takes the hose to fill a 5-gallon bucket. Make sure that the hose is set at the same flow rate that you will use when you irrigate. **Use this equation:**

300 ÷ (__seconds to fill a 5-gal. pail) = __ gal. per min.

For example:

If it takes 45 seconds to fill a 5-gallon pail, then:

300 ÷ 45 seconds = 6.7 gal./min.

Once you know the flow rate of the hose in gallons per minute and the number of gallons to apply, you can determine how many minutes to run the hose.

Bear in mind that it is difficult to return accurately and repeatedly to any faucet setting other than fully open. Fully open settings may apply water too quickly for heavier soils (those higher in clay content) to absorb, leading to runoff. An excellent way of controlling hose applications is to add a control device (fig. 5.5) between the faucet and the hose. You can set the device to stop the flow after the desired number of gallons is applied. Because this type of device measures the actual amount of water applied, you do not have to rely on opening the faucet at a consistent lev-

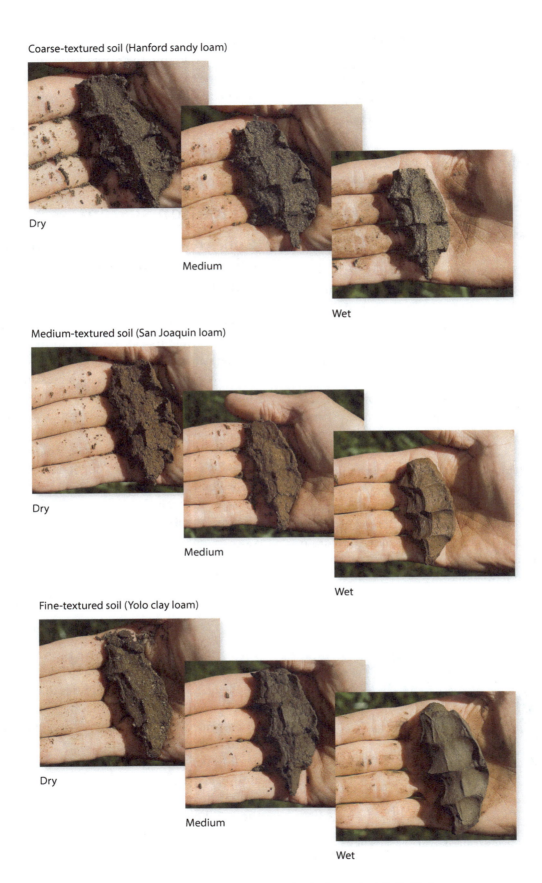

Coarse-textured soil (Hanford sandy loam)

Dry

Medium

Wet

Medium-textured soil (San Joaquin loam)

Dry

Medium

Wet

Fine-textured soil (Yolo clay loam)

Dry

Medium

Wet

Figure 5.4. Determining soil texture and moisture by the feel method. *Photos:* Jack Kelly Clark.

el each time you water the tree. An alternative hose control device is one that works like a kitchen timer. While this type works well, you need to set the discharge rate yourself based on the water needs of the trees.

If you have no other irrigation system to irrigate surrounding vegetation, all of the tree's irrigation requirements will need to be supplied by the garden hose. Even if no other vegetation surrounds the tree (for example, turfgrass irrigated with automatic sprinklers), it is beneficial to use the hose periodically for deep watering. Keep turfgrass or ground covers at least 6 inches away from the tree trunk to keep water competition to a minimum.

Garden hoses have several advantages. They are simple and inexpensive. The need for maintenance is low. They represent an effective method of keeping trees alive under drought and water restrictions. Also, an irrigator who depends on garden hoses may be more aware of where the water is being applied and of overall tree health.

Garden hoses have disadvantages as well. They are time and labor intensive—and, unless they are controlled with timers, the irrigator must remember to turn the water off.

Soaker hoses

A soaker hose (fig. 5.6) is a specialized type of drip irrigation that is effective for irrigating newly planted trees and small trees. Water slowly seeps through tiny pores along the hose under very low water pressure, encouraging deep water penetration and reducing the chance of runoff. Soaker hoses longer than 75 feet do not function well because pressure is lost before water reaches the end. Increasing the water pressure in soaker hoses that are too long is not a solution because it can lead to breakage and bursts. It is a good idea to cover soaker hoses with mulch.

Leave soaker hoses in the sun to soften them. Once they are pliable, wrap them in concentric circles around young trees throughout the canopy and slightly beyond the drip line, keeping the trunk dry.

A backflow prevention device and a flow meter are recommended. Backflow prevention, in fact, may be required by plumbing code. Like other drip systems, soaker hoses need to be monitored regularly for clogging and damage.

Due to the design of soaker hoses, they must be used only on flat ground if they are to provide even watering.

Soaker hoses are inexpensive and easy to install. They require low levels of maintenance. Their runoff potential is low because they deliver water slowly.

Figure 5.5. This flow control device shuts the water off based on the number of gallons applied. This model can also be set to shut off after a set period of time. *Photo:* Chuck Ingels.

Figure 5.6. A soaker hose can be useful in irrigating narrow plantings. *Photo:* Chuck Ingels.

Fine-tune sprinkler irrigation by using the "water balance approach"

The water balance method is used successfully by many large-scale growers who use sprinkler irrigation—and it works well for backyard growers too. The volume of water applied during each irrigation remains constant and is based on the water-holding capacity of the soil. The irrigation frequency varies, based on changes in reference evapotranspiration. By using the CIMIS network or soil moisture sensors to keep track of daily reference evapotranspiration, you can replenish water based on a set soil moisture depletion (research has found that 50% often works well). Each irrigation refills the soil profile completely, with an extra 20 percent provided for efficiency loss.

Example:

A mature, standard-size (large) fruit tree growing in loamy soil occupies 300 square feet, has a rooting depth of 3 feet, and a daily water use (evapotranspiration) of 0.25 inch per day in July.

How much water should be applied (net)?

3 ft. rooting depth × 2 in. of available water per ft. (loam) = 6 in. of available water.

How much total water should be applied per application?

6 in. × 50% depletion = 3 in. (net amount of water to apply) + 20% (to counter system inefficiency) = 3.6 in.

What is the duration of each irrigation?

Use the catch can test described in this chapter to measure how long it takes your sprinkler system to apply 1 inch of water. Multiply that number by 3.6 inches to determine how long to water. With an application rate of 1 inch per hour, it would take 3.6 hours to apply 3.6 inches of water.

How often should the irrigation occur?

3.6 in. of water ÷ 0.25 (average in./day) = 14 days (or, twice during July)

They work well for young trees with relatively small root systems and they reduce evaporation if covered by mulch. As with garden hoses, they do a good job of providing supplemental water when trees' needs are not supplied adequately by other systems, especially during drought.

On the other hand, soaker hoses are not well suited for irrigating mature, standard-size trees with large root systems and higher water needs—that is, soaker hoses longer than 50 to 75 feet don't work well. Also, soaker hoses may get plugged up.

Permanent sprinklers

Permanent irrigation sprinklers are installed in the ground and operate when the watering cycle is initiated, either manually or by an automatic controller and solenoid valve(s). Many home growers use pop-up sprinkler heads that automatically rise when irrigating and return underground when the water is turned off. Choose a system with heads that don't wet the foliage and trunk of trees, which can lead to disease problems. Low-angle sprinklers and pop-up sprinklers that can be adjusted manually are recommended ways to avoid these problems.

Fruit trees should be irrigated on their own dedicated valves. Sprinklers should be programmed so that irrigation frequency and duration match their needs rather than those of other landscape plants.

Among the advantages of permanent sprinklers is that their water application rate is fairly easy to determine via can tests that supplement the information supplied by the sprinkler manufacturer. This is especially necessary as systems age and become less efficient. In addition, permanent sprinklers can be automated using solenoid valves and an electronic controller, which allows users to irrigate early in the morning, when evaporation rates are low. Moreover, due to their higher application rates, permanent sprinklers are often better suited to irrigating mature, large trees than are drip systems.

There are issues to take into consideration when using automatic sprinklers, however. They must be regularly adjusted so that the recommended amount of water—based on season and age and stage of development of the trees—is applied. In addition, sprinklers that operate when no one is home or no one is awake may develop leaks and other damage that go undetected. To avoid these problems, periodically turn on the sprinklers manually and observe and address any problems.

Drip and microsprinkler systems

Drip and microsprinkler irrigation systems operate under low pressure (fig. 5.7), apply water to a localized area, and are well suited to irrigating trees. These systems are extensively used in commercial orchards. The discharge rates of drip emitters range from half a gallon to 4 gallons per hour. It is important to add enough emitters to adequately irrigate maturing trees, and to move the tubing and emitters outward as root systems expand.

Because microsprinklers have higher flow rates (6–50 gal/hr, or more) than drip systems, only one or two microsprinklers are required per tree. Microsprinklers' larger orifice size reduces clogging, as well. The wetting pattern of microsprinklers (20–30 ft.) is well suited for use in orchards.

There are many effective drip irrigation system layouts. However, layouts need to be adjusted as trees mature. For example, while newly planted trees, up to 1 year old, may be adequately irrigated with one emitter on each side of the trunk (see fig. 4.19), more emitters need to be added as trees age. While punch-in emitters can be used for young trees, tubing with built-in, evenly spaced emitters (in-line emitter tubing) and no external parts that can be damaged are recommended. A single ring of tubing is adequate for a young tree but a larger ring needs to be added 1 or 2 years later, as roots expand beyond the drip line of the tree. Ensuring uniform soil moisture throughout the entire rooting zone is ideal, and requires an adequate number of emitters as trees mature. (Note, however, that adding too many emitters may result in insufficient pressure at the end of the line.) As you design a system, review University of California publications, consult with irrigation specialists, or refer to irrigation manufacturer guides to make sure that the valve, pipe, and tubing sizes will accommodate predicted flow rates.

The advantages of drip and microsprinkler systems include the fact that their efficiency rates are higher than those of sprinkler systems because they apply water directly to the root zone. In addition, due to low flow rates, runoff of water, fertilizers, and pesticides is minimized. Drip emitters can be placed underneath mulch, minimizing evaporation. Drip and

Figure 5.7. In-line drip tubing has built-in emitters and is available in different flow rates and emitter spacings (A). A microsprinkler system puts out more water with less tubing than an in-line drip tubing system (B). *Photos:* Chuck Ingels.

microsprinkler systems are easily expanded and moved outward as trees mature and enlarge their root systems. These systems often reduce weed growth because the soil surface is kept dry. Also, young trees are well adapted to the more frequent, longer irrigations provided by drip irrigation.

Drip emitters and microsprinklers, however, with their small emission openings, must be monitored. Plugged emitters must be cleared, especially when nonpotable water is used. Drip irrigation systems can be damaged by animals, insects, digging, and human activity. Tree roots may grow over drip lines buried under mulch, making repairs difficult. Mulch also makes it difficult to check soil moisture levels. A large tree that requires 50 gallons of water per day, and that is irrigated by drip emitters that produce 1 gallon of water per hour, requires multiple emitters and several hours of run time. Drip systems require less running time for younger, smaller trees than for larger, older trees.

Tying it all together: Tips for effective irrigation

Irrigating the entire root zone

Water should be applied to the entire root zone, starting several inches outward from the trunk and extending throughout (and slightly beyond) the tree canopy. The trunk should be kept dry to reduce disease incidence and to conserve water. Applying water slightly below the current root zone encourages deep rooting, which anchors and stabilizes maturing trees.

As trees age, drip lines, soaker hoses, sprinklers, and microirrigation systems need to be adjusted to apply water to a larger area of soil. When watering with a garden hose, the same principle applies: Water farther outward as your trees mature. If you are using a permanent sprinkler system that cannot be moved, water by hand the outer areas of the tree canopy that are not irrigated by the sprinkler.

Make sure water is reaching the desired 2 to 3 feet in depth during each irrigation by pushing a metal or plastic rod (fig. 5.8) into the soil. It will easily penetrate wet soil while downward movement into dry soil will meet resistance. For sandier soils, do this 1 day after irrigating—or, for soils higher in clay, 2 days after irrigating.

If you have access to a soil sampling tube or an auger (see fig. 4.4), you can evaluate soil moisture by using your hand as a measuring device.

Water cycling (cycle and soak) to reduce runoff

Water cycling helps prevent runoff of soil water, which is often laden with fertilizers and pesticides. Runoff can pollute our waterways in addition to wasting water. Runoff is common on heavy soils, on those higher in clay, and on slopes, especially when sprinkler systems with high application rates are used.

Water cycling involves irrigating your trees two or more times in succession—with later irrigations

coming before soil has dried out after earlier irrigations—to ensure that the entire rooting area is irrigated and runoff is avoided. Each cycle should run as long as possible—until runoff begins. You may need to apply three or four cycles, back to back, to satisfy the water needs of your trees, especially during summer. Each additional cycle promotes deeper water penetration, encouraging deep rooting. (Water cycling is different from applying small amounts of water every day that don't penetrate deeply enough to irrigate the entire root system.)

Monitor the health of your trees. Healthy, vigorously growing trees are a positive sign that your irrigation management practices are correct. Drought-stressed trees will stop growing and may eventually start to lose leaves. Leaves will wilt and older leaves may droop. Trees receiving too much water may show similar symptoms because many roots may

Figure 5.8. By pushing a metal rod into the soil, you can judge how deeply the soil has been wetted (in this photograph, a handle has been welded onto the rod). You will be able to push the rod easily into moist soil, but not into dry soil. *Photo:* Chuck Ingels.

have died from inadequate aeration and waterlogging. In both cases, it is important to check the water status of the soil and the health of the roots, as well as the health of the upper portion of the tree. Healthy roots are light colored (sometimes white) under the bark and generally exhibit signs of new growth. Dying roots may be brown, with no new growth, and they often have an unpleasant smell. Note that even high-quality, well-drained soils can be overwatered. This can produce excessive shoot growth that is difficult to control and may impair fruit production—especially if too much nitrogen is also applied.

Irrigating during a drought or amid water restrictions

During drought, water restrictions may be imposed. These restrictions might limit the days when irrigation can occur or the amount of water that can be applied during a given time. In such situations, making sure that available water is used efficiently can save your trees.

Keeping your trees alive amid drought or water restrictions should be a priority. In addition to producing food, trees help mitigate impacts of climate change by providing shade and cooling urban heat islands. They also provide benefits such as reducing soil and water erosion, providing habitat, and enhancing biodiversity. Older trees absorb carbon dioxide and store appreciable amounts of carbon in their wood. The benefits provided by trees are greatest when they mature, so ensuring their health and longevity is important. Lawns, flowers, and other nonfood plants are much more dispensable. They can "catch up" or be replanted if sacrificed in favor of trees during dry periods. While tree fruit production may suffer if water restrictions prevent optimal irrigation, a few deep waterings early in the morning, when evaporation is minimal, will keep them alive during spring and summer.

Continue to water your trees if you remove your lawn. If you let your lawn go dormant, severely restrict its water supply, or remove it to conserve water, remember to water any trees that were dependent on water from the sprinkler irrigation used to water the lawn. Remembering that tree roots extend beyond the drip line of the tree and may need supplemental irrigation if turf is removed can save your trees. Deep watering the entire root system of your trees once or twice a month in the morning using a garden or soaker hose will keep them alive.

To preserve trees during water restrictions or under drought conditions, when water may not be available, maintain a 3-to-4 inch layer of organic mulch (wood chips, for example) to reduce evaporation. In fire-prone areas, use less-combustible products such as rocks, pebbles, or decomposed granite, maintaining a mulch layer 2 to 3 inches thick. In addition:

- Give trees a deep soaking every 2 to 4 weeks, depending on water availability, tree size, and soil type (sandier soils dry out faster than those with more clay).
- Whitewash the exposed scaffolds to prevent sunburn.
- Soak the soil under trees at least once or twice during the season.
- Closely monitor and control spider mites and other pests that may build up when water is insufficient.
- In case of severe drought or severe water restrictions, you may need to remove all fruit and prune trees heavily (to branches of 2–3 in. thick) as a last-ditch effort to save trees. Pruning should be done in early spring, if drought or water restrictions are foreseen, to reduce the potential for branch diseases in wetter climates.

Summary

Irrigating home orchards effectively is both a science and an art. The experience you gain from monitoring the health of your trees—coupled with simple and useful tools such as the "feel test" to estimate soil moisture and irrigating based on historical evapotranspiration, the age of your trees, and the tables provided in this chapter—will help you keep your trees healthy and productive while you also conserve water. Newer approaches that use precision irrigation methods and smart, weather-based technology can further enhance irrigation efficiency and effectiveness.

Reference

Jones, D. W., R. L. Snyder, S. Eching, and H. Gomez-McPherson. 1999. California Irrigation Management Information System (CIMIS) reference evapotranspiration. Climate zone map. Sacramento: Department of Water Resources. https://wwwcimis.water.ca.gov/Content/pdf/CimisRefEvapZones.pdf

Further reading

Hanson, B., L. Schwankl, and A. Fulton. 1999. Scheduling irrigations: When and how much. Oakland: UC Agriculture and Natural Resources Publication 3396.

Hartin, J. S., and B. Faber. 2015. Water management. In D. Pittenger, ed., California master gardener handbook. UC Agriculture and Natural Resources Publication 3382. 83–108.

Irrigation Association. 2016. Landscape drip irrigation design and management. 3rd ed.

Schwankl, L., B. Hanson, and T. Prichard. 1997. Micro-irrigation of trees and vines: A handbook for water managers. Oakland: UC Agriculture and Natural Resources Publication 3378.

Schwankl, L., and T. Prichard. 1999. Drip irrigation in the home landscape. Oakland: UC Agriculture and Natural Resources Publication 21579.

Snyder, R. L., B. L. Lanini, D. A. Saw, and W. O. Pruitt. 1987. Using reference evapotranspiration (ETo) and crop coefficients to estimate crop evapotranspiration (ETc) for trees and vines. Oakland: UC Agriculture and Natural Resources Publication 21428.

Snyder, R. L., W. O. Pruitt, and D. A. Shaw. 1987. Determining daily reference evapotranspiration (ETo). Oakland: UC Agriculture and Natural Resources Publication 21426.

Vossen, P., and D. Silva. 2015. Temperate tree fruit and nut crops. In D. Pittenger, ed., California master gardener handbook. Oakland: UC Agriculture and Natural Resources Publication 3382. 459–536.

Chapter 6

Fertilization

Maxwell V. Norton and Chuck A. Ingels

Deciduous fruit trees require several nutrients for optimal growth and fruit production. Elements required in relatively large amounts (macronutrients) include nitrogen, phosphorus, potassium, calcium, magnesium, and sulfur. Elements required in relatively small amounts (micronutrients) include iron, manganese, zinc, boron, copper, chlorine, and molybdenum. These nutrients are absorbed primarily by the roots from the soil, although some may also be absorbed through the leaves or other plant surfaces.

In order to be absorbed by the roots, nutrients must be dissolved in water in a plant-available chemical form, usually in an inorganic (mineral) form—in other words, as an ion, an atom, or group of atoms carrying an electrical charge. Nutrients in such a form can be dissolved in soil water and are referred to as "available." For example, roots absorb most nitrogen in the form of nitrate (NO_3^-) and some in the form of ammonium (NH_4^+). They absorb potassium in its ionic form, K^+. As soil microorganisms decompose organic matter, they release nutrients as plant-available forms. Other nutrients become available through chemical reactions in the soil. We supply plant-available forms by applying organic and synthetic (chemical) fertilizers. The nutrients obtained in any of these ways are indistinguishable to plants. Fertilizers vary in their nutrient release rates and other properties.

Nutrients and their roles in plant development

Although deciduous fruit trees require nutrients for tree growth and fruit production, those grown in backyard settings—in typical sandy loam to clay loam soil, with proper irrigation—may need little fertilizer, once established. However, crop harvest removes nutrients—which, for subsequent crops, must come either from the soil or from added fertilizer. Nitrogen is the principal nutrient lacking in most soils. Other nutrient deficiencies, when encountered, are generally limited to potassium, iron, and zinc—and, on rare occasions, boron. When a nutrient is lacking and yield is reduced, there may be no visible symptoms of nutrient deficiency. This "hidden hunger" can be ascertained through tissue tests, although such tests are usually not needed in home orchards.

Macronutrients

Nitrogen (N)

Fruit trees use nitrogen in large amounts. Nitrogen is taken up by the roots from soil. Most of the nitrogen in soil exists in an organic form in living organisms and decaying organic matter. This organic nitrogen is slowly converted to plant-available inorganic forms, mostly nitrate, as soil microorganisms decompose the organic matter. Nitrate is mobile and moves with water in the soil. It can easily leach out of the root zone, especially with overirrigation in sandy soils; the use of excess nitrogen fertilizer can lead to leaching of nitrate into groundwater.

Depending on location in California and soil conditions, backyard fruit trees may not need annual applications of nitrogen. However, in sandy soils in the southern San Joaquin Valley and in Southern California, mature trees may benefit from an annual application of up to 1 pound of nitrogen per tree per year. If you suspect nitrogen deficiency, watch for yellowing of leaves, particularly the older leaves, because nitrogen is mobile in plant tissues and is drawn toward fruit and new shoot growth. Yellowing of leaves can have a variety of other causes, however, including drought, poor soil condition, and waterlogging. If you do need to fertilize, divide the total nitro-

gen requirement for the year into two or three smaller quantities applied during the growing season, particularly if soils are sandy. Too much nitrogen will
cause the tree to produce excessive new growth,
which will shade the lower parts of the tree and can
lead to fewer fruit, poor fruit color and flavor, and
delayed maturity. Excess nitrogen also increases the
tree's susceptibility to insect pests and diseases and
can lead to nitrate pollution of groundwater.

Phosphorus

Phosphorus deficiency has very rarely been observed
in California fruit or nut trees, except in some Sierra
Nevada foothill soils. It is available to plants primarily in the form of phosphate ions. Phosphorus reacts
very readily with many elements in the soil and in
doing so it can become unavailable to plants. It is
most available at a soil pH of 6.0 to 7.0.

Potassium (K)

Potassium is abundant in most California soils but it
is often in an unavailable form, as part of soil particles and rock. This is especially true in soils that contain large amounts of clay, which binds potassium.
Potassium does not readily leach out of the soil. It is
taken up by plant roots as a positively charged ion
(cation), K^+; unlike nitrogen and phosphorus, it is
not synthesized into complex molecules, but remains
a simple ion in solution in the plant.

Calcium

Calcium is abundant in California soils and is absorbed by roots in an ionic form (Ca^{2+}). Calcium
does not readily leach out of the soil. Its deficiency in
deciduous fruit trees is rare. Calcium has a strong influence on pH—that is, acidity or alkalinity of soil. In
many areas of California, natural waters also contain
high levels of calcium. Excess calcium carbonate
(lime) in the soil raises the soil pH and can induce a
disorder known as lime-induced chlorosis, in which
the ends of shoots turn yellow as a result of iron or
zinc deficiency, itself caused by high pH. High calcium levels can also induce magnesium deficiency.
Consistent watering can help with calcium deficiency.

Magnesium

Magnesium deficiency is rare in fruit trees in California. Magnesium is not easily leached from the soil.

Like calcium, it is taken up from the soil in the form
of an ion (Mg^{2+}). In areas with soils derived from ser-
pentine, high magnesium levels can induce calcium
deficiency symptoms, such as apple cork spot and
bitter pit. Foliar or soil-applied calcium may be needed to correct a magnesium-induced calcium
deficiency.

Sulfur

Deciduous fruit trees are only rarely deficient in sulfur in California. Sulfur exists in soil organic matter
and is released as sulfate (SO_4^{2-}) as soil microorganisms cause decomposition.

Plants absorb sulfur mainly through their roots,
but they can also absorb it through leaves and other
plant surfaces. Gardeners can add elemental sulfur to
the soil to lower the soil's pH. Adding sulfate materials like gypsum will not lower soil pH, except in very
specific situations (involving high-sodium, or sodic,
soils). Adding too much sulfur can lower pH below
its optimal level.

Micronutrients

Iron

Iron deficiency, which can be relatively common in
deciduous fruit trees in California, is usually caused
by waterlogged, compacted, or alkaline soils. Roots
absorb iron primarily in an ionic form (Fe^{3+}); it can
also be absorbed by leaves. Although iron is one of
the most abundant elements in many soils, most of it
is bound in minerals and so is unavailable to plants.
A plant's ability to absorb the small amount of iron
that actually is available can be greatly reduced by
poor aeration (too much water in the soil), a soil pH
value above 7.5, or physically damaged or diseased
roots. Iron is not mobile in the soil or in plant tissues.
Thus, iron deficiency symptoms are expressed in new
growth rather than older foliage.

Manganese

Deciduous fruit trees in California rarely suffer manganese deficiency. Roots absorb manganese from the
soil in its high-pH ionic form (Mn^{2+}); it is relatively
immobile in the soil and in plant tissue.

Zinc

Zinc deficiency is fairly common in fruit trees in California. Zinc is taken up by a tree's roots and absorbed through its leaves in an ionic form (Zn^{2+}). Like iron, manganese, and many other minerals, zinc combines readily with other elements. Relatively little free (ionic) zinc is available to plants in most California soils. Many factors can reduce its mobility in soil, such as a low level of zinc in the soil or a high pH.

Zinc is immobile in plant tissue. Although plants use zinc in small amounts, a deficiency can be immediately noticeable on new leaves and can severely damage buds, twigs, and stems. Zinc-deficient leaves are often small and have interveinal chlorosis, and may be white in color.

Boron

Most California soils have an adequate or even excess supply of boron, and its deficiency is relatively uncommon in fruit trees. Deficiencies may occur in very sandy soils and Sierra Nevada foothill soils. Boron is immobile in deciduous fruit tree tissues. An excess of boron (boron toxicity) can be a problem in arid regions of the state or where irrigation water contains boron. Boron toxicity has been observed on the west side of the San Joaquin Valley, in the Cache Creek watershed in Yolo County, and in many parts of Central and Southern California. Boron is not easily leached out of the root zone but may be leached out of a soil whose internal drainage is good if plenty of low-boron water is applied.

Soil fertility management

A good soil has an appropriate balance of mineral nutrients, organic matter, living organisms, air, and water (see chapter 1, "Climate and soils"). Maintaining soil fertility largely consists of maintaining this balance and correcting it when necessary.

Nutrient recycling

In a mature backyard landscape, little or no fertilizer may need to be added to trees and shrubs each year if you recycle leaves, clippings, and prunings back into the soil. In the home landscape, many nutrients are naturally recycled: As leaves, twigs, and other plant debris are decomposed by soil microorganisms, the nutrients tied up in them are released into the soil to

be taken up by plants. The recycling process can take from a few weeks to several years. You can increase the rate of the process by adding ground-up or chopped prunings, leaves, and clippings to the soil as mulch. This returns many nutrients to the soil to be used again by the trees. Over time, you can increase the soil's overall fertility in this way. However, as noted above, nitrogen may need to be added because fruit harvest removes this nutrient, and woody plant parts recycled as mulch contain little of this nutrient.

Salinity

Soil *salinity* (salt level) refers not only to common table salt (sodium chloride), but to many chemical compounds in which positively charged ions, such as sodium, calcium, or magnesium combine with negatively charged ions, such as chloride, sulfate, or bicarbonate. High levels of salts in the soil can break down the soil's structure, raise its pH, reduce its ability to support plants, and even, at high levels, kill plants.

Plants absorb salts through their roots and leaves. Salts occur naturally in soils; other sources include synthetic (chemical) fertilizers, manures, manure-based composts, poor-quality water used for irrigation, and de-icing materials used by road departments in cold-winter areas.

Many California soils in low-rainfall areas have naturally high salinity, since salts accumulate through mineral breakdown but have not been transported to lower soil levels via percolation of rain. In all soils, the excessive use of fertilizers, composts, or manures, and irrigation with poor-quality water, can raise salinity to damaging levels. Salinity injury symptoms may appear as poor growth or leaf symptoms, but more-severe salt damage leads to burning of leaf tips and margins (fig. 6.1). If you suspect salinity injury, a soil sample from the root zone can be tested by a laboratory. Such analyses are inexpensive and are often included in a routine agricultural soil test. It is also possible to use simple, inexpensive soil salinity meters from garden centers to give an idea of potential problems, but for definitive results a laboratory test is preferable.

However, you should try to rule out other causes first. The best way to avoid adding to problems related to salinity is to prevent them: Apply fertilizers sparingly and in the proper amounts, exercise caution when applying manures and compost made

Figure 6.1. Marginal necrosis of almond leaf margins caused by excessive soil salinity. *Photo:* Jack Kelly Clark.

from manure, irrigate with good-quality water, and irrigate to the needs of the plant.

As mentioned above, salts come from a variety of sources, which can include irrigation water, fertilizers, manure, compost, and the soil itself. Salt levels in river water and well water can be either low, medium, or high. For example, municipal water from the Sacramento River Delta and water from the Colorado River may be high in salts, depending upon the pumping location and the time of year. (Total salts is not the same thing as water hardness. *Water hardness* is descriptive of the amount of calcium, magnesium, bicarbonates, and carbonates in the water.) The best water, of course, is rainwater. Capture as much of it on your property as you can.

If high salinity is found or develops in a soil, watering practices need to be evaluated. No chemical or material added to the soil can correct it, and products specifically marketed to eliminate it are not effective. The only practical remedy is to leach (drain) the salts out of the root zone using good-quality (low-salt) water, but even this can only be done if the soil at the site has good drainage. Rainwater is the best water available for keeping salt levels low. Try to keep rainwater on your property rather than losing it to the storm drain system.

Soil pH

The acidity or alkalinity of a substance is expressed as its pH on a scale of 0 to 14. Acid soils have low pH values (less than 7); alkaline soils have high pH values (greater than 7). The optimal pH for deciduous fruit trees is between 6.0 and 7.5. A very low (acidic) pH, below 5.5, reduces the availability of calcium,

magnesium, phosphorus, nitrogen, and other nutrients; encourages aluminum and manganese toxicity; and makes trees more susceptible to certain fungal and bacterial diseases. An exception is blueberries, which require a very acidic soil (pH 4.5 to 5.5). A very high (alkaline) pH, in excess of 7.5, reduces the availability of iron, zinc, copper, and manganese.

Keeping the soil at the proper pH helps maintain your soil's fertility because nutrients will continue to be available. You may find it useful to have your soil tested before you plant, especially if large numbers of trees are to be planted, since preplant treatments are much easier to accomplish than postplant treatments. If the soil pH is too low (acidic), you can raise it by incorporating lime, dolomite, or wood ashes into the soil. If the pH is too high (alkaline), you can lower it by incorporating soil sulfur followed by irrigation, which causes a rapid (6-month) change in pH value. Fertilizers and organic-matter application will also cause pH to fall gradually until it reaches an equilibrium. For more information, consult your local UC Cooperative Extension office.

The type of nitrogen to use is affected by whether your soil is typically acidic (low pH) or basic (high pH). Table 6.1 shows the soil's reaction to the fertilizer (that is, the fertilizer's effect on soil pH). You can influence the pH of your soil by choosing a fertilizer to which your soil will react in a certain way. Ammonium sulfate, which acidifies the soil more than many other fertilizers, benefits acid-loving plants like blueberries, azaleas, camellias, and hydrangeas.

Types of fertilizer

Compost, mulch, and organic, and synthetic fertilizers

In this section, we use the terms *organic* and *inorganic*. *Organic*, in chemistry, means that a molecule contains carbon, whereas *inorganic* means that a molecule does not contain carbon. Naturally occurring compounds may be either inorganic or organic.

In vernacular use, *organic* implies a derivation from a living or once-living source. In this section, we use *organic* mostly in this sense.

Composts, mulches, and organic fertilizers constitute an important part of fertility management in backyard fruit culture. Their nutrients are released

Table 6.1. Examples of synthetic fertilizers for soil application

Fertilizer	Formula	Nitrogen (N %)	Phosphorus (P_2O_5 %)[†]	Potassium fertilizer* (K_2O %)[‡]	Effect on soil pH	Comments
Ammonium sulfate (sulfate of ammonia)	$(NH_4)_2SO_4$	21	0	0	strongly acidic	
Calcium nitrate	$Ca(NO_3)_2$	16	0	0	basic	also a source of calcium
Potassium chloride (old term: "muriate of potash")	KCl	0	0	60	neutral	high hazard from chloride
Potassium nitrate	KNO_3	13	0	44	slightly basic	
Potassium sulfate (old term: "sulfate of potash")	K_2SO_4	0	0	50	almost neutral	
Superphosphate	$Ca(H_2PO_4)_2$	0	20	0	neutral	
Urea	$CO(NH_2)_2$	45	0	0	moderately acidic	
12-12-12	—	12	12	12	varies, usually acidic	
16-16-16	—	16	16	16	varies, usually acidic	

Source: Adapted from Faber et al. 2002, p. 56.

Note: "—" indicates that information is not available.

*Other synthetic materials used as fertilizers include zinc sulfate ($ZnSO_4 \cdot H_2O$, 36% zinc) and chelates of iron and zinc. Chelation increases the stability of the nutrients in the soil, making them available to plants for longer periods of time.

[†]Phosphoric acid (P_2O_5) actually contains 43% phosphorus. The percentages given for the oxide can be converted to percentages of the element by multiplication: $P = P_2O_5 \times 0.43$.

[‡]Potash (K_2O) actually contains 83% potassium. The percentages given for the oxide can be converted to percentages of the element by multiplication: $K = K_2O \times 0.83$.

slowly during the growing season and converted into a form that the tree can use. Compost, mulch, and organic fertilizers supply the same nutrients as synthetic fertilizers. The difference between them is that the nutrients in synthetic fertilizers are more concentrated and are released more quickly, whereas composts and mulches, in addition to supplying nutrients, may also improve the soil's tilth and water penetration. Also, the cost per pound of nutrient is usually less for synthetic fertilizers than for organic materials. Composts and mulches also serve to recycle waste. Because organic fertilizers release their nutrients slowly, they are not useful in treating acute nutrient deficiencies; faster-release or more-concentrated materials should be used for this purpose. Compost, mulch, and organic fertilizers can be used in conjunction with synthetic fertilizers. When correcting a nutrient deficiency, check the guaranteed analysis of any fertilizer to make sure it has the nutrients you need.

Compost is made of partially decomposed organic material and is often incorporated into the soil, where its nutrients gradually become available to roots—but it can also be used as a mulch on the soil surface. It is usually low in nutrient content (single-digit percentages); its principal value is improving soil structure and tilth. You can make your own compost using waste materials from your house, yard, and garden. Publications on making compost are available at your local UC Cooperative Extension office. Make sure that the compost is fairly well decomposed before you incorporate it into the soil. Plant-based compost may contain most or all of the nutrients needed for tree growth. However, compost alone may not supply enough nitrogen for optimal tree growth.

Mulch, strictly speaking, is not a fertilizer—it is any material put on top of the soil to conserve moisture, suppress weeds, encourage beneficial organisms, reduce erosion, and perform other useful functions. Yet applying organic mulches such as chopped leaves, clippings, twigs, and other organic waste to the soil can help soil by improving its tilth, encouraging beneficial organisms such as earthworms, and reducing the number of weeds that compete with trees for nutrients. Mulch reduces evaporation of water from soil. Also, over time, the bottom of the mulch layer—the part that touches the soil—will decompose and gradually become part of the soil, much like a compost. You can make mulch at home by chopping leaves, clippings, tree prunings, and other yard waste and spreading them on top of the soil.

Organic fertilizers are commercially produced materials that include various manures or organic concentrates, such as bone meal or fish meal (table 6.2). Purchased on a retail basis, organic fertilizers are more expensive per unit of nutrient than synthetic fertilizers. Manures, which often are mixtures of composted animal waste and plant matter, can be used to supply nitrogen and other nutrients to trees, but they must be used with caution because they may contain weed seeds and high levels of salts. Manures, depending on the sources, have varying levels and ratios of nutrients and could be viewed as soil amendments because organic matter is added. Manures usually do not have a guaranteed analysis printed on the bag. The nutrient content of fresh manure is usually higher than in bagged products.

Synthetic (inorganic) fertilizers

Synthetic fertilizers—also known as inorganic, chemical, mineral, or commercial fertilizers—are typically salts (see table 6.1). The nutrients they contain (nitrogen, phosphorus, potassium, and so on) are the same as those found in organic fertilizers. Synthetic fertilizers, however, are made by concentrating naturally occurring minerals or through synthesis (for example, taking nitrogen from air) into a fertilizer compound. For the most part, the nutrients in synthetic fertilizers are rapidly available to plants, although slow-release synthetic fertilizers are available.

Synthetic fertilizers are sold in bags or packages that must be labeled with the name of the chemical

Table 6.2. Approximate analysis of some organic fertilizers*

Fertilizer	Nitrogen[†] (N %)	Phosphorus[‡] (P_2O_5 %)	Potassium[§] (K_2O %)
Straight manures and composts (some store-bought materials are blends of manure and compost)			
Chicken (dry)	2.0–4.5	4.6–6.0	1.2–2.4
Dairy (dry)	0.6–3.5	0.5–1.1	2.4–3.6
Horse (fresh)	0.7–3.0	0.3–1.2	0.5–2.2
Poultry (dry)	2.0–5.0	1.0–2.3	1.6–2.3
Poultry (fresh)	1.0	0.9	0.5
Sheep (dry)	3.0–5.0	0.4–1.6	2.0–4.0
Sheep (fresh)	1.1	0.4	1.0
Steer (dry)	1.0–2.5	0.9–1.9	2.4–3.6
Organic concentrates			
Bat guano	10.0	3.0	1.0
Bone meal	3.0	15.0	0.0
Cottonseed meal	6.0	0.4	1.5
Dried blood	13.0	1.5	2.5
Feather meal	12.0	0.0	0.0
Fish meal	10.0	6.0	0.0
Soybean meal	7.0	1.2	1.5
Wood ashes[¶]	0.0	2.0	6.0

Source: Faber et al. 2002, p. 59.

*For more extensive information, see Chaney et al. 1992. Analysis reported in this table is an average for primary nutrients without accounting for losses caused by leaching or decomposition. One cubic foot of air-dry manure weighs about 25 lb.

[†]Analysis based on dry weight except for fresh manures, which contain about 65% to 85% water.

[‡]Analysis based on dry weight except for fresh manures, which contain about 65% to 85% water. Phosphoric acid (P_2O_5) actually contains 43% phosphorus. The percentages given for the oxide can be converted to percentages of the element by multiplication: $P = P_2O_5 \times 0.43$.

[§]Analysis based on dry weight except for fresh manures which contain about 65% to 85% water. Potash (K_2O) actually contains 83% potassium. The percentages given for the oxide can be converted to percentages of the element by multiplication: $K = K_2O \times 0.83$.

[¶]Burning eliminates organic matter and forms inorganic compounds.

form of the nutrient and must have a guaranteed analysis; that is, the label must state the percentages of nutrients that the package contains. The analysis generally consists of three numbers that describe the chemical content of the fertilizer: The first represents the percentage of nitrogen, the second represents the percentage of phosphorus as P_2O_5, and the third represents the percentage of potassium as K_2O. For example, ammonium nitrate contains 34 percent nitrogen by weight and has no phosphorus or potassium, so it is labeled "34-0-0." The numbers do not add up to 100 percent because the plant nutrients are bound to other atoms in the fertilizer molecules. There is no "filler" in a fertilizer such as 34-0-0 or 16-16-16 that might make the numbers add up to 100.

A "complete" synthetic fertilizer contains some amount of all three nutrients. The term *complete* does not mean that the fertilizer supplies all of the nutrients needed by a plant nor that nutrients are present in the correct relative amounts—only that all three are present. For example, a "complete" fertilizer need not contain zinc or iron, although both are required for plant growth. Since complete fertilizers are mixes, they are named after their analysis, such as "16-16-16," instead of after the chemicals they contain.

Take special care in the use of synthetic fertilizers because they are more concentrated than organic fertilizers. Since most synthetic fertilizers are salts, they can increase the salinity of the soil if misapplied and they can burn leaves or fruit if they come in contact with them. Also, when you apply one nutrient, you may reduce the tree's ability to take up some other nutrient; for example, excess phosphorus can tie up zinc and magnesium may compete with calcium. Too much nitrogen can cause excessive growth, while ammonium sulfate or sulfur may increase the soil's acidity to damaging levels.

However, these distinctions among fertilizer types are not as simple as presented here. For example, mined minerals—such as greensand, a potassium source—is slow release. In terms of its chemistry, it is inorganic (no carbon), although it is a natural product. Bat or bird guano is high in nitrogen and salts, and behaves like a synthetic fertilizer, to which it is similar in chemical properties.

Nutrient deficiencies and toxicities

Plants can be harmed by receiving too little of a nutrient (deficiency) or too much of a nutrient (toxicity). In most California backyard environments, deciduous fruit trees may develop obvious nutrient deficiencies or toxicities, although in many locations, iron or zinc deficiencies can be observed. The most commonly deficient nutrients are nitrogen, iron, zinc, and potassium. Deficiencies of boron, manganese, and magnesium can also occur. Other nutrient deficiencies are rare. Iron deficiency symptoms are common, but they may not result from a lack of iron in the soil. Instead, the symptoms may result from excess soil moisture, which prevents the roots from taking up sufficient iron. Iron deficiency symptoms can also be an indication of high soil pH.

Diagnosing nutrient deficiencies and toxicities

Many nutrient deficiencies and toxicities produce relatively distinctive visual symptoms on leaves and shoots (table 6.3). A good place to begin diagnosis is with an attempt to eliminate other causes of the symptoms, such as disease (see chapter 11, "Integrated pest management for backyard orchards"), too much or too little water, or damage from wind, sun, heat, or cold (Costello et al. 2003). If the plant is healthy and no other causes of damage are apparent, determine whether the problem affects new growth or old growth first. Nitrogen and potassium are mobile in the plant, so deficiencies in these nutrients affect older leaves first. Zinc and iron are immobile in plants, so deficiencies in these tend to affect younger leaves first. Also, consider the location or pattern of symptoms—for example, whether leaves are turning brown on the tips and edges or are yellowing between the leaf veins. Symptoms of several nutrient deficiencies are shown in figures 6.2 through 6.7.

Even with the most careful examination, nutrient deficiencies and toxicities cannot be conclusively diagnosed on the basis of visual symptoms alone; laboratory analysis of plant tissues (leaves and petioles) may be needed as well. Tissue analysis may be too expensive for the backyard orchardist. Soil analysis is inexpensive and can be helpful, since pH, salinity,

Table 6.3. General symptoms of nutrient deficiency and toxicity in deciduous fruit and nut trees

Nutrient	Deficiency symptoms	Toxicity symptoms
Nitrogen (N)	Deficiency symptoms are similar for peach and plum, showing pale green leaves near the terminal of shoot and yellow leaves at the base. In peach and nectarine, leaf midribs and stems are characteristically red. As the season progresses, red and brown spots develop in leaves. Shoot growth and leaf size are reduced, but not so much as with zinc deficiency. Premature leaf drop often occurs. Fewer flower buds are produced for the next season and if very severe, the resulting fruit may be smaller and have more color.	Excessive growth of dark green leaves; few fruit; delayed maturity of fruit; reduced fruit size and quality; leaf tips and margins may turn brown and die.
Phosphorus (P)	Leaves on peaches and nectarines are dark green, eventually turning bronze and developing a leathery texture. A purple or red coloration appears on the leaves, petioles, and young shoots. Leaf size may be reduced and premature defoliation may occur, beginning with the basal leaves. Yield and fruit size are reduced. Fruit are more highly colored and ripen earlier but exhibit surface defects.	Slow growth, stunting, and purplish or dark green leaves, eventually turning bronze and developing a leathery texture (sometimes with cupping), chlorosis between leaf veins (interveinal) and at leaf edges (marginal). Extremely rare.
Potassium (K)	Slow growth; pale green leaves; leaves curl and roll upward along margins; leaf tip and marginal browning ("burn") and necrosis. Symptoms usually do not show up until midsummer and often are first observed in the middle of the shoot. Older leaves may fall off. You may observe fewer flower buds and fruit. Fruit is often smaller. On pears and walnuts the leaves may have a bronze color. Apples often have burning on the edge of the leaves. In almonds the tip of the leaf will curl up.	None, but excess K can cause Mg deficiency symptoms.
Calcium (Ca)	Reduced terminal (end) growth of shoots; may have twig dieback and leaf drop; chlorotic patches may develop on leaves before they fall; pits on apples, pears. Very rare.	—
Magnesium (Mg)	Marginal chlorosis leaving an inverted V-shaped pattern around the midrib; leaves curl upward along margins; marginal yellowing with green area along midribs of leaves; older leaves are affected first and it then progresses out the shoot. Tree usually remains vigorous and yield and fruit size usually are not affected. Very rare.	—
Sulfur (S)	Similar to nitrogen deficiency, generally showing on young leaves first. Very rare.	—
Iron (Fe)	Loss of chlorophyll, leading to interveinal chlorosis (veins remain green); young leaves affected first; twig dieback; reduced growth and leaf drop in severe cases. The ends of shoots often turn a bright gold color and may even turn white.	—
Manganese (Mn)	Interveinal and marginal chlorosis (no sharp distinction between veins and interveinal areas as with iron deficiency); chlorosis develops into a herringbone pattern; in contrast to other plants, fruit trees show symptoms on older leaves first. Unless severe, shoot growth, yield, and fruit size are unaffected.	—

Table 6.3. General symptoms of nutrient deficiency and toxicity in deciduous fruit and nut trees, continued

Nutrient	Deficiency symptoms	Toxicity symptoms
Zinc (Zn)	Leaves remain very small ("little leaf"); decrease in stem length; rosetting of terminal leaves, interveinal chlorosis on young leaves; fewer fruit buds form; delayed bloom; smaller crop; twig dieback after first year. Terminal leaves will have a wavy margin. Small leaves may form rosettes on the shoot tips and young spurs.	—
Boron (B)	Death of terminal growth; growth of many shoots at the end of twigs ("witches' broom"); thickened, curled, wilted, chlorotic leaves; young leaves affected first; soft, necrotic spots on fruit; reduced flowering.	Small necrotic (dead) spots on underside of leaves; yellowing of leaf tip; edges of leaves turn blackish and die. Cankers may develop along midrib, petiole, and young twigs. Rare except in arid inland areas with water containing high levels of boron. Fruit can be distorted and have sharp, sunken areas. Peach and nectarine are very sensitive.

Sources: Costello et al. 2003; Faber et al. 2002; Johnson and Uriu 1989; Perry and Asai 1983.

Note: "—" indicates that information is not available.

Figure 6.2. Symptoms of nitrogen deficiency on a peach tree, showing overall yellowing of leaves, including the veins. *Photo:* Jack Kelly Clark.

Figure 6.3. Phosphorus deficiency symptoms of pear, showing cupping of leaves. *Photo:* Jack Kelly Clark.

and levels of potentially toxic elements such as boron, sodium, and chloride can be determined. Soil analysis does not, however, indicate the levels of nutrients in plants themselves. (Commercial laboratories will tell you how they prefer you to collect and handle plant tissue and soil samples.) UC Cooperative Extension offices do not provide tissue or soil testing but can direct you to laboratories in your area.

Using fertilizers

Different fertilizers release nutrients at different rates. If a tree is acutely deficient in nitrogen, an application of compost or organic fertilizer will not solve the problem quickly and the nitrogen deficiency may lead to overall tree decline. But do not overfertilize. Besides wasting your money and time, an excess application of fertilizer can harm trees, the soil, and the overall environment. Follow all instructions on the fertilizer label regarding timing, rates, mixing, method of application, and disposal of unused material.

Calculating how much fertilizer to apply

Fertilizer recommendations are often given in terms of the amount of the needed element rather than the amount of the fertilizer product required. In table 6.4, however, we indicate the amount of fertilizer required, so no further calculations are needed. To de-

Figure 6.4. Potassium deficiency symptoms of prune, with pale green yellowing of the leaves and a curling inward (boating). Sometimes burning along the margins and tips also appears. *Photo:* Harry Andris.

Figure 6.5. Zinc deficiency, showing the classic "little leaf" symptom. *Photo:* Jack Kelly Clark.

Table 6.4. Approximate amounts of fertilizer to apply per year to correct a deficiency*

Deficiency and fertilizer type	Dosage to correct deficiency			
	Large fruit trees	Small fruit trees	Large nut trees	Small nut trees
Nitrogen	*pounds per year*			
Actual nitrogen	1.0	0.5	2.0	1.0
Ammonium sulfate	4.8	2.4	9.5	4.8
15-15-15	6.7	3.4	13.3	6.7
16-16-16	6.6	3.1	12.5	6.3
16-20-0	6.6	3.1	12.5	6.3
20-27-5	5.0	2.5	10.0	5.0

Apply half of the nitrogen in midspring and the rest right after harvest.

Deficiency and fertilizer type	Dosage to correct deficiency	
	Large fruit and nut trees	Small fruit and nut trees and bushes
Potassium	*pounds per year*	
Potassium sulfate applied to clay soil	15	8
Potassium sulfate applied to sandy soil	7	4

Deficiency and fertilizer type	Dosage to correct deficiency
Zinc	
Zinc sulfate	2 oz per gallon of water as a foliar spray in early to mid-November. Thoroughly soak all the leaves on the trees. This will cause the leaves to burn and drop off, but this will not hurt the tree.

*Trees younger than four years old should receive the small tree rate. For other specialty fertilizers not listed here, follow the label directions.

Table 6.5. Approximate weight of ammonium sulfate fertilizer and actual nitrogen held in some commonly available containers that you can use for measuring

Container	Ammonium sulfate (21-0-0) fertilizer	Actual nitrogen
	ounces	
6.5 fl. oz. tuna can	8	1.7
14 fl. oz. soup can	16	3.4
12 fl. oz. frozen juice can	14	2.9
24 oz. coffee can	70	14.7

Figure 6.6. Iron deficiency symptoms include a characteristic interveinal chlorosis, with sharply defined green veins. It usually occurs in soil that has a high pH or is overwatered. *Photo:* Jack Kelly Clark.

termine how much of a particular fertilizer it would take to apply a given amount of the needed element, divide the amount of the element by the percentage of that element in the fertilizer. For example, assume that you need to apply 1 pound of actual nitrogen using ammonium sulfate fertilizer. The analysis of ammonium sulfate (as printed on the bag) is 21-0-0, meaning that it contains 21 percent nitrogen (or 0.21 lb N for every 1 lb of fertilizer), 0 percent phosphorus, and 0 percent potassium. The calculation would be

1 lb. N ÷ 0.21 lb. N in fertilizer = 4.76 lb.,

which is about 4 pounds 12 ounces of fertilizer. Similarly, when using dry chicken manure pellets containing 4 percent nitrogen and 3 percent phosphorus and potassium, 25 pounds would be required to supply 1 pound of nitrogen. The 25 pounds of fertilizer would also provide 0.75 pounds of phosphorus and potassium (25 lb × 0.03).

Soil application

Nitrogen, phosphorus, and potassium fertilizers are usually applied to the soil in a dry (granular or powdered) form. Spread the fertilizer evenly on the soil, avoiding clumps and uneven spots, in a circular pattern around the tree. For a mature tree, apply no closer than 2 feet to the tree trunk. Rather, sprinkle around it sparingly. After spreading the fertilizer, it helps to rake it into the top inch or so of soil. For individual trees, you can apply the fertilizer in a narrow band around the tree, near the drip line (figs. 6.8–6.9). When fertilizing a young tree, do not concentrate the fertilizer on top of the root ball.

Nitrogen fertilizers are best applied in the spring and summer, when uptake of water and nutrients is greatest.

Figure 6.7. Manganese deficiency symptoms, showing interveinal chlorosis and with broad green bands around the veins. It is usually caused by high-pH soil. *Photo:* Harry Andris.

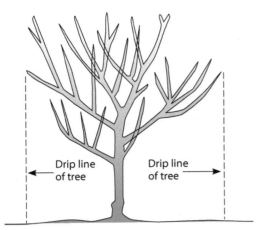

Figure 6.8. Location of the drip line or canopy edge of a tree. This is a good area for applying fertilizer and water. *Source:* Ingels et al. 2007.

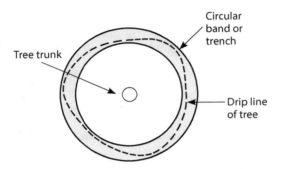

Figure 6.9. Location of the circular band or trench around the drip line in which you can apply fertilizer. *Source:* Ingels et al. 2007.

Water the fertilized soil thoroughly to move the nitrogen into the tree's root zone. You can also place fertilizer material right under a drip irrigation emitter so the applied water can dissolve it and carry it into the root zone (see fig. 6.9). In larger home orchards with extensive drip lines, fertilizer is not needed under every emitter.

Fertilizing through the irrigation water

Many farmers and greenhouse growers routinely apply soluble fertilizers through the irrigation system. Devices that introduce fertilizer into the water stream, known as fertilizer injectors, can be used in the home garden as well. This process is called *fertigation*, and it lends itself well to the use of drip irrigation.

If used properly in an efficient irrigation system, fertigation can be an effective way to apply fertilizers accurately. Roots grow mainly where water is applied

and fertigation places the fertilizer where the roots are. Therefore, less fertilizer is needed. However, there are potential drawbacks to fertigation. If the water source is high in cations and carbonate, precipitates may clog emitters. Also, with large or sloping sites, the water's distribution uniformity may be poor. In that case, the fertilizer uniformity will also be poor.

Choosing the right injector and fertilizer materials requires detailed study because injectors and irrigation systems vary greatly. The wrong injector or fertilizer can lead to insufficient water flow, resulting in poor uniformity in distribution of water, insufficient or excess applied nutrients, clogging, or other problems. If additional drip lines are added after the system is set up, you should consider increasing the water flow.

Materials that may be injected in fertigation systems include organic, dry, and liquid fertilizers. Not just any fertilizer can be injected, however—it must be soluble. The label may indicate if it is suitable for injection. Soluble fertilizers that are dry must first be mixed with water to form a solution.

Foliar application

Micronutrient fertilizers (mainly iron and zinc) can be applied to a tree's leaves. The usual method is to spray them on in a liquid form. Check the guaranteed analysis of nutrients on the label. Verify that the formulation is safe for application to leaves (foliar application) and dilute it according to instructions. Foliar applications are best made in the spring before hot weather causes leaves to become thick and waxy. If the leaves are heavily coated with dust, wash the tree off and let it dry prior to application. Spray the fertilizer evenly and make sure that all leaves are fully wetted. The spray should be applied to the point where the liquid begins to run off. Foliar sprays provide an immediate but short-term response; they are often used in conjunction with soil-applied fertilizers. Some people use various organic foliar sprays, such as fish and kelp products, to add small amounts of nutrients, vitamins, minerals, and hormones. Little formal research has been conducted to determine the value of such treatments. Do not combine foliar fertilizers with pesticide sprays, since some combinations can damage leaves.

Zinc and potassium

As stated earlier, trees and shrubs in a mature yard may need little in the way of routine fertilizer applications, especially in cooler climates and in locations with loam or clay loam soils. Very sandy or gravelly soils have low nutrient content and low nutrient-holding capacity, so trees planted on these soils may benefit from application of certain nutrients.

Other than nitrogen, the elements most likely to become deficient in many parts of California are zinc and potassium; zinc sulfate and potassium sulfate, applied every other year, may prevent deficiencies. Because zinc and potassium are immobile in the soil, you have to apply them in a concentrated band through which the roots can grow. You can also apply nitrogen fertilizer in the same band. The band

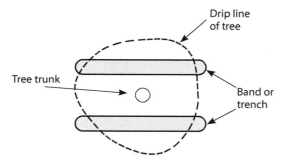

Figure 6.10. Location of straight bands or trenches for fertilizer application. *Source:* Ingels et al. 2007.

does not need to extend all the way around the tree. It can be as short as a foot or two in length on two sides of a small tree (fig. 6.10) or four sides of a large tree.

The amount of nitrogen to apply depends on the condition of the tree. If the tree is growing well and its foliage is dark green, no extra nitrogen is needed. If growth is weak and leaves are uniformly pale, the tree may need more nitrogen, although other factors can also cause these symptoms. Follow the guidelines in tables 6.4 and 6.5.

Reference

Costello, L. R. 2003. Abiotic disorders of landscape plants. Oakland: UC Agriculture and Natural Resources Publication 3420.

Further reading

Chaney, D. E., L. E. Drinkwater, and G. S. Pettygrove. 1992. Organic soil amendments and fertilizers. Oakland: UC Agriculture and Natural Resources Publication 21505.

Faber, B., L. Clement, D. Giraud, and D. Silva. 2015. Soil and fertilizer management. In D. Pittenger, ed., California master gardener handbook. Davis: UC Agriculture and Natural Resources Publication 3382. 37–82.

Geisel, P. M., and C. L. Unruh. 2001. Compost in a hurry. Oakland: UC Agriculture and Natural Resources Publication 8037.

Ingels, C. A., P. M. Geisel, and M. V. Norton, tech. eds. 2007. The home orchard. Oakland: UC Agriculture and Natural Resources Publication 3485.

Johnson, R., and K. Uriu. 1989. Mineral nutrition. In J. H. LaRue and R. S. Johnson, eds., Peaches, plums, and nectarines: Growing and handling for fresh market. Oakland: UC Agriculture and Natural Resources Publication 3331. Ch. 13.

Chapter 7

Training and pruning

Chuck A. Ingels, Ted DeJong, Louise Ferguson, Janine Hasey,
Katherine Jarvis-Shean, Craig Kallsen, and Maxwell Norton

A fruit or nut tree must eventually support the weight of a potentially large fruit or nut crop. In general, when a tree is young, we prune for structure; when it is mature, we prune for fruit size and quality. Proper training in the first few years of a tree's development creates a strong scaffold and branch structure—and makes various cultural practices such as fruit thinning, pest management, and harvesting easier. Table 7.1 lists training systems, including open-center, central-leader, modified central leader, espalier, and "fruit-bush" training.

Pruning is the most important training practice, though bending branches and tying or staking them into position can also be helpful. Mature trees are pruned to reduce tree height, improve sunlight penetration into the lower portions of the tree, rejuvenate fruiting spurs, and reduce the amount of fruit thinning that the tree will need. Pruning is commonly done during the dormant season (winter), as well as from midspring through summer, but can be done at any time of year. Table 7.1 lists the amount of pruning that is generally conducted on various fruit and nut species.

Before they were domesticated, fruit trees grew without training or pruning. Many fruit-tree species produced small fruit and were more like bushes than trees. Modern tree varieties (cultivars) bear relatively heavy crops at an early age, with no training or pruning after planting—but the weight of the fruit can bend or break the main branches, resulting in a poor tree structure. Fruit will also be small in size.

This chapter describes some basic concepts regarding training and pruning—and also provides advice on specific training and pruning methods. Whenever you do any work to train your trees, be sure to observe the effects over subsequent weeks or months. Remember that mistakes are for learning, and they can usually be corrected.

Fundamentals of pruning fruit trees

Bearing habits of fruit and nut trees

Proper pruning requires that you know the types of branches or shoots upon which a particular species of fruit is produced. For example, you should only make heading cuts on persimmon if you desire strong main branches. This is because heading cuts in persimmon involve cutting off the new bearing shoots that originate from near the tips of 1-year-old branches (fig. 7.1A). Species such as apple, pear, and cherry produce spurs (short shoots specialized for fruiting) (fig. 7.1B). Spurs should be retained—and sometimes reinvigorated by thinning and shortening them. Peach and nectarine trees produce flowers and fruit on long 1-year-old branches ("hangers") (fig. 7.9C). Table 7.1 shows the bearing habits of various fruit and nut species.

Tools and techniques for making pruning cuts

Use pruning loppers to cut shoots and small to medium-size branches. There are two types of pruning loppers: bypass and anvil (fig. 7.2). Both types have a single blade, but on bypass loppers the blade bypasses the jaw or hook, which keeps the branch in place while the blade shears past it. Anvil loppers have a straight blade that cuts down against a flat surface. Bypass loppers are generally easier to use and better for cutting because they cut more cleanly and cause less damage to the bark of larger branches than do anvil types. Use a sharp pruning saw for branches too large to be cut with loppers (generally, branches with a diameter greater than 2 in.). Keep pruning tools sharp. Dull tools make rough cuts that can tear bark. Tearing inhibits wound repair and promotes damage by insects or disease.

Table 7.1. Fruiting wood characteristics and pruning of fruit and nut trees

| | Location of fruiting buds on | | | | | | |
| | Long branches | | Short branches or spurs | | Approximate life of bearing spur or branch | Type of training system | Amount of pruning for mature trees |
Type of tree	Laterally	Terminally	Laterally	Terminally			
Almond	minor		major		5 years	open center	light (thinning)
Apple		minor		major	8–10 years	central leader, modified central leader, open center, espalier, or fruit bush	moderate
Apricot	minor		major		3 years	open center or fruit bush	heavy
Cherry	minor		major		10–12 years	open center or fruit bush	light to moderate
Chestnut		minor		major		modified central leader	light (thinning)
Fig*	major		minor		bears on 1 year and new shoots	open center, modified central leader, or fruit bush	various
Peach/ nectarine	major		minor		1–2 years	open center, perpendicular V, or fruit bush	heavy
Pear, Asian	major	very minor		major	6–8 years	modified central leader, open center, espalier, or fruit bush	moderate to heavy
Pear, European	minor	minor		major	8–10 years	modified central leader, open center, multiple leader, espalier, or fruit bush	moderate
Pecan		major		major	fruit spikes borne on tips of new shoots	central leader	light (thinning)

open center

central leader

modified central leader

fruit bush

espalier

| Type of tree | Location of fruiting buds on | | | | Approximate life of bearing spur or branch | Type of training system | Amount of pruning for mature trees |
| | Long branches | | Short branches or spurs | | | | |
	Laterally	Terminally	Laterally	Terminally			
Persimmon[†]	major	major	minor	minor	bears on new shootsthat grow near tips of 1-year-old branches	modified central leader or open center	light (mainly thinning)
Pistachio	major		minor			modified central leader or open center	light
Plum, European	minor		major		6–8 years	open center or fruit bush	moderate
Plum, Japanese	minor		major		6–8 years	open center	heavy
Pomegranate	minor		major		bears on short, new shoots	modified central leader of fruit bush	moderate
Quince	major	minor			bears on new shoots	modified central leader or open center	light (mainly thinning)
Walnut, teminal-bearing varieties[‡]		major		major	bears on tips of new shoots	modified central leader	light (mainly thinning)
Walnut, lateral-bearing varieties[‡]	major	major	major	major	bears on tips of new shoots	modified central leader	light to moderate; heavier if little shoot growth

*Figs bear fruit laterally on both 1-year-old branches and current-season's shoots.

[†]Persimmon fruit are borne laterally on new shoots that grow from 1-year-old branches. Fruiting shoots originate mainly from terminal buds and lateral buds near the tips of branches.

[‡]See chapter 3 for bearing habits of walnut varieties.

Figure 7.1. Examples of bearing habits: persimmon, which bears on new shoots (A); Asian pear spurs, which should be thinned (B); 1-year-old peach fruiting branches (C). *Photos:* Chuck Ingels.

Figure 7.2. Bypass lopper (A) and anvil-type hand pruner (B). Many gardeners prefer bypass loppers; anvil loppers are mainly used on small branches. *Photos:* Chuck Ingels.

To remove an entire branch, cut just beyond the branch collar (the slightly raised area on the main branch at the point where the branch to be cut is attached) (fig. 7.3). Never cut into or behind the branch collar, since doing so limits the ability of the tree to seal the wound. Remove branches more than 2 inches in diameter in two steps, using a sharp saw.

Figure 7.3. Pruning cut made just beyond the swollen branch collar. Cutting into the collar would inhibit callus formation and wound healing. *Photo:* Chuck Ingels.

First, make an undercut about one-quarter of the way through the underside of the branch near its point of attachment, but outside the branch collar. Then remove the limb with a cut on the upper side of the branch just outside the first cut. For larger branches (more than 3 in.), use a three-step cut (Hodel and Pittenger 2015, 316).

Wound emulsions, paint, or other materials are not necessary—in fact, studies have shown these materials do not help trees to seal pruning cuts. Leave pruning cuts open to the air to dry out and form callus tissue (new wood).

For more information on pruning, see Hodel and Pittenger 2015, 314–320; Ingels et. al 2002; and Vossen and Silva 2015, 503–509.

Apical dominance and the effects of heading versus thinning cuts

Proper pruning requires an understanding of the way trees respond to different types of cuts. Tree growth is controlled in part by plant hormones that are produced primarily in the apical meristems (cells that make up the actively growing shoot tips) and the leaves. The plant hormone auxin (indoleacetic acid) is produced in the shoot tips and new leaves and moves down the shoot, preventing or delaying the growth of lateral buds (see chapter 2, "Growth and development"). Auxin also influences the rate of growth and the angle of branches. The phenomenon by which the shoot tip controls growth below is called apical dominance. Some species, such as cherry and pear, exhibit strong apical dominance; shoots of these species grow strongly upright, usually with few lateral branches, especially on young trees. Some other species, especially peach, have little apical dominance, so lateral branching readily occurs.

A *heading* cut, in which a branch or shoot is shortened (fig. 7.4), removes the upper portion of the branch or shoot (which regulates growth lower on the branch). Lateral buds are then freed from the effects of auxin and the buds just below the cut respond with rapid shoot growth. This response is sometimes desirable—for example, when developing scaffold branches on young trees. Often, however, excessive shoot growth from too many heading cuts will result in dense branching and thus shading of lower fruiting branches.

A *thinning* cut entirely removes a branch or shoot at the point of its attachment to a larger branch (fig. 7.5). Because a thinning cut does not leave a stub or short branch, it does not stimulate vigorous shoot growth. It does, however, enhance sunlight penetration into the canopy.

Branch spreaders to reduce pruning

The training of trees can be improved and accelerated by spreading undesirably positioned upright shoots and branches with toothpicks, clothespins, sticks, pruned whip branches, or purchased spreaders—rather than by removing or heading the shoots and branches (fig. 7.6). For larger branches, spreader boards can be made by notching the ends of laths or by inserting finish nails into the ends of ¾- to 1-inch-square sticks (fig. 7.7). A branch that is trained to grow into a particular position will remain in that position for the life of the tree. Spreading branches when they are young also widens the angle of branch attachment, making the branch connection stronger. Spreaders are particularly useful with central-leader training to reduce the possibility that a branch will become codominant with the central leader (central-leader training is a system in which the trunk is encouraged to form a central axis, with branches distributed laterally around it). If a branch needs to be repositioned, you can also pound a stake into the ground and use it as an anchor to tie the branch in the desired location (fig. 7.8). Spreaders, stakes, and strings can be removed once the desired branch position is achieved—in about a year, or sometimes sooner.

Summer pruning versus dormant pruning

The timing of pruning influences a tree's response to pruning. Dormant pruning is the most invigorating because it allows the carbohydrates the tree has stored in the roots and wood for the winter to be allocated to fewer growing points. Pruning in early spring just after shoot break can slightly reduce vigor and also reduces apical dominance, thereby stimulating growth below the pruning cuts. Pruning from midspring through summer removes actively growing and photosynthesizing leaves. It can reduce tree

Figure 7.4. A heading cut leads to the vigorous growth of shoots from buds just below the cut, as shown. With apically dominant species such as cherry, shown here, only the top two or three buds usually grow, and the shoot growth is upright. Growth of the lowest shoot is often weaker and more horizontal. *Photo:* Chuck Ingels.

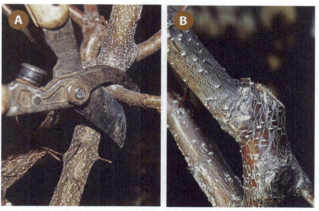

Figure 7.5. Thinning cuts: removal of branch back to a main branch (A) and cutting off a branch just above a lateral branch that is at least one-third the diameter of the main branch (B). *Photos:* Chuck Ingels.

Figure 7.6. A plastic spreader (red) and sticks were used to spread branches on this genetic dwarf apple. *Photo:* Chuck Ingels.

Figure 7.7. This pear tree developed an upright, narrow shape that cannot be corrected solely by pruning. An open center was developed by using spreaders. In illustrations of this type, trees are shown before pruning (green) and after pruning (brown). Adapted from Micke et al. 1980.

Figure 7.8. Using stakes to bend and tie branches to spread them. *Photo:* Chuck Ingels.

vigor and subsequent growth to some extent because the tree has already expended valuable carbohydrate reserves on shoot and leaf growth.

Summer pruning of mature deciduous fruit trees is used to remove excessively vigorous shoots that shade lower fruiting branches. It can be done any time from midspring through summer. Thinning cuts are preferred to avoid stimulating even more growth. Summer pruning, however, can lead to sunburn in warm areas of California.

Use both summer and winter pruning to manage vigor and crop load. Proper summer training and pruning can reduce the amount of dormant pruning needed, while winter pruning, which takes place while leaves are absent, allows a clear view of the tree's framework, so any remaining crowded or unwanted branches can be removed.

In wetter areas, avoid making large cuts in the lower portion of trees in winter and early spring because wood-rotting fungi may infect wounds. Make large cuts low in the tree only from late April through August, and never when rain is predicted. This especially applies to apricots and cherries, which are susceptible to infection by branch-killing diseases, including Eutypa dieback and Botryosphaeria dieback (see chapter 11, "Integrated pest management for backyard orchards"). These diseases are less prevalent in very dry regions and in much of Southern California. Infection occurs on wounds made during wet weather from fall through winter, causing branch dieback and severe gumming at pruning wounds. It is thus best to prune apricot and cherry trees after harvest in the summer (July or August) so that at least 6 weeks of dry weather are likely to follow the pruning. (Pruning in August will result in less subsequent regrowth than will pruning in July). Be sure to leave enough foliage to cover limbs. Alternatively, you can prevent sunburn by painting limbs exposed to hot afternoon sun with tree paint, whitewash, or a 50:50 mixture of white latex paint and water (see chapter 4, "Orchard design and planting and care of young trees").

No matter which training method you choose, consider doing some pruning in the spring and summer to train young trees and shorten the time needed to reach full fruit production. When necessary, bend and stake shoots of young trees to grow in the desired direction during the spring and summer. Bending branches in this manner is a quicker way to develop the scaffold structure than heading the branches and waiting for new lateral branches to form.

Controlling size of fruit and nut trees

Full-sized and trees on dwarfing rootstock

Full-sized trees on standard rootstocks can potentially grow to heights of 16 to 18 feet for most stone fruit and 25 to 30 feet for most other species. Trees on dwarfing rootstock vary depending on the rootstock but can generally grow to about 10 to 20 feet tall. Pruning of both standard and semidwarf trees keeps trees smaller, but the greater the dwarfing, the less the vegetative vigor and—therefore—the less effort required to keep them small.

Unfortunately, there are only a few species of fruit trees on reliable dwarfing rootstocks available to homeowners, mainly for semidwarf apples and quince. Also, for some European pear varieties, the more size-controlling selections of Old Home x Farmingdale rootstocks are available. The Gisela rootstock series provides varying degrees of dwarfing for cherry.

Citation rootstock has a 15 to 20 percent dwarfing effect on the stone fruit trees apricot, aprium, pluot, and plumcot but has been demonstrated to be incompatible with peach and nectarine. Several UC-patented semidwarfing rootstocks in the Controller series are compatible with peach and nectarine but are difficult to find in retail nurseries. To date, there are no dwarfing rootstocks for almond, Asian pear, persimmon, fig, pomegranate, walnut, pecan, or chestnut.

Genetic dwarf trees

Genetic dwarf trees may grow to 8 to 10 feet tall and wide at maturity, with compact branches and dense fruiting points and foliage. They provide an adequate amount of fruit for a single family and also make beautiful landscape trees (fig. 7.9). Excellent genetic dwarf selections are available for some species (mainly stone fruit) but are very limited for others. Peach and nectarine cultivars have been bred to include a dwarfing gene that produces a tree with short internodes; the tree grows to about one-third the size of a normal tree (fig. 7.10). Mutations of standard apple

cultivars that have compressed growth and an abundance of fruiting spurs are called spur-type trees.

Genetic dwarf and spur-type trees are usually grafted onto a standard rootstock. They bear fruit of normal size but may set more fruit per given area because the shoots have shorter internodes and compressed fruit buds. Because fruit set can far exceed the reduced canopy's capacity to size the fruit, be sure to thin dwarf trees properly (see chapter 9, "Fruit thinning").

Utilize thinning, and if necessary, reduction cuts to allow light penetration into the lower canopy. The lower and interior fruiting branches tend to die quickly if shaded by dense growth (see the discussion of thinning cuts, below).

Figure 7.9. Genetic dwarf peach and nectarine trees can be featured in the landscape and are especially showy during flowering. *Photo:* Chuck Ingels.

Figure 7.10. Genetic dwarf peach, showing short internode distance (A) and standard-size peach, showing longer internodes (B). *Photos:* Chuck Ingels.

Types of training systems

A tree's growing habit determines how it is trained. Young cherry, plum, and pear trees produce very upright growth. To promote a more spread-out canopy, bend the scaffold branches outward while they are still flexible or cut them back to outside lateral branches (see figs. 7.6 and 7.7). Trees in the stone fruit group, such as apricot, peach, and almond, have a spreading growth habit and tend to produce lateral branches without heading. With these species, it is often necessary to remove flatter-angled branches and leave more upright branches, thus maintaining the upward, outward growth pattern.

Open-center or open-vase system

In the open-center or open-vase system, the center of the tree is kept free of large branches and vigorous upright shoots through careful pruning. This allows sunlight to reach the lower fruiting branches. Open-center pruning is commonly used for almond, apricot, cherry, fig, nectarine, peach, pistachio, plum, and prune trees. Apple, pear, and pomegranate trees can also be trained to this system.

First growing season (year 1)

You may be able to hasten the development of an open-center tree in the first growing season after planting by choosing and promoting scaffold branches (main structural branches) that developed after the initial heading after planting (see chapter 4, "Orchard design and planting and care of young trees")—but only if growth is adequate. In late spring of the first growing season after planting, select three or four shoots to become the primary scaffold branches and pinch back all other strong shoots to about 4 to 6 inches long (fig. 7.11). Scaffold branches should ideally be spaced several inches apart vertically and distributed evenly around the trunk, with the lowest branch about 12 to 18 inches above the ground. Branches should have a wide angle of attachment to the trunk; narrow-angle branches tend to split off in later years with the weight of the fruit. If a shoot or branch grows in the wrong direction, consider tying or staking it into the correct position rather than cutting it back and waiting for a properly positioned shoot to grow.

Cut back the selected future scaffold branches on vigorous trees to about 2 to 3 feet long in midsummer—or when they have grown long enough to promote side branching and develop secondary scaffold branches. Remove poorly positioned, comparably sized shoots as necessary, but leave well-positioned, small, noncompeting lateral shoots for future fruit production and to supply carbohydrates and provide shade for the trunk and main branches. Those shoots may also replace damaged scaffold branches. Bend and stake branches when necessary. Leave some small lateral branches along these scaffold branches and the trunk for early fruiting, tree growth, and sunburn protection. After initial pruning, avoid excessive summer pruning, which can stunt young trees.

First dormant season after planting (year 2)

Follow the same procedure as described above if scaffold selection was not completed the previous sum-

Figure 7.11. Peach tree in first growing season before summer pruning (A). Unwanted shoots were headed back or removed and three well-spaced shoots were selected to become the primary scaffold branches (B). *Photos:* Chuck Ingels.

Figure 7.12. This unpruned 1-year-old peach tree had numerous potential scaffold limbs arising from its trunk. With pruning, three limbs were left, spaced about 120° apart around the trunk and several inches apart vertically. These scaffold limbs were headed slightly to promote branching at the desired points during the next growing season. *Source:* Ingels et al. 2007.

mer. Select three or four primary scaffold branches distributed evenly around the trunk and, if possible, spaced 6 inches apart vertically on the trunk (figs. 7.12–7.14).

Avoid selecting scaffold branches that are directly above or below one another along their length; a branch vertically angled 45 to 60° from the point of attachment is the most desirable. Avoid upright limbs that have narrow, acute angles of attachment, which tend to be weak at the point of attachment and can later split or break from the tree. Flat or horizontal limbs are also less desirable as scaffold limbs, but they may be used if needed.

If the tree grows poorly the first year after planting, head back the primary scaffolds severely—to three or four buds—to promote vigorous growth the next year. Then correct the causes of the poor growth, which often involve poor soil condition, lack of adequate weed control, or improper watering.

Figure 7.13. Some trees do not have three desirable scaffold limbs. In such cases, a branch arising from a primary scaffold can be selected to fill in the space and provide another scaffold limb. On this tree, the third scaffold limb was selected by cutting off weak limbs in the center of the tree and leaving a strong outside branch. *Source:* Ingels et al. 2007.

Figure 7.14. So that it would develop an open center, this 1-year-old Japanese plum tree was pruned to leave outside, spreading limbs, and was headed to promote branching at the desired locations. *Source:* Ingels et al. 2007.

Developing mature trees (years 3–5)

Head the primary scaffold branches in the dormant season to encourage the growth of succeeding tiers of secondary scaffold branches. If lateral branching has occurred naturally, the primary scaffold branch can be cut off just beyond the laterals. Depending on tree vigor and shape, allow one to three secondary branches to develop from each primary scaffold (figs. 7.15–7.16). Remove all other strong branches; they can compete with the selected scaffold branches and block sunlight to lateral fruiting branches and spurs. Competing branches can be removed in either the dormant or the growing season.

Continue training trees in subsequent dormant seasons to direct scaffold growth upward and outward and to fill open spaces with fruiting branches (figs. 7.17–7.19).

By the end of year 4

By this time, there should be three or four primary scaffolds supporting five to seven secondary scaffolds at about eye level. A few additional tertiary-level branches can be added above the secondary branch tier to fill the periphery of the treetop, keeping the center of the tree open to permit light infiltration to

Figure 7.15. Many branches had to be removed from this vigorous, 2-year-old peach tree. Low and horizontal limbs were cut off and vigorous, moderately upright limbs were selected for permanent secondary scaffolds and headed at 2 to 3 feet long. *Source:* Ingels et al. 2007.

Figure 7.16. This 2-year-old almond tree had too many limbs. They were removed during pruning to leave two secondary scaffolds on each primary limb. No heading cuts were made and many small lateral branches were left for fruit wood. *Source:* Ingels et al. 2007.

lower fruiting wood. (An exception is almond trees from which nuts are shaken rather than hand-harvested.) The center can thus fill in somewhat because spurs low in the tree are less important.

Mature trees (years 5 and up)

A major goal of pruning during the mature years is to ensure that ample sunlight reaches the lower spurs so the crop can be harvested closer to the ground. This is especially important for pome and stone fruit cultivars.

Pruning mature open-center fruit trees involves keeping the center free of vigorous, upright shoots during the growing season (fig. 7.20), reducing tree height, and thinning out branches to reduce crowding (figs. 7.21–7.22).

During the dormant season, thin out older spurs of spur-bearing species (except almond). Remove old spurs to keep remaining spurs productive and to produce larger fruit (see table 7.1 to determine spur life). For peaches and nectarines, which bear on 1-year-old wood, select and keep half of the 1-year-old lateral fruiting branches that originate close to main branches. Head any selected branches longer than about 18 inches by one-third (fig. 7.23). Remove

Figure 7.17. This 4-year-old peach tree should bear a substantial crop in its fifth year. Fruit wood was thinned out to adjust the crop load and reduce fruit thinning. *Source:* Ingels et al. 2007.

Figure 7.18. This 3-year-old plum tree was pruned by thinning the tertiary scaffolds to one or two per secondary scaffold. All interfering branches in the center of the tree were removed. By pruning to outside branches, the weight of leaves and fruit next summer will help spread this naturally upright-growing tree. *Source:* Ingels et al. 2007.

Figure 7.19. This 4-year-old almond tree was pruned by thinning out undesirable growth in the center as well as those limbs that had not assumed an outward-upward direction. Note that because a heavy nut set is desired on almond trees, little thinning of the young lateral branches was done. Larger interfering branches in the lower part of the tree were removed. *Source:* Ingels et al. 2007.

2-year-old fruiting branches or cut them back to healthy 1-year-old branches unless you want to retain them as new structural branches. If needed, circle a strong rope around the scaffold branches toward the top of the tree to support the branches as they bear the weight of the fruit (fig. 7.24).

Perpendicular V system

The perpendicular V system, developed by University of California researchers at the Kearney Agricultural Center near Fresno, is used for peach and nectarine. The tree canopy is trained into a V shape, wider at the top than bottom, that is perpendicular to the row (if there is one). The main advantages of this system are close spacing (allowing for multiple varieties in a smaller space) and ease of management. This system resembles the open-center system in that the center is kept open through the growing season, but in this system only two primary scaffold branches are developed and no secondary or tertiary branches are created. All of the fruiting branches grow directly off the two main scaffolds or off short branches that arise from the scaffolds.

Begin by planting bare-root trees 5 to 6 feet apart in the row. A north-south row orientation works best because it allows both sides of the V to receive equal sunlight as the sun moves across the sky. Head the trees at about 12 to 18 inches. Place two bamboo stakes in the ground in a V shape and, as shoots grow, tie one strong shoot to each stake (fig. 7.25). Remove or cut back all other branches that grow from the trunk. Make sure that the angle of attachment of the two branches is wide; this will help

Figure 7.20. This vigorous, upright shoot that grew in the center of an open-center peach tree was removed in May. You need to remove these shoots because they shade lower fruiting branches, rendering them unproductive. *Photo:* Chuck Ingels.

Figure 7.21. Mature peach and nectarine trees require thorough thinning of the 1-year-old (bearing) wood. *Source:* Ingels et al. 2007.

Figure 7.22. Pruning of mature Japanese plum trees consists mainly of removing the 1-year-old, vigorous, upright branches. Some 1-year-old branches are left to develop spurs, while some of the old, weak spurs are removed. *Source:* Ingels et al. 2007.

Figure 7.23. This figure shows one way to prune a peach fruiting branch. A dormant 2-year-old branch was headed the previous winter and fruited the previous summer, bending it downward. Two new shoots grew in the summer, one on the fruiting branch and one on the scaffold branch (A). After pruning, the older wood was cut off to promote 1-year-old fruiting wood near the scaffold branch (B). *Photos: Chuck Ingels.*

strengthen the branches for the weight of the fruit. Continue to direct the growth of the two shoots upward and outward, allowing lateral shoots to grow off of them. These will be next year's fruiting branches and their leaves will shade the scaffolds to prevent sunburn. Do not allow vigorous upright shoots to grow in the middle or to become codominant with the scaffold branches.

In subsequent years, continue to develop the two scaffold branches and keep them topped at the desired final height, usually about 8 to 10 feet (fig. 7.26). Remove or cut back competing upright shoots once or twice during the growing season. While lateral fruiting branches should continue to provide adequate protection from sunburn, take care to protect bare and exposed west- or south-facing branch surfaces from the hot afternoon sun. Paint any exposed surfaces with tree paint or a 50:50 mix of white latex paint and water to prevent sunburn and borer infestation. Scaffold branches should be strong enough to support the weight of the fruit, but circling a rope around them near the top of the tree will provide extra support.

During winter, thin and shorten lateral fruiting branches; remove competing leaders; and maintain the desired tree height. Sun-exposed 1-year-old branches arising from scaffold limbs should produce fruit, as well as several new shoots, the following season. After harvest, cut back the lateral branches to leave 1-year-old branches arising from or near the

Figure 7.24. You can tie a strong rope around the tree to reduce propping and limb breakage. *Photo: Chuck Ingels.*

Figure 7.25. Developing perpendicular V trees. After planting, place one bamboo stake in each direction of desired growth and grow one shoot on each stake. Continue to direct shoots upward and outward and remove or cut back competing upright shoots, but leave lateral shoots to develop fruiting branches. *Photo: Chuck Ingels.*

Figure 7.26. Four-year-old peach and nectarine trees trained to the perpendicular V system and topped at about 8 to 10 feet. Note the lateral fruiting branches that arise from the scaffold branches. *Photo:* Chuck Ingels.

scaffold branch. Head branches longer than about 18 inches by about one-third their length (see fig. 7.23). As in previous years, remove about half of the 1- and 2-year-old wood from the tree during the winter.

Central-leader and modified central-leader systems

Some tree species naturally grow, or are easily trained to grow, as a single, central trunk (the leader), with lateral branches growing outward and upward from the trunk. In true central-leader training, the leader remains the only vertical growing point, whereas in modified central-leader training, the leader is eventually removed, or loses dominance after lower branches are established. Apples, pears, and tall trees such as pecans and walnuts are particularly well suited to central-leader training, and persimmon can be easily adapted to the method.

Central-leader training

Apples and pears are often trained by forming three or four tiers of lateral branches along the leader, with three or four branches per tier (fig. 7.27). Beginning in the growing season and continuing during dormancy, select the central leader, spread the desired scaffold branches, and head back (and later remove) any other vigorous upright shoots that compete with the central leader. Create the first tier of four lateral branches by tying or staking branches outward at an angle of about 45 to 60° from vertical after the branches have grown 2 to 3 feet long. Head the cen-

tral leader just below the growing point when it has grown about 2 to 3 feet past the first tier, usually in the first dormant season after planting. Also, head the first-tier scaffold branches (fig. 7.28). Heading the central leader may be unnecessary if trees branch out at the desired locations on their own. Heading scaffold branches may also be undesirable in some cases—for example, when dwarfing apples.

During the next season, train a second tier of four branches outward from the leader. These second-tier branches should be offset vertically from those of the first tier; bend and tie branches in the proper direction if necessary. Allow the most vigorous upright shoot to continue its growth as the central leader.

In the following season, head the central leader to create a third tier of scaffolds in the manner described above. Avoid bending branches of upper tiers directly over branches of the lower tiers. Maintain a pyramidal shape by keeping lower branches longer than upper branches. This ensures that sunlight continues to reach the lower branches (fig. 7.29).

Once the desired tree height is reached (no more than 8 to 10 ft.), cut the leader back to a slightly angled lateral branch. The entire training process will take about 4 to 6 years, depending on tree vigor and spacing. Central-leader trees can be created more simply by allowing lateral branches to grow singly up and down the leader rather than in distinct tiers, as long as the branches do not crowd or shade each other (see figs. 7.5 B and C). Remove, shorten, or bend upper or closely spaced branches to prevent or eliminate shading of lower branches.

Encourage spur development and some side branching of the main lateral branches. Prune in the summer to remove vigorous upright shoots, or head them back to only three to six buds— unless a longer shoot is needed to protect fruit that is exposed to very hot afternoon sun. Summer heading of upright shoots can create fruit-bearing spurs on less vigorous trees, such as those grafted to dwarfing rootstocks. On standard-sized trees, heading can encourage the growth of another set of vigorous shoots, especially just below the cut. Remove the more vigorous of these shoots and prune the less vigorous ones back to create more spurs. These upright branches can also be removed in the dormant season.

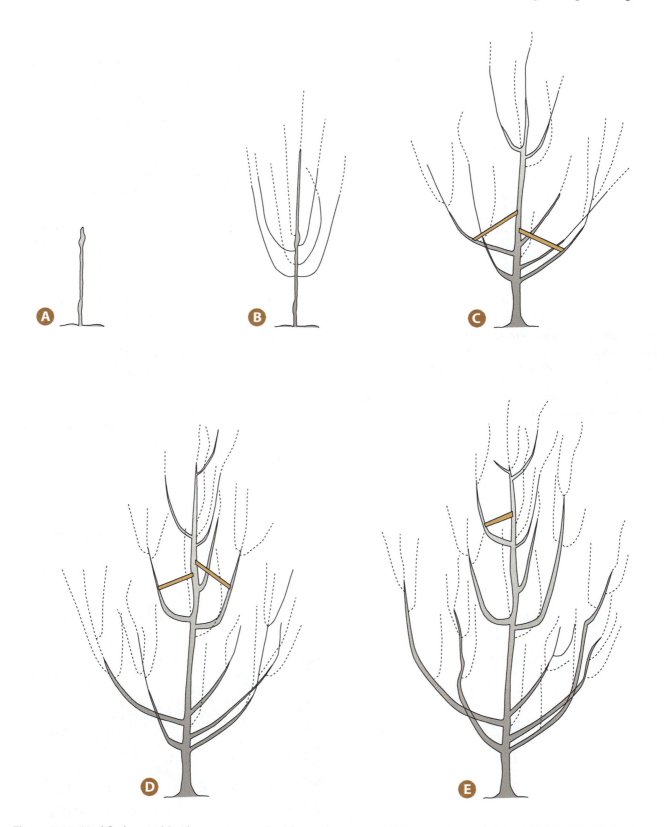

Figure 7.27. Modified central-leader pruning method for apple or pear (fruiting spurs are not shown). Dashed lines indicate branches that are to be removed. Bare-root tree at planting time (A). First tier of scaffold branches and reestablished central leader (B). First tier of branches staked into desired position as second tier of branches is established (C). Branches developed in the third (D) and subsequent (E) years are spaced evenly around and up the central leader. The leader is removed at a predetermined height. Note the 45–60° angle of branch attachment formed by using spreaders. *Source:* Ingels et al. 2007.

Figure 7.28. Apple trees are often trained to the modified central-leader system. The first year's branches of this apple tree were thinned out to four scaffold limbs and the central leader was maintained. All scaffold limbs and the central leader were headed back with approximately one-third of last year's growth removed. *Source:* Ingels et al. 2007.

Figure 7.29. The uprights and interfering branches of this 4-year-old apple tree have been continually thinned out and the central leader maintained. Spreader boards are often used to achieve wider angles of later branches. *Source:* Ingels et al. 2007.

Modified central-leader training

In this system, the central leader is allowed to grow until five to seven widely spaced lateral branches form. The dominance of the leader then fades beyond this point and multiple coequal limbs are allowed to form. This system is common for large trees, especially walnut and chestnut.

Fig, persimmon, and pistachio trees can be trained to a modified central leader that is essentially a delayed open center (fig. 7.30). Scaffold branches with vertical spacing are created along the trunk; structurally, these branches are stronger than an open center. The center does not need to be kept open as with a peach tree, but spaces should be created to allow light into the lower canopy. This prevents lower fruiting branches from becoming shaded and dying, forcing fruit production into the upper canopy.

Begin forming a modified central leader by first forming a central leader with up to five scaffold branches, distributed both around the tree and vertically along the leader. Vertically space the scaffolds about 6 to 12 inches apart. Prune mature fig, persimmon, and pistachio trees, as described later in this chapter.

"Fruit-bush" system

Fruit bushes have worked well for many home gardeners. Trees of any species—whether standard (full-size) trees or trees on dwarfing rootstock—can be trained as fruit bushes. Producing fruit bushes is eas-

Figure 7.30. These fig trees were grown with delayed open-center training. With each tree, scaffold branches were developed off the short leader and the open center was developed low, but the center was not kept open on top. *Photo:* Joe Connell.

Figure 7.31. Recently pruned apricot fruit bush, which is being maintained at about head height. *Photo:* Chuck Ingels.

Figure 7.32. When training the young fruit bush, you can use hedge shears to cut the shoots by about half. Some selective shoot thinning will also be needed to prevent crowding and shading of lower fruiting branches. *Photo:* Chuck Ingels.

ier if you start with dwarfing rootstocks because they grow somewhat less vigorously than semidwarf and standard trees. Dwarfing rootstocks, however, are not available for all species. Benefits of the fruit-bush system are the ability to manage trees without a ladder and to grow multiple species and varieties in a relatively small area. The main drawback is that crop yields are often lower than those produced through other training systems.

Fruit bush–trained trees are kept small by periodic summer pruning (fig. 7.31). Begin pruning newly planted trees in the first growing season, when new growth is about 2 to 3 feet long, usually in late April or May. Cut the new growth in half with hedge-trimming shears, giving the tree a uniform, bushy appearance (fig. 7.32). Cut subsequent new growth in half in late June or July (fig. 7.33). You may need to cut vigorous new growth (for apricots, plums, and plum-apricot hybrids) once or twice more during the season. Thin out the excess shoots resulting from these hedging cuts to allow sunlight to reach the lower branches during the summer. Thin out additional crowding branches in the dormant season when they are easier to see. Continue cutting new growth in the same manner in the second year until the trees reach 5 to 7 feet tall, or a height at which you can easily prune the top.

Pruning in subsequent years involves cutting off any shoots growing above the tree's permanent height in May and again in July or August (fig. 7.34).

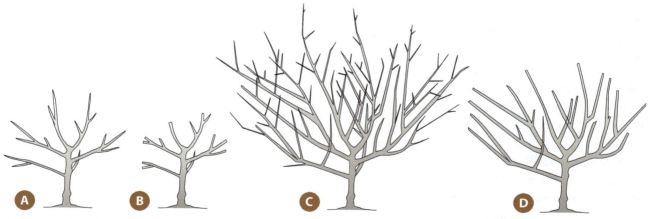

Figure 7.33. Fruit-bush pruning method (leaves removed to show structure). New growth early in first growing season, from late April to early May (A). Initial heading of new growth (B). Subsequent new growth after heading (June or July, with some shoots removed to allow light penetration) (C). Additional growth headed back in summer and some branches thinned out (D). Growth may require pruning one or two more times during the first growing season. Continue heading back each year until the tree reaches the desired height. *Source:* Ingels et al. 2007.

Highly vigorous trees may require a third pruning. Rapid, dense growth can be especially challenging with plums and apricots. Periodically thin out crowding branches, especially at the top of the tree, and remove nonproductive fruiting wood in early spring, when you can see which branches have no flowers. After the third year, it may be necessary to open up the center of the tree, creating a combination of a fruit bush and an open-center tree.

Espalier training

Espalier (pronounced "es-PAL-yay" in English) is a French word derived from the Italian *spalliera*, meaning "something to rest the shoulder (*spalla*) against." As a fruit tree–training system, *espalier* refers to forming trees into a two-dimensional flat plane, usually against a wall or fence, or along a freestanding trellis. It also refers to a tree that has been trained on such structures. Training trees in this manner can be considered a form of horticultural art, but it also has significant horticultural advantages that are utilized by both amateur and commercial growers.

While there is evidence of its use in ancient Roman and Egyptian times, espalier training of fruit trees began in earnest in sixteenth-century Europe. Its purpose was to form walls or dividers while also producing fruit. In Britain's North American colonies, an espalier was a latticework or wall support upon which trees were trained, sometimes defining the boundary of a garden or creating a focal point. Today, trellis-trained apple and pear orchards in Europe and the US Pacific Northwest often provide higher production and lower labor costs than orchards with large, widely spaced trees. Examples of espaliered trees and trellised orchards are shown in figure 7.35.

A major benefit of fruit-tree trellis structures is that they can fit into the narrow spaces of smaller home lots, as long as there are at least 6 to 8 hours per day of summer sun. Training trees into narrow fruiting walls increases sunlight capture for efficient production and facilitates fruit thinning, pruning, and harvest. Other important benefits are better spray coverage and greater ease of covering trees with bird netting to reduce damage by birds and squirrels—or with row cover material to reduce damage by sunburn or by certain insect pests, such as spotted wing drosophila. Like fruit bushes, espalier-trained trees tend to be smaller than those produced with

Figure 7.34. Vigorous shoots of cherry-plum fruit bush to be removed in late April (A). The height of pruning is the permanent height of the tree. Completed pruning of fruit bush (B). *Photos:* Chuck Ingels.

other training methods, meaning that they potentially require less water.

Species differences

Espalier training is used for apples, pears, and Asian pears, mainly because most varieties of these fruit reliably produce long-lasting fruiting spurs (see table

Figure 7.35. Espaliered pear on trellis. *Photo:* John F. Karlik.

Advantages of trellis structures

- Good use of narrow spaces in the landscape
- Narrow fruiting wall allows good sunlight penetration into entire canopy
- Efficient crop production
- Potential heat capture in winter on south-facing walls
- Improved pest management

Disadvantages of trellis structures

- Increased costs for trellis
- Increased time for training and detailed pruning and tying
- Specialized knowledge needed to prune
- Challenging to manage fast-growing trees and trees that fruit on long shoots or branches
- Narrow canopy may increase sunburn and branch borers

7.1) and fewer vigorous shoots. Non–spur bearing species can be challenging candidates for espalier training but, with proper pruning and adequate space, can produce fruit for many years. Summer pruning of peaches and nectarines is essential because they bear fruit laterally on 1-year-old sun-exposed branches (see fig. 7.23B). Encourage 1-year-old lateral branches on persimmon because most fruit is produced on shoots originating near the ends of these branches. Keep persimmon trees' strong upright shoots in check. Figs require adequate space for growth to provide room for two crops, the first produced laterally on last year's (1-year-old) growth in early summer and the second on long current-season

shoots in late summer. Pomegranates are borne on new shoots arising from short spurs; growth of standard varieties may be excessive and dwarf varieties may be much easier to grow. Citrus, though not covered in this publication, can be easily espaliered. Citrus trees are usually grown in informal or fan shapes.

Since vigorous espaliered fruit trees can easily outgrow their space, it is important to use dwarfing rootstocks whenever they are available in retail nurseries. Most nurseries carry semidwarf trees, which can vary greatly in their dwarfing (for example, M7 apple rootstock is much more dwarfing than M111).

Genetic dwarf trees can also be used in smaller spaces, and may take years to fill out a large trellis.

Structural support

Support structures for espalier training can vary greatly, from an existing building or fence to a free-standing wire trellis. Wires can be attached to structures. Ideally, though, they should be self-supporting and should be kept several inches to several feet away from buildings or fences to allow for maintenance. Avoid using shaded north-facing walls. South-facing walls can provide warmth in the cool season in coastal areas—and for citrus in winter in frost-prone areas. Fully exposed east-facing or west-facing walls also work well—but in hot climates, you must protect the foliage and fruit of sensitive species like cherry and Asian pear from sunburn.

Trellis orientation

A self-supporting trellis (that is, one not supported by a fence or wall) in full sun is the ideal structure for maximum production. North-south orientation is usually best, providing plenty of sun on alternate sides of the canopy in the morning and afternoon. Using an east-west orientation means that the north side becomes shaded, though shading effects can be reduced by maintaining a narrow canopy. East-west orientation may also reduce branch sunburn in the hottest climates, compared to a north-south orientation. Various trellis angle patterns can be used to produce desired sunlight effects.

Tree and row spacing

Expected tree vigor depends on desired spacing within a trellis row. Trees can be planted relatively close together (5–8 ft. apart) if they are grown in poorer soil, in cool climates, or on highly dwarfing rootstocks, or if they are partially shaded. Standard or minimally dwarfing trees may benefit from being planted 10 to 12 feet apart. Figs, apricots, plums, and plum hybrids are vigorous and large trees that may require even wider spacing. Spacing between adjacent trellis rows should be about the same as the height of the trellises—that is, 8-foot-tall trellises should be at least 8 feet apart.

Posts and wires

Support the wires on long-lasting posts made of wood, metal, or another durable material. Posts for chain-link fencing and 4-by-4-inch wood posts are both often used, but T-posts, large metal poles, and other items are used as well.

Wood posts should be pressure-treated lumber or redwood; pressure-treated wood decays more slowly. As for fence posts, reduce the potential for wood rot by supporting the posts with concrete that is placed in the hole and extended above the soil and mulch line.

Posts for chain-link fences are long lasting, but they make it a bit more difficult to add crossarms to attach irrigation tubing (see below). Metal posts should also be set in concrete but the concrete does not need to extend above the soil because the metal will not rot. The depth to which any post is set depends in part on the height of the trellis, but a typical depth is generally 2 to 3 feet.

A trellis designed for horizontal T training has three to four wires, spaced 2 feet apart, on which shoots are trained to become scaffold branches. Other training methods may be best with 12- to 18-inch wire spacing to facilitate training and shoot tying. Use wire no thinner than 14 gauge (the larger the number, the thinner the wire). Twelve-gauge wire offers strong, long-lasting support. Alternatively, vinyl-coated cable can be used. With posts for chain-link fences, wires are attached with tension bands, and turnbuckles are used on the end posts. With wood posts, wires are directed through holes. On end posts, wires are attached to turnbuckles, which in turn hook onto screw hooks or screw eyes attached to the posts. The use of turnbuckles allows wires to be tightened periodically to keep them from sagging.

There are two ways to support posts to prevent the posts from bending inward due to the weight of the fruit and tightening of turnbuckles. For chain link–fence posts, add a top rail. For wood posts, the top rail poles can be inserted into holes ½ to ¾ inch deep, made with a hole saw slightly wider than the pole. When concrete is fully dry, the posts are bent outward slightly to insert the poles into the holes. Ensure that the poles are inserted deeply so they will not fall. Tighten turnbuckles after the poles are inserted. Alternatively, the top wire—or an additional wire on the end posts—can angle down and be tied to a secured earth anchor or to an existing structure.

Crossarms can be added for installing wires and drip lines on either side of the trellis to increase the spread of the wetted area. Attach tubing to the wire with clips or spiral-cut drip-tubing pieces. This method makes it easy to see if emitters are functioning and allows for applying fertilizer under the plug-in emitters. The wire can also be used for training low fruiting branches.

Tools and supplies

Espalier training requires much tying of young shoots—and then removal of ties from older shoots and branches. The simplest and most convenient tying gadget is a reusable plant-tie band that stretches and latches around itself for temporary tying. These bands can be kept in a multiple-pocket tool belt while the user prunes and ties shoots. The most commonly used sizes are lengths of 3, 4, and 6 inches. Plant-tie bands can be found online and at some specialty horticultural supply stores. Green tie tape with a ½-inch width can supplement or substitute for tie bands. While plant-tie bands can usually be removed with one hand—specifically, by grabbing and pulling the loop over the rubber hooks—removing green tie tape is easiest with a pair of scissors or a knife.

Summer pruning

Espalier trees should be summer pruned during the growing season beginning in April or May and continuing through mid-to-late summer to prevent shading of lower and interior fruiting branches. In areas with wet springs, pruning should occur exclusively in the summer because branch disease organisms may enter pruning wounds in the dormant season; this is especially true with cherry and apricot and with large cuts in general.

Espalier training methods

Fruit trees are amenable to many espalier training methods, ranging from highly productive to artistic. New shoots of young trees can be bent and tied in various ways, or redirected by using heading cuts to force shoots.

Choice of training method depends in part on tree species, desired tree shape, and predicted ability to manage the tree. Main structural branches can be up-

right (in the palmette style, for example), horizontal (horizontal T, for example), or angled. Fan patterns are easiest to develop, as selected shoots are simply directed upward or outward and new shoots are allowed to fill in open areas. The horizontal T method is excellent for pome fruit and some other spur-forming species. Angling and arcing methods may provide the dual benefit of reduced shoot growth and increased flower bud and fruit formation—bending a short shoot or branch from the vertical often achieves both.

Some examples of espalier methods are described below.

Horizontal T (horizontal cordon)

Head the trees at planting to about the level of the lowest wire. Direct the uppermost shoot of each tree upward toward the next wire after spring growth begins. Allow the two strongest lateral branches to grow outward and upward at a 45 to 60° angle, tying each shoot to a bamboo stake, then bending them later to the horizontal before tying them to the wires (fig. 7.36). Shoots of vigorous trees will usually continue their growth if you simply tie them to the wire as they grow. Head back the vertical leader of vigorous trees to just above the second wire in the same growing season; otherwise, make this cut during the following dormant season. Continue training new shoots in this manner in following years as the uppermost shoot reaches each successive trellis wire.

During the growing season, head upright, vigorous shoots that begin to grow from the horizontal

Figure 7.36. For young espalier-trained trees, it is best to train the new shoots upward and outward at an angle along a stake to provide optimal growth and fruit spur formation. Once they reach the end of the stake, tie them down to the wire.

Figure 7.37. Espalier-trained Asian pear with main branches directed outward and then upward (A). The tree in spring, 2 years later (B). The tree in early summer (photo taken from a ladder) (C). Note the strong trellis needed to support the tree. *Photos A–B:* Chuck Ingels. *Photo C:* Jack Kelly Clark.

branches to three or four buds each after they have grown about 8 to 12 inches. If left unheaded in-season, these shoots will become tall whips and will shade out and kill the spurs; a single, late corrective action will only reinvigorate growth. When pruned in-season, apples will often form spurs or short shoots that end in terminal flower buds. Renew spurs on older trees by thinning and pruning off old or unproductive sections, leaving the younger wood. To prevent shading and spur death in the lower canopy, do not allow the top tier to grow wider than lower tiers.

Palmette verrier (candelabra)
Palmette is a system in which most spurs are formed on upright cordons produced from short, lateral branches. In the palmette verrier method, lateral cordons are separated vertically; the bottom cordon is widest and the top cordon is narrowest (fig. 7.37A).

The greatest selection of shoots for training is often developed by allowing a tree headed at bare-root planting time in winter to go unpruned the first year. Cut back strategically placed 1-year-old branches to two or three buds in the second winter. The central branch can be left longer to begin the next cordon tier. Select new shoots and direct them outward along the wires and upward on temporary, thin, bamboo stakes tied to the wires. There are variations to the palmette method.

Spurs begin to form along these upright shoots the following year, and most of the vegetative growth occurs at the top (figs. 7.37B and C). Once fully developed, any strong upright shoots are removed with spring and summer pruning, and vigorous side shoots are thinned, shortened, or both. It is necessary to keep some shoot growth in hot areas to prevent fruit sunburn. This may allow the canopy to get wider. Production may be reduced as the canopy thickens over time, especially on the north side. It may then be necessary in mid-to-late spring to cut the upright scaffolds back severely and recreate the structure with shoots that grow from the cut branches.

Fan shapes
A fan-shaped example follows: A Stella cherry tree is 11 feet wide by 8 feet tall and is angled from northwest to southeast. Shoots that grow after planting the bare-root tree are directed upward and outward in a fan shape. Shoot tying continues in year 2, and unwanted shoots are cut at the base. No heading cuts are used unless multiple shoots are desired for branching. Training continues in this manner. Growth-reducing pruning after the trellis is filled out becomes important to prevent the shading of spur leaves. Pruning involves cutting, to the base, lateral shoots and shoots that grow above the top of the trellis. Over time, spurs must be rejuvenated by cutting back to new spur growth or thinning spurs after harvest. Structural branches can also be renewed by cutting off one to three of the thickest branches each year and redirecting shoots to take their place.

Peach and nectarine trees do not lend themselves well to espalier training because of their strong vegetative growth and because they bear on 1-year-old branches that must receive sun exposure to be productive. However, with knowledge and persistent effort, they can be grown on espaliers and produce large crops. The overall goal is to produce a narrow fruiting wall so no branches or shoots are excessively shaded. This is done, mostly or solely, with spring and summer pruning.

One training method is the two-scaffold fan, in which two main branches are developed and the upright shoots that grow on the scaffolds are tied to wires. For this method, we discuss a single tree, at the Fair Oaks Horticulture Center, trained over a 4-year period. The trellis is 11 feet wide by 8 feet tall, slightly skewed from an east-west orientation. It gets some morning sun on one side and afternoon sun on the other. There is less shoot growth, and consequently less pruning, in cooler regions. Vegetative growth on varieties maturing late in the season (August or September), like the O'Henry peach discussed below, is easier to manage than on early-maturing varieties because the fruit demand much of the tree's carbohydrates. Shoot growth is therefore less pronounced, and minimal in late summer. The O'Henry tree was pruned five times in year 2 between early April and mid-July, three times in year 3, and twice before the August harvest—followed by renewal pruning immediately after harvest in year 4.

Year 1 of espalier training. Cut the trunk of bare-root trees to about 12 to 18 inches tall after planting to position the two main (scaffold) shoots as low as possible. Select and train two of the new growing shoots upward and outward along the trellis. Slowly lower them to just above horizontal as they grow, initially keeping them more upright to allow vigorous shoot growth until the two shoots are fully extended. The lower portion of the shoots may stiffen if left too long. Train upward some of the lateral shoots growing along the main scaffolds, spacing them about 6 to 8 inches apart to fill in below the scaffolds. Flower buds that form during the first summer should produce fruit in year 2, as well as moderate vegetative growth.

For potted trees purchased from a nursery in spring or summer, cut all but two low shoots off and train these two outward as discussed above. An alternative method, if the lowest shoots are well above 1 to 1.5 feet, is to allow the tree to grow in the first year and then cut the trunk to 12 to 18 inches in the winter. Train two new shoots as described above, bearing in mind that ensuing growth will be even more vigorous than a bare-root tree in its first year. A third method is to plant the tree at an angle, which lowers the height of the shoots. Choose the two lowest, best-positioned shoots that will become scaffolds. Plant high enough to ensure that the scion portion of the trunk will never have contact with soil or mulch, even as the trunk expands.

Year 2. Prune up to five times during spring and summer to manage vigorous growth. Since peaches and nectarines lack apical dominance, shoots growing from lateral buds on the upright shoots may quickly become dense and shade interior branches.

Thin fruit in April to somewhat closer than the typical 6 inches apart. In this way, with as much fruit as possible allowed to remain, vegetative growth is slowed. Early thinning under less optimal growing conditions—for example, in cooler climates or poor quality soil—will ensure adequate shoot growth.

Numerous lateral shoots will grow on the main upright shoots during the growing season. Cut the upright shoot off just above the lowest lateral shoot; this lateral shoot is then tied to the wire and maintains the upright shoot growth. Shoots should be spaced about 6 to 8 inches apart and kept free of lateral shoots. If lateral shoots are simply pruned off and the upright shoot is left to grow, no shoots will grow and no flowers will form at those nodes. Continually cutting to the lowest lateral also slows the overall growth and size of the tree.

Year 3. Continue filling the trellis with upright, single shoots spaced about 6 to 8 inches apart. Maintain space between upright shoots and keep the canopy narrow along the trellis. As in the previous year, cut vigorous shoots to the lowest lateral. Leave many of the short lateral shoots in the lower canopy for next year's fruit. Cut unwanted shoots back to a whorl of buds; the buds rarely grow and the leaves help protect the branch from sunburn.

Year 4. Several hundred flowers should have formed, resulting in 250 to 350 fruit growing to maturity. If weather events greatly reduce or eliminate fruit in spring, vegetative growth will be exceptionally vigorous. Perform spring and summer pruning to remove or cut back lateral shoots to a whorl of buds, and top the tree to maintain tree size. Remove upright shoots above the top of the trellis back to the branch from which they grew, and leave them unheaded.

Fruit form and mature on lateral branches that grew as shoots the previous year. After harvest, remove or cut back branches that have become shaded and are no longer fruitful. The entire canopy has also become crowded with older wood by this time.

There are a few potential options for managing trees starting in about year 4. One is to cut off all upright branches after harvest. Begin replacing branches by leaving and loosely tying up several vigorous upright shoots originating from the lower canopy. After harvest (mid-August for the O'Henry peach), cut most large branches back to the point where they can be replaced by acceptable upright shoots and tie these shoots upward. Alternatively, severely cut back one side of the tree every other year. A second strategy involves removing only the thickest or oldest branches and directing new shoots to replace them. This strategy reduces the loss of so many fruiting branches in one season. The disadvantage, because the new shoots will be partially shaded by the remaining branches, is reduced fruit production.

Sunburn

Maintaining a narrow fruiting wall may expose branches to afternoon sun on south- and west-facing sides in hot climates. Branch sunburn can occur on either north-south or east-west trellises, but is usually more severe on the former. After spring or summer pruning, and before sunburn occurs, paint exposed branches with white, water-based latex paint.

Growing cherries and Asian pears on an east-west orientation or on an east-facing wall or fence may be helpful as cherry leaves, as well as Asian pear leaves and fruit, may be more susceptible to leaf burn on hot west-facing sides.

Pruning of specific species

Persimmon

Prune young persimmon trees during the training years to hasten early development to maturity. Persimmon trees bear heavy fruit loads at the ends of the branches and also have fragile wood that may break with wind. Long, vigorous shoots should therefore be tipped or headed during the growing season to promote branching and create a strong structure on the young tree.

A central-leader or modified central-leader shape with wider branch angles is best for persimmons in hot climates. Because persimmon fruit sunburn easily, an open vase shape is only suitable for cooler climates. Angle branches to between 45 and 90° to avoid the splitting that will occur with narrow angles and heavy crop loads. Branches co-originating from about the same location on the trunk may split out.

Persimmons bear on wood that grew the year before. The three or four "mixed" buds on a 1-year-old persimmon branch produce the flowers and eventually fruit; thus, perform light annual pruning after the tree is mature. Heavy dormant-season pruning stimulates strong vegetative shoot growth that may fail to develop flowers and fruit until the following season. An effective technique for balancing the crop is, during harvest, to cut out the branches that bore fruit that year, using a thinning cut at the base of the branch.

Persimmon branches quickly become weak or die if they receive insufficient sunlight. Maintain an open canopy using annual reduction cuts to allow sunlight to penetrate and filter through the leaf area.

Pomegranate

Pomegranates grow naturally as bushes from the profuse suckers that grow from root crowns. If a pomegranate tree is left untrained it will develop naturally into a large umbrella-shaped shrub.

Create an aesthetically pleasing and productive tree by selecting one trunk and training to the open-center or modified central-leader system. Remove all suckers growing from the crown and the base of the trunk. In very cold areas, develop multiple trunks in case one or more trunks are killed by frost.

Standard pomegranate trees can become quite large and spreading, requiring the use of ladders for fruit harvest. Strive to achieve and maintain a tree height of 8 to 10 feet.

After a few years, the density of the branches will make it hard for light to penetrate the canopy and the tree will become less fruitful. Prune annually to avoid overcrowding. Use thinning cuts in late spring and again in summer to remove or thin the many vigorous upright shoots that would otherwise quickly grow, shading the lower fruiting wood. Also remove any crowded, crossing-over, and dead or damaged branches and large interior branches. Trees maintained in this manner produce less fruit than minimally pruned trees, but all of the fruit is reachable from the ground or from a small ladder.

Pomegranate trees produce long thorns that can puncture the eyes or skin, so wear protective gloves and eyewear when pruning.

Fig

Fig trees naturally become rounded to a bell shape, making subsequent training difficult. Fortunately, young trees can easily be trained into nearly any shape or size. The branch structure can be developed to provide a jungle gym for climbing or limbs for sitting.

A large, rounded shade tree with a single trunk or multiple trunks conforms well to modified central-leader or open-center training. Figs can also be espaliered to a wall or trellis with horizontal wires about 2 feet apart. For best fruit production, grow espaliered figs on a southwest-facing wall. In climates with very cold winters, fig trees may be killed back to the ground so they can be trained as bushes and may require only light annual pruning. Little or no pruning results in outer branches hanging down with the weight of the fruit. Trees will become rounded to a bell shape, and subsequent training can be difficult.

Fig trees need to be trained correctly, with severe pruning, to produce large amounts of fruit harvestable from the ground. Head the trunks of bare-root trees at 18 to 24 inches. For container-grown trees planted during the growing season, make the heading cut the winter after planting if no low branches are present. The first primary scaffold branches should be 12 to 18 inches above ground so that any well-positioned branches at this height can be saved as scaffolds. Head these three to five well-positioned primary scaffold branches to produce secondary scaffolds in the second dormant season. Prune mature trees to 5 to 6 feet tall each winter. Allow them to spread outward to make more growing points (this also controls shoot vigor), but allow entry points into the center of the tree to facilitate harvesting and pruning.

Bearing habit will dictate successful pruning. Most fig varieties bear two crops—the first in early summer (known as the breba crop) and the main or second crop, in late summer and fall. The later crop usu-

ally has more fruit than the first crop, but they are a bit smaller. Buds for the breba crop form in the fall along the branches formed that growing season, overwinter as expanded buds, and bear fruit on branches that, by that time, are 1 year old. The second crop forms in the summer on the current season's shoots.

Severe winter pruning to reduce tree size can eliminate or severely reduce the first crop, but a substantial second crop will usually form no matter how severe the winter pruning. As a general rule, thin out the canopy by about one-third during dormancy to produce a sufficient first crop.

Summer pruning is generally unnecessary, though some thinning of shoots may be warranted to reduce crowding of short trees. In hot growing areas, also head back tall shoots that have resulted from severe winter pruning. Heading back these long shoots just after the breba crop is harvested will reduce the second crop but maintain tree height and sunlight. One summer pruning technique to produce earlier-maturing fruit of a higher quality on size-controlled trees involves removing the growing tip after five or six leaves have developed in the spring (tipping). This interrupts vegetative growth and diverts the plant's energy into fruit development until vegetative growth can resume. Take care not to summer prune more than one-third of the leaf cover; otherwise, you risk sunburning previously shaded bark. Whitewash any exposed branches.

Experiment in your own climatic conditions to find local limits for how early or late you can summer-prune. If a crop is desired, allow enough time after pruning for the new shoots to develop buds. Doing so will maximize double cropping and allow for the new growth to harden and survive low temperatures.

Almond

Almond trees should be trained to the open-center system. The initial training is similar to that for peach and apricot, but because almonds are shaken from trees rather than picked, they require far less maintenance after the first few years.

Head trees to 2 to 3 feet after planting. This leaves enough trunk space to vertically stagger the scaffold branches. Remove crossing limbs, rootstock suckers, and shoots that are too low to be scaffolds during the first growing season. Otherwise, just let the tree grow and wait until the first dormant season to do significant pruning.

The most important winter pruning decision is selecting three to four strong, well-anchored scaffolds that won't break or split from the trunk in future years. First remove branches that would obviously make bad scaffolds—those that cross the middle or have very narrow or wide attachments. Then select scaffolds from the remaining branches.

The ideal angle for strong attachment to the trunk is 45 to 70° from the vertical. Narrow branch angles will develop bark that creates a wedge in the scaffold crotch, preventing strong attachment. Branches wider than 70° from the vertical may not support heavy crop weight.

Space scaffolds evenly around the trunk to give them room to attach to the trunk and distribute the crop weight. Select three to four scaffolds spaced 90 to 120° apart when viewed from above, providing room for limb growth and strong branch attachment. Space scaffolds evenly around the tree and 3 to 6 inches apart, up and down the trunk if possible. After choosing the scaffolds, remove all competing branches from the trunk. Leave short lateral branches coming off the scaffolds to become the first fruiting branches.

The next step is to prune the selected primary scaffolds, with the goal of directing next season's growth . Head scaffolds to 3 feet from the trunk on less vigorous trees and to 4 feet on more vigorous trees. Cuts should be made 1 to 2 feet below the branch tip. Any area of concentrated buds that creates heavy, bushy growth, should be cut off.

During the second dormant season, continue to shape the structure of the tree upward and outward to create strong architecture and to fill the available space with canopy as quickly as possible. First remove crossing branches, central vigorous branches in the center, and branches that would become an unwanted primary scaffold if not removed. Then select secondary scaffolds from the remaining branches. Select two to three strong and well-spaced secondary scaffolds per primary scaffold. The branches should be vigorous, with upward and outward growth, and should be evenly spaced around the canopy.

The architecture of the tree is largely established by the third dormant season. This is the time to transi-
tion from training to minimal maintenance pruning. Remove limbs that are broken or may threaten the shape you have already established, such as crossed limbs and competing limbs that may interfere with scaffold attachment. Once the structure of the tree has been established, almond tree pruning in a home orchard primarily involves removing dead or diseased branches to prevent the disease from spreading into the trunk.

Walnut

Young walnut trees need very little pruning, if any, to keep them growing or to produce an adequate nut crop. They will grow vigorously as long as the trees are managed properly, especially where adequate irrigation is concerned. The goals are to develop a tree whose strong scaffolds can bear heavy nut crops without breakage of limbs—and a tree that requires the least pruning possible, other than some thinning cuts. Unheaded walnut trees tend to grow with a central leader, and with primary branches naturally well spaced along the trunk and at wide angles. In contrast, heading the trunk at the first dormant pruning produces a tree with a modified central leader.

Year 1. Head bare-root trees four to six buds above the graft union at planting, or leave them unheaded. Where wind is a problem, pound an 8-foot stake into the ground 10 to 12 inches away from the tree at planting. Place the stake opposite the side toward which the prevailing wind blows the tree. The goal during the first growing season is to train a single trunk that grows 7 to 12 feet tall. The leader will become the trunk; tie it loosely to the stake so there is some movement when the wind blows. Lower side shoots may be pruned back to 1 to 2 feet so as not to compete with the leader, unless there is more trunk growth than needed.

Year 2. Remove (thin out) competing leaders and lower limbs (below 3 to 4 ft.) in the first dormant season. The trunk (central leader) can be left unheaded. The central leader and primary scaffold branches grow during the second season.

Year 3. In the second dormant season, remove lower branches (below 3 to 5 ft.), depending on where you want the lowest branch. Remove competing leaders, limbs with a narrow angle of attachment, or limbs directly over one another. Leave scaffold branches unheaded. Unheaded trees will grow short side shoots on primary branches during the third season.

Year 4. No pruning is needed in the third dormant season unless low-hanging branches interfere with safety or maintenance. Unheaded limbs will extend during the fourth growing season.

Year 5 and beyond. Scaffold limbs can be left unheaded in the fourth dormant season; thinning is unnecessary. Pruning of mature trees is confined to removing dead wood or limbs that interfere with maintenance. Trees should be structurally strong and well balanced.

Pistachio

Pistachios for the home orchard are usually sold as potted trees. Retail nursery trees are typically unheaded, and may or may not have branches for training. If a tree with no branching is purchased during the growing season, head the tree at 18 to 24 inches in the winter.

Pistachio trees demonstrate strong apical dominance. Left untrained, they will produce long shoots with little branching that will bend over and trail to the ground. To encourage branching, pistachio trees require intensive training the first 4 or 5 years after planting. Pistachio trees may be trained using the open-center or modified central-leader methods. The open-center method usually requires heading the main trunk so that several lateral shoots push in the lower portion of the tree. Heading is necessary to obtain suitably located lateral shoots for training into scaffolds. Select three or four primary scaffold branches that are distributed evenly around the trunk. In the case of the modified central-leader system, primary scaffold branches are spaced about 6 to 10 inches apart vertically along the trunk. In this case, the central leader is fairly short, resembling the delayed open-center system described earlier.

Shoots that grow from the trunk or leader will form the primary scaffold branches. When these shoots are about 15 inches long, cut them to 12 to 14 inches. After these heading cuts are made, you can head the subsequent shoots (secondary scaffold branches) back to 12 to 14 inches if they reach 15 inches in length by late spring or early summer. Otherwise, wait until winter to head back secondary scaffold branches. Tertiary and subsequent branches should only be pruned in the winter because summer pruning can result in weak and spindly growth. Tertiary and subsequent branches are left longer than the primary and secondary branches. Commercial growers normally cut them back to a length of 22 inches or somewhat longer—again, to stimulate lateral branching.

Continue this process of winter pruning for several years until the framework of the tree is established, always heading back subsequent branches of young trees to 30 inches or less to promote lateral branching, until the desired tree height is reached. Keep the center of the tree fairly open in order to admit sunlight for flower bud formation and fruiting.

Usually, once you establish the basic framework of the tree, only light pruning is necessary. However, pistachio is an alternate-bearing tree. In years of light nut production, numerous long shoots may form at the top of the tree and outer canopy that will require heading back to maintain upright tree growth. Both male and female flower buds begin to appear during the fourth or fifth year after planting. The flower buds of both male and female trees are longer and plumper than the vegetative buds. To stimulate lateral shoots, ensure that some vegetative buds are present below your pruning cuts. Also, as the trees move from juvenility to nut production, watch for side shoots with flower buds (called spurs). Do not prune off the new spur growth. The spurs will produce most of the nuts, especially when the trees reach maturity. As the old spurs become shaded and die, new spurs will be produced on younger growth higher in the tree. As the tree becomes mature, relatively few vegetative buds form laterally on shoots (most buds are flower buds), so heading cuts do not always stimulate lateral branching.

If at some point you want to encourage rejuvenation of the tree, regrowth is usually satisfactory when you prune the tree back fairly severely using both heading and thinning cuts.

Restructuring older trees

Restructuring fruit bushes or other small trees

Mismanaged fruit trees produce most fruit in the top of their canopies. This can lead to broken branches and greater difficulty in managing the crop. Sufficient sunlight is required to keep lower fruiting branches alive and productive, especially in late spring through summer. Use appropriate training methods and summer pruning to ensure sunlight and production throughout the trees.

If interior shading results in lack of fruiting branches in lower scaffold limbs (known as blind wood), it may be feasible to head the limbs to recreate the tree structure. This technique is best done on smaller trees that are no older than 10 years old, although large, older trees may also respond (see the following section). Head once the rainy season ends in April or May to avoid branch dieback diseases, especially in regions with wet springs. To prevent limb sunburn in hot areas, paint the limbs and trunk with tree paint, or white latex paint mixed 50:50 with water, shortly after making the cuts.

Renewing large, overgrown trees

Very tall, neglected fruit trees are common in residential yards. Most fruit must be picked from ladders—or simply isn't picked. These overgrown trees are difficult to prune or spray and the weight of unthinned fruit often causes higher branches to break. Neglected trees are also frequently invaded by diseases, borers, and other insect pests.

Consider the following questions before deciding to prune an overgrown tree:

- Do you want the fruit that the tree produces?
- Are new, improved varieties of the tree available, with desirable characteristics such as dwarfing or disease resistance?
- Would you rather have a different type of fruit tree in the same location?
- Would you rather have a shade tree instead of a fruit tree?
- Are there serious disease or insect problems on the trunk or main limbs?

If you decide to keep the existing overgrown fruit tree, use one of these three basic pruning strategies:

1. Maintain the tree's height, making mostly thinning cuts.
2. Reduce tree height slowly over 3 years.
3. Drastically cut back all main branches, leaving only one or two temporary scaffold limbs.

If you must cut large limbs, wait until about late April to allow the cut tissues to begin to seal more rapidly in warm, dry weather and to reduce the chances of decay in the large wounds (see "Method 2," below). If the pruning will cause branches to be exposed to prolonged periods of hot afternoon sun (common after severe pruning), protect the branches from sunburn by painting them with tree paint, whitewash, or a 50:50 mixture of white interior latex paint and water.

Method 1: Maintain the tree's height and make mostly thinning cuts

This method assumes that a tree is structurally sound and no taller than you can easily manage with a moderately tall ladder (12 ft. or shorter). Depending on your objectives for the neglected tree, branches will probably need to be removed, especially in the upper canopy.

First, prune out dead, diseased, or broken limbs; branches that cross or rub against each other; and crowded limbs and branches growing toward the interior of the tree. Thin enough of the remaining canopy to allow sunlight to penetrate to the lower wood. If excessive pruning allows branches to become exposed to afternoon sun, paint them white as discussed above. Choose a height to prune to each year and remove branches that grow beyond the height at which you are able to pick the fruit safely from a ladder. Summer prune yearly to remove new, vigorous shoots, especially in the upper canopy.

Method 2: Reduce the tree's height slowly over a 3-year period

For structurally sound trees, winter prune to lower the height by one-third annually over a 3-year period to reach a final desirable height.

Avoid making major cuts during summer, as remaining shoots may be damaged when you remove the branches, tree growth may suffer excessive vigor loss, and exposed branches can sunburn and attract borers. Cut branches back to a lateral branch that is no larger than one-third the size of the main branch to avoid leaving large stubs. Remove or head back newly created water sprouts once or twice during the summer to prevent shading of the lower fruiting wood. Thin additional branches as needed to allow some sunlight to penetrate into the canopy.

Since it will be difficult to develop new limbs from the trunk, it may be better to simply remove trees that lack low branches.

Method 3: Drastically cut back most of the main branches

This is an extreme method for reducing tree height in a single season. In this method, large branches are headed or cut back to lateral branches. A good time for this type of major pruning is April or May, when active growth and drier weather are beginning. Cuts are made somewhere below the desired height of the tree in order to allow for new growth. Bear in mind, however, that large cuts will likely not callus over, so wood decay will eventually set in and kill the tree.

Not all fruit trees can resprout from large lower branches. Those that can are apple, pear, citrus, and avocado. The inability of buds low on the tree to grow through the thick bark may prevent older stone fruit trees (peach, cherry, apricot, and nectarine) from resprouting. Many trees of all species may lack small, low branches or twigs from which to form a new framework. If no main branches lower than 6 to 8 feet from the ground exist, methods 1 or 2—or complete removal of the tree—may be preferable, since a major cut low on the tree would leave just a stump.

Preserve and cut back even the smaller lateral branches that are located in reasonable places. These laterals, along with shoots that arise from buds on the main branches, will form the framework for the new, smaller tree. Shoots growing from adventitious (latent) buds will form weak connections. They may break off later if allowed to grow long. However, these branches will likely remain strongly attached if the tree is kept small. Paint all exposed scaffold branches with tree paint, whitewash, or a 50:50 mixture of white interior latex paint and water to prevent sunburn.

Method 3 removes a great deal of leaf area while leaving in place a large root system. Leave one or two smaller main limbs, or a large side "nurse limb," unpruned. These limbs will absorb the tree's growth energy and provide foliage so photosynthesis can continue. Remove the nurse limb or cut it back the following year after new branches have arisen from the cut limbs.

A follow-up program of summer pruning and dormant pruning is essential to reshaping the tree in the manner you desire. If you want to grow one or more different varieties instead of the variety of the existing tree, consider topworking (grafting) the tree to a different variety. Topworking can be conducted at the time that you cut the main branches (see chapter 8, "Budding and grafting").

References

Hodel, D. R., and D. Pittenger. 2015. Woody landscape plants. In D. Pittenger, ed., California master gardener handbook. 2nd ed. Oakland: UC Agriculture and Natural Resources Publication 3382. 303–335.

Ingels, C., P. M. Geisel, and C. L. Unruh. 2002. Fruit trees: Training and pruning deciduous trees. Oakland: UC Agriculture and Natural Resources Publication 8057.

Vossen, P. M., and D. Silva. 2015. Temperate tree fruit and nut crops. In D. Pittenger, ed., California master gardener handbook. 2nd ed. Oakland: UC Agriculture and Natural Resources Publication 3382. 459–536.

Further reading

Aldrich, T. M., D. E. Ramos, and A. D. Rizzi. 1982. Training young walnut trees by the modified central-leader system. Oakland: UC Agriculture and Natural Resources Publication 2471.

Brickell, C., and D. Joyce. 2017. Pruning and training: The definitive guide to pruning trees, shrubs, and climbers. Revised new edition. New York: DK Books.

Harris, R. W. 1999. Arboriculture: Integrated management of landscape trees, shrubs, and vines. 3rd ed. Englewood Cliffs, NJ: Prentice-Hall.

Ingels, C., and P. M. Geisel. 2014. Fruit and nut tree pruning guidelines for arborists. Davis: UC Agriculture and Natural Resources Publication 8502.

Ingels, C. A., P. M. Geisel, and M. V. Norton, tech. eds. 2007. The home orchard. Oakland: UC Agriculture and Natural Resources Publication 3485.

Westwood, M. N. 2009. Temperate zone pomology: Physiology and culture. 3rd ed. Portland, OR: Timber Press.

Chapter 8

Budding and grafting

Chuck A. Ingels and Pamela M. Geisel

Budding and grafting are methods of plant propagation that allow the home orchardist to join two or more different pieces of plant tissue within one plant so they grow together as one plant. In woody plants, the top of the plant—the scion—is *grafted* as a herbaceous or woody stem onto the root system and stem of another plant, the rootstock. *Budding* is the insertion of a bud into the rootstock. Both methods are asexual methods of plant propagation that allow both components to retain their unique characteristics. However, rootstocks and scions can influence one another in multiple ways. For example, a specific rootstock may be used to induce better cold tolerance in a scion, avoid a soil disease that a scion is susceptible to, or enhance the quality or yield of the fruit, flowers, or foliage that the scion produces. In summary, grafting and budding are used to combine different plant materials to produce a better single plant.

These simple techniques allow you to grow more than one variety, and in some cases more than one species, of fruit on a single tree. For example, if you have space for only one cherry tree and you also need a pollinizer variety, you can bud or graft one or more other cherry varieties onto the single tree. Budding and grafting can also be used to extend the period of fruit harvest from a single tree—that is, you can grow several peach and nectarine varieties with different harvest times on the same tree. The home orchardist will most often use budding and grafting to add one or more varieties or species to an existing tree. You can also use budding and grafting to repair an existing tree that has been injured, or to change from one variety to another. These are the same practices commonly used in wholesale nurseries to propagate new plants grown on a rootstock.

To successfully produce the grafted or budded tree that you wish to grow, the scion must be graft-com-patible with your tree or rootstock. Generally, different varieties of the same species (for example, one cherry variety added to another) are compatible. If grafted properly, they readily unite and grow as a single plant. Different species (for example, a peach grafted onto a plum) may be incompatible because they may grow together poorly. In other cases, the graft union may fail entirely. Even though budding and grafting are ancient techniques, the underlying physiological and structural reasons for plant-graft incompatibility are poorly understood. Table 8.1 gives a list of graft compatibilities for selected deciduous fruit and nut trees. However, consulting a knowledgeable UC Advisor, Master Gardener, nursery employee, or professional for more information on grafting compatibility for your tree is advisable.

Potentially, a decision to bud or graft can be hazardous to the tree and even to the future of a commercial crop. Diseases are easily transferred from plant parts. The scion that you removed from the donor tree may be infected with disease-causing organisms such as fungi, bacteria, viruses, and viroids. The donor plant material may appear healthy but diseases might still be present that can cross the bud or graft union, infecting the entire tree. Insects and mites, or their eggs, may be transferred in this way as well. Severe diseases have crossed country, state, and quarantine boundaries by means of grafting and budding. Laws have been passed regulating grafting and budding of some plant species. For example, it is probably illegal for a home orchardist to use uncertified citrus plant material to bud or graft a tree in California. Fortunately, certified disease-free citrus budwood is available from the California Citrus Clonal Protection Program, ccpp.ucr.edu/onlineOrdersV2/. Regardless of the plant species, the use of certified disease-free budwood is always recommended. For

Table 8.1. Grafting compatibilities of common deciduous fruit and nut trees

Rootstock	Almond	Apple	Apricot	Cherry	Peach and nectarine	Pear	Plum (European and Japanese)*	Quince	English walnut
					Scion				
Almond	S	I	U	I	P†	I	P	I	I
Apple	I	S	I	I	I	U	I	U	I
Apricot	U	I	S	I	P‡	I	P§	I	I
Cherry:									
Mazzard	I	I	I	S	I	I	I	I	I
Mahaleb or Stockton Morello	I	I	I	P	I	I	I	I	I
Peach	S	I	P	I	S	I	P	I	I
Pear	I	U	I	I	I	S	I	U	I
Plum:									
Myrobalan	U	I	P	I	U	I	S	I	I
Marianna 2624	P¶	U	S	I	U	I	S	I	I
Quince	I	U	I	I	I	P#	I	S	I
Walnut: Northern California black or Paradox	I	I	I	I	I	I	I	I	S

Key:

S = Satisfactory for grafting.

P = Partly satisfactory for grafting: most cultivars grow and fruit normally on this rootstock, although some cultivars and some trees do not make satisfactory or permanent graft unions.

I = Incompatible combination for grafting: the grafts either do not grow or growth is weak and short-lived.

U = Unsatisfactory for grafting, although grafts may grow for a time.

Source: Geisel 2002, p. 114; Hartmann and Beutel 1994, p. 26.

*In general, many European and Japanese plums may be grafted on most European plums. Although many Japanese cultivars do well on other Japanese cultivars, European cultivars are not successful on Japanese stocks. Peaches, almonds, and apricots may sometimes be grafted on Japanese and European plums with reasonable success, but as a rule the grafts will fail to grow or do not grow satisfactorily.

†Peach trees are sometimes short-lived and become dwarfed on almond rootstock.

‡Many peach varieties fail to grow well on apricot rootstock.

§Some Japanese plum cultivars are compatible with some apricot rootstocks. In contrast, most European plums are not compatible with apricot rootstocks.

¶Some almond cultivars (such as Nonpareil) do not make a satisfactory union with Marianna 2624, so an interstock of Havens 2B plum must be used to work such cultivars on this stock. Other cultivars (such as Ne Plus Ultra and Mission) make reasonably satisfactory unions with Marianna 2624.

#Some pear cultivars (such as Old Home and Hardy) make good unions with quince, while others (such as Bartlett) do not and must be double-worked using one of the compatible pear cultivars as an interstock.

some plant species, your county UC Cooperative Extension Advisor, Master Gardener or commercial nursery may have or know of disease- and insect-free sources of budwood. One such example might be an annual scion exchange at a local chapter of the California Rare Fruit Growers, crfg.org.

As briefly explained earlier, in both budding and grafting, parts of two plants are united to grow as one plant. The scion is the part that is removed from one plant and attached to another; the new growth from the scion remains true to type rather than blending genetically with the rootstock. The rootstock (also called stock) is the plant to which the scion is attached. A union forms when the stock and scion form a tissue connection of the vascular cambium (or cambium), a thin layer of actively dividing cells located between the inner wood and the bark of a tree (see chapter 2, "Growth and development"). Undifferentiated callus cells form at the union, and these soon differentiate into new vascular tissues that permit the passage of nutrients and water between the stock and the scion.

With budding (also called bud grafting), the scion is a single vegetative bud from the desired plant. In grafting, the scion is a section of a 1-year-old branch that contains two or more vegetative buds. Your choice of whether to use budding or grafting will depend on the plant species, age and size of the stock, the time of year, and your comfort level and history of success with the method. Some plant species are much easier to propagate by one method or the other. Some people prefer budding because it requires smaller cuts and can be done using either of two techniques. Grafting is generally limited to winter and early spring, but some people prefer it because it is more versatile in that it can be used on 1-year-old wood or wood that is several years old. We suggest the reader consult a reference for information about grafting or budding methods and timing for the specific plant combination intended.

Grafting supplies

Knives

Many types of grafting knives are available from mail order catalogs, nurseries, and farm supply stores. Folding knives are the safest because the blade, which must be kept very sharp, is only out when you are making the cuts. Some folding knives have two blades: one used for grafting and the other for T-budding (fig. 8.1A). The single, straight blade is used for most grafting methods as well as for chip budding, but it is not well suited for making the long T-cut on the stock in T-budding. Knives designed primarily for T-budding have a substantial curve at the end of the blade and a bark lifter opposite the blade (see fig. 8.1A). A similar type has a single blade with a very slight curve at the tip and a bark lifter on the opposite side (fig. 8.1B). This blade can be used for both grafting and budding, but again, the long T-cut on the

stock is somewhat easier with a more curved blade. Another type of folding knife has a simple curved blade on one side and a bark lifter on the other (fig. 8.1C). Nonfolding budding knives (fig. 8.1D) and grafting knives (fig. 8.1E) are also available. You can also make a grafting knife at home by grinding down a strong household knife into the correct shape.

Always keep the blade very sharp, using a sharpening stone or another sharpening tool. A sharp blade is safest because it consistently makes clean cuts, without the sudden "give" that may cause you to cut yourself. Make sure to bevel the blade on one side only, as with bypass loppers and hedge shears. The

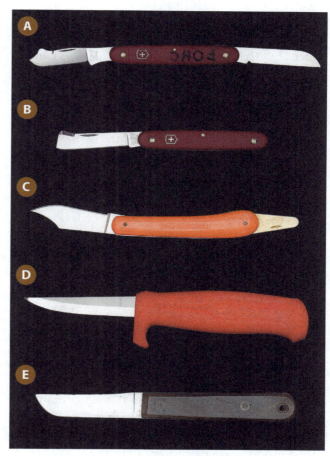

Figure 8.1. Some of the knives available for budding and grafting. Knife with two folding blades: a straight blade (left) for grafting and a T-budding knife (right) with a curved tip and a bark lifter (A). These blades are also available singly on some models. Rosebudding knife combining the T-budding and grafting blades into a single folding blade (B). Making a longitudinal cut (see fig. 8.4C) is slightly more difficult with this blade than with the more curved blade in (A), above. Budding knife with separate folding blade and bark lifter (C). Simple (nonfolding) budding knife (D). Simple (nonfolding) grafting knife (E). *Photos:* Jack Kelly Clark.

straight, nonbeveled side enables the grafter to make long, straight cuts. Most grafting knives are beveled for right-hand use. Left-handed pruning knives are less available.

Because you have to keep the blade of a grafting knife very sharp, there is potential for serious injury when grafting. Unless you are an experienced grafter, never cut toward unprotected fingers. Always cut away from your body. Avoid pushing hard with the grain of the wood, as the knife may suddenly "give" and slice into your flesh or into a branch that you don't want to cut. With some methods—such as the long, sloping cut used in whip, bark, and cleft grafting—your thumb may be perilously close to the blade, so you should make sure to wear a thumb protector or suitable glove. Gloves generally increase safety, but they may be cumbersome. Always close folding knives or sheath nonfolding knives when they are not in use. If you do cut yourself, seek prompt medical attention. Have a first aid kit available when you are grafting.

Wrapping and waxing materials

Different types of wrapping and waxing products are available to hold grafts in place and to provide an airtight seal. The type of wrap to use depends on which grafting method you use and the size of the wood. Wraps include cloth and plastic grafting tape, with or without one sticky side; parafilm stretch tape, which sticks to itself; and rubber strips, also called budding rubbers or budding strips (fig. 8.2). Some products, especially parafilm tape and rubber strips, begin to break down within a few weeks, so you usually will not have to cut them off later. Other tapes may not break down before branch thickening occurs, so you may have to cut them to prevent branch girdling.

Waxing is necessary with several grafting methods, especially if the wrap does not form an airtight seal. Most products are paste-like or creamy even in cold weather, but others must be softened by working them with your warm hands. When properly used, any sealing product designed for grafting should form an adequate seal, but remember to check for cracks at least once a week for a few weeks and to reseal if cracks form.

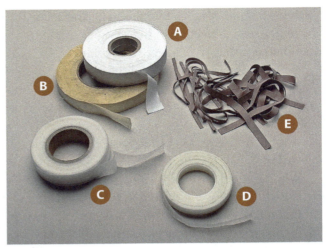

Figure 8.2. Various types of wraps used in budding and grafting. Plastic tape with no adhesive (A). Cloth tape with one adhesive side (B). Parafilm tape with perforations for easy removal (buddy tape) (C). Parafilm tape (D). Rubber strips (E). *Photo:* Jack Kelly Clark.

Key points for budding and grafting

- Use disease-free scions and rootstock.
- Position the scion so that at least a portion of the cambium of the scion touches the cambium of the rootstock—the more contact, the better.
- Use a sharp budding or grafting knife or other sharp, single-beveled knife (that is, sharpened on one side only).
- Keep scions cool after you collect them and during the grafting; using wet newspaper over ice water in a cooler is a good method.
- Make clean, straight cuts, and have extra scion wood available.
- Do not leave cut surfaces exposed to sunlight or wind—or at least keep such exposure to a minimum.
- Do not touch the cut surfaces and do not allow them to dry out.
- Label each graft with the variety name, and later mark or paint where the graft was made.
- If you use wax, make sure to rewax whenever cracks appear.
- If necessary, cut binding strings or tapes once the grafts or buds have joined.
- Stake new shoots if necessary; remove suckers and unwanted shoots that shade out desirable shoots growing from the graft.

Budding (bud grafting)

There are two primary methods of bud grafting. Historically, T-budding has been the most widely used technique for grafting fruit trees and some ornamentals, but chip budding is increasing in popularity because some people find it easier and more successful. T-budding is usually performed in the spring and early summer. Chip budding can be used from midsummer through fall, as well as during the dormant season.

T-budding

When T-budding, you insert a shield-shaped piece of the desired (scion) variety into a T-shaped cut in the bark of the stock. For this reason, the method is sometimes called shield budding. T-budding is best done with a specially designed budding knife (see fig. 8.1). If no budding knife is available, you can use instead a previously unused single-edge razor blade or a very sharp knife such as an X-ACTO hobby knife.

Because T-budding involves cutting and peeling back the bark of the stock, you have to do it when the bark is slipping (when it can easily be peeled away from the wood), which happens most when the tree is actively growing. Depending on the species, the bark of a 1-year-old branch can begin slipping as early as late February in Southern California, and later as you go north. Bark may continue to slip through early fall. Bark of a water-stressed tree does not slip easily.

T-budding is usually done on the current season's shoots, but it can also be done on 1-year-old branches. The shoot or branch should be at least as thick as a pencil at its base.

Details related to when and how to T-bud or chip bud may influence the success achieved with different plant species (fig. 8.3). A general description of the methods follows.

1. To collect budwood, cut off a vigorous current-season shoot that is about ¼ to ⅜ inch (6–10 mm) thick from the bud source tree. This shoot is called the bud stick, or budwood. Immediately cut off the bud stick's leaves by cutting the leaf stalks (petioles) in half; this reduces water loss through the leaves and also provides you a short handle (the half stem) by which to hold the bud after it is removed. In addition, cut off the top portion of the bud stick, where there will be buds that are not mature enough to graft. If you will not graft the buds immediately, wrap moist paper towels or newspaper around the bud stick and put it in a plastic bag. Keep it refrigerated, preferably at 36 to 40°F (2–4°C), until you use it; it will remain viable for 2 to 3 weeks when cut and stored in this manner.

2. Choose a current-season shoot on the stock tree whose circumference is the same as or slightly larger than that of the scion shoot. If budding to a young rootstock tree or a rootstock sucker, choose an area on the trunk about 6 to 12 inches above the ground. Make a transverse cut through the bark only, running about halfway around the shoot. Then finish the capital T by making a longitudinal cut perpendicular to the first cut and extending downward about 1.5 inches (38 mm). (Some people prefer to make an inverted T, with the longitudinal cut extending upward from the transverse cut. In this case, the bud cuts [see step 3, below] would also be reversed.) Use the bark lifter on the budding knife (a butter knife will work, too) to separate the bark from the wood on both sides of the second cut, beginning at the top and working downward. Avoid using a sharp blade for lifting: It will tend to cut the bark rather than lift it.

3. Hold the scion bud stick by the bottom and remove a lower bud from the scion in the following manner. Beginning about half an inch below the bud, make a shallow cut beneath the bud, cutting toward the top of the bud stick. Continue the cut upward to just over half an inch above the bud, cutting about one-third to one-half the thickness of the shoot. Then make a horizontal cut about half an inch above the bud, through the bark only. Remove the bud by squeezing the sides of the cut bark just above the bud. This squeezing should separate the bark from the wood, taking the bud with the bark. Only a sliver of wood will remain attached to the bud stick.

Depending on the plant species, it may be necessary to include the wood sliver with the bud rather than remove the bark from the wood. If you do this, make sure you are grafting onto stock that is larger than the bud stick in order to ensure good contact between the edge of the bud piece (the cambial area)

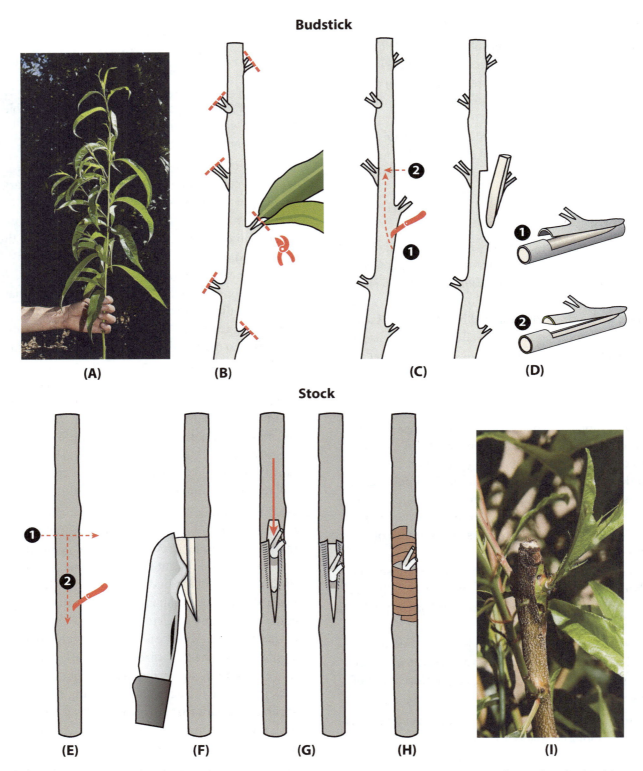

Budstick

(A)   (B)   (C)   (D)

Stock

(E)   (F)   (G)   (H)   (I)

Figure 8.3. T-budding method: Preparing budstick: Vigorous shoot removed from tree (A). Remove leaves from budstick but leave petiole portion remaining for handling (B). Undercutting the bud on the budstick (C1). Horizontal cut through the bark of the budstick (C2). Bud shield removed from budstick wood (D1). Optional method of including the wood with the bud (D2). Preparing stock: Transverse cut through the bark of the stock (E1). Longitudinal cut through the bark of the stock (E2). Using the bark lifter to separate the bark of the stock from the wood (F). Inserting the bud shield into the T cut on the stock (G1). Bud shield inserted under the flaps of the T cut (G2). Wrapping and final tie-off of rubber strip around the stock to secure the bud shield (H). New shoots (I).

and the cambium of the stock. The larger stock is usually necessary because the flat surface of the scion's wood sliver is being placed against the round surface of the stock.

1. Hold the bud by the leaf stalk and insert the point (bottom) of the bud shield into the T-cut on the stock. Gently slide the bud shield downward until the top cut of the bud piece is just under, and is touching, the top of the T-cut. If necessary, use the flat part of the knife to help push the bud into place. The bud should be centered between the bark flaps. Check the bud orientation to insure it is inserted upright.

2. To secure the bud, firmly wrap the cut areas with a rubber strip or parafilm tape around the bud, beginning at the top and working downward. Begin and end the wrapping by tucking the ends of the rubber strip or tape under the wrap. With a rubber strip, it is not essential to completely cover the cut area; that is, there can be some space between the spiral wraps of rubber strip, as long as the bark flaps firmly cover and seal the bud piece. If you are using parafilm tape, pull the tape as you wrap it to stretch it tightly over the cut areas, but preferably not over the bud. However, with citrus, to prevent the bud from drying out, the entire bud is included in the wrap, and the parafilm is removed in about 10 days. Within a few weeks, you can cut the branch off above the bud to force the shoot to grow.

Chip budding

Chip budding is a method that is often used at times of year when you cannot use T-budding because the bark is not slipping. These times include late summer to early fall, as well as the late dormant season. When the bark is slipping, in spring and early summer to midsummer, T-budding is often used instead.

Grape growers sometimes plant rootstocks in the vineyard, let them grow all summer, and then use chip budding in the fall on the young rootstock plants. A bud of the desired variety is grafted at the base of each vine and then covered with soil for several weeks to keep the bud cool and moist. The method for chip budding is as follows:

1. For chip budding (fig. 8.4), choose budwood about ½ to ⅜ inch in diameter and choose a rootstock

that is the same size or slightly larger, but no bigger than about ¾ inch in diameter. If you are chip-budding in the summer or fall, your bud stick should be a current-season shoot with a base that is starting to turn brown and woody. Choose only healthy shoots that were exposed to substantial sunlight on the tree. Immediately remove the leaves from the bud stick, leaving a petiole stem to hold the bud.

2. Remove a "chip" with a bud from the budstick, then

    a. Make the first cut about 0.5 inch below the bud, transversely across the shoot or branch and at a downward angle of about 45 degrees. Sometimes a narrower angle may be better because it permits the bud to fit more deeply into the stock, allowing a tighter fit.

    b. Start the second cut about 1 inch above the first, cutting downward under the bud until your cut intersects with the first cut. The bottom of the chip is V-shaped.

3. Remove a chip of similar size from the stock.

4. Place the chip with the scion bud into the cut you have made in the rootstock.

5. For best success, the chip should match the cut in the stock in size and shape so the bud chip's cambium layer matches with that of the stock. If the cut on the stock is wider than on the bud chip, place the chip to one side or the other so the cambium layers match on that side.

6. Securely wrap the cut areas with parafilm tape and rubber strips. If you use a rubber strip alone, seal all cut edges with grafting wax, but avoid waxing over the bud.

Determining whether the bud graft has taken

You can tell that the graft was successful if the bud remains plump and the bark piece remains green. To be certain, you can nick the bark of the bud patch with a knife: If it is green underneath, the graft was successful (although the bud could still be dead); if brown, the graft was not successful.

Forcing bud growth

Buds that are grafted in late summer through early fall should not be forced to grow until the following

Budstick

Stock

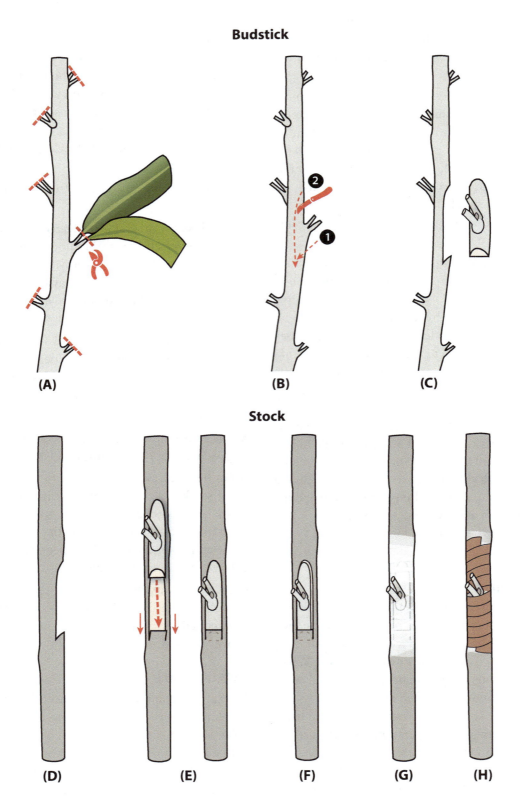

Figure 8.4. Chip budding method: Cherry budstick with leaves being cut off but petiole portion remaining for ease of handling (A). Transverse cut across scion below bud. Lengthwise cut on scion intersects with the end of the first cut (B). Removed chip (C). Identical cuts being made in stock (D). Chip of desired variety inserted into cut on stock (E, F). Cambium layers of chip of a smaller size than the stock cut should match on one side (cambium layer of stock can be seen on cut surface). Wrapping with parafilm tape; double-wrap the parafilm, but use a single layer on the bud (G). Budding rubber secured over the parafilm (H).

spring; otherwise, fall frost may kill the tender, young shoots. You can, however, force buds grafted from early spring through midsummer to grow about 2 to 3 weeks after grafting, or when you are confident the graft was successful. To force a bud to grow, cut off the shoot or branch onto which the bud was grafted, about ¼ inch above the top of the cut. As the desired shoot grows, remove any competing shoots nearby that might shade it.

If you don't want to cut the branch off above the bud, you can sometimes force the bud to grow by girdling or notching (also called scoring) the branch above the bud. To girdle a branch to stimulate bud growth, remove a strip of bark about ³⁄₁₆ to ¼ inches wide and running crosswise, no more than halfway around the branch, just above the top cut of the bud graft (fig. 8.5). You can girdle any time from early spring (after the bark begins to slip) through early summer. The practice is most successful on current-season or 1-year-old wood, but it often works on older wood as well. The girdled strip will quickly callus over after the bud begins to grow.

If a bud was grafted in late summer or early fall, notching can be used in late winter (before the bark is slipping) to force the bud to grow. Pull a saw or round "rat-tail" file in a single stroke across the branch just above the bud, filing through the bark only (fig. 8.6). Girdling and notching work by interrupting the downward movement of the plant hormone auxin through the phloem. Auxin is a plant hormone that is produced in the shoot tips and leaves and moves down the phloem, preventing the growth of lateral buds (see chapter 2, "Growth and development"). When you interrupt the flow of auxin, the bud or buds immediately below the girdle or notch temporarily cease to be influenced by the auxin and will usually grow into a vigorous shoot.

Figure 8.6. Notching with a saw above a bud to stimulate a vigorous shoot for a headed branch (A). The method is usually done at or before bud swell, but it can still work at this point. After notching with saw (B). Notching above a dormant grafted bud with a ⅛-inch rat-tail file (C).

Figure 8.5. Girdling above a grafted bud may force it to grow without heading the branch or trunk. Here, two vertically separated half-girdles were made in the spring on the trunk of this young cherry tree, forcing new shoots to grow below the cuts. *Photo: Chuck Ingels.*

Grafting of scion and stock of the same size

Grafting, which includes topworking (see "Grafting of scion onto larger stock [topworking]," below), consists of attaching a 1-year-old vigorous scion branch (often called a whip) with two or three buds to the stock, rather than attaching only a single bud. In order to reduce the time the graft is exposed to the elements, most grafting methods are used in the later dormant period but before bud swell. However, bark grafting must be performed in early spring when the bark is slipping—but a dormant scion branch must be used. Special grafting tools are available for this purpose and will be discussed below, but you can use any small, sharp knife—preferably one that is beveled on one side only.

For all methods in which a scion is grafted onto a 1-year-old stock of the same size, you generally do not need to try to match cambium layers because they usually match up naturally. You just need to be sure the two sticks truly are the same size and that, when fitted together, they are snugly aligned to appear as one continuous branch. Hold the scion up to the stock to determine where diameters are the same size and where the cuts will be made.

Whip grafting with scion and stock of the same size

Whip grafting (fig. 8.7), also known as whip-in-tongue grafting, is often used on 1-year-old rootstock wood that is about ¼ to ¾ inch in diameter. For best results, the scion and rootstock should be about the same diameter. The practice can also be successful when the stock is larger than the scion as long as the cambiums of the stock and scion match on at least one side. Whip grafting usually provides excellent cambial contact and results in a strong graft union. The method for whip grafting is as follows:

1. For whip grafting, collect the scion wood in the dormant season before buds begin to swell. Graft it immediately or wrap it with moist paper towel or newspaper and store it in a plastic bag in the refrigerator for later use.

2. Make a sloping cut 1 to 2 inches long at the top of the rootstock and a matching cut at the base of the scion. The straightest cut is made with one swift movement rather than rocking or slicing with the knife. The cut will be longer with larger-diameter wood and shorter with smaller-diameter wood.

3. Make a cut downward into the stock starting about one-third of the distance from the tip; the cut should be about ¼ to ⅜ inches long. The cut goes with the grain of the wood. Avoid splitting below the cut, and avoid cutting at an angle, or the remaining tip will be flimsy. With the knife still in place, slightly twist the knife away from the tip of the stock to create an opening. Bending the knife in this manner makes it easier to interlock the stock and scion. Make a similar cut in the scion, one-third the distance from the tip. There is potential for injury here: Use caution when making these cuts.

4. Slide the two vertical cuts together so the pieces interlock tightly.

5. Wrap the union tightly with parafilm tape or grafting tape. Wax the union if the wrap is not airtight. If the tape is airtight (for example, if parafilm tape is used), no wax is needed. The scion's shoot growth may be delayed in comparison with the stock.

Cleft grafting with the same size scion and stock

Cleft grafting can be used for grafting onto a larger stock—this is called topworking (see next section)—or onto a scion and stock of the same size. Where scion and stock are the same size, there is no advantage in using cleft grafting instead of whip grafting. Moreover, the diameter of the wood used and the timing of the graft, in the latter portion of the dormant season, are the same. People who have difficulty making the vertical cuts of the whip graft may find cleft grafting easier, although making cleft grafting's long, uniform scion cuts can be challenging as well. The cleft-grafting method for scion and stock of the same size is as follows:

1. For cleft grafting (fig. 8.8), collect the scion wood in the dormant season before buds begin to swell. Graft it immediately—or wrap it with moist paper towel or newspaper and store it in a plastic bag in the refrigerator for later use.

2. Find an area on the stock with a diameter similar to that of the scion (see fig. 8.7). In that area, cut

the stock straight across with hand pruners. Make the cleft cut through the center of the stock ¾ to 1¼ inch deep, depending on the scion thickness (see fig. 8.8A).

3. Remove any obvious flower buds from the two scion buds (see figs. 8.8B–C). Make a long, sloping cut on one side and a similar cut on the other side,

creating a point when viewed from the side (see figs. 8.8D–E). Ensure that the cuts are straight, preferably by making the cuts quickly, in one movement. Create a long point and "carve" only if necessary. The overall length of the two cuts should be about ⅝ inch to 1 inch, depending on the scion's thickness.

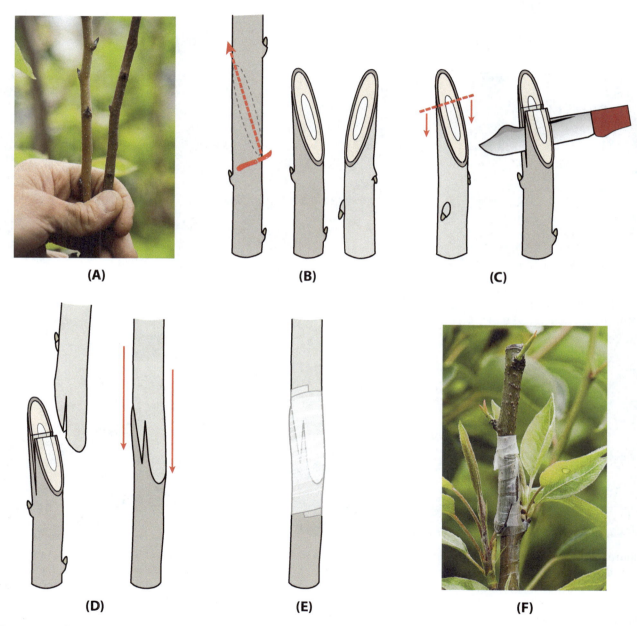

(A)   (B)   (C)

(D)   (E)   (F)

Figure 8.7. Whip grafting method: Pear scion wood, collected in January and stored in refrigerator until early April (A), is (B) matched in size with 1-year-old branch (left). Beginning the long, sloping cut (exercise caution). Matching cuts of the stock (left) and scion (right). Downward cut through the wood of both the stock and the scion, one-third of the distance from the tip (C). Gently twist the knife away from the tip to create an opening; try not to split the wood. Slide the scion into the stock so the cuts interlock and cambium layers match (D). Union wrapped with parafilm tape (E). Shoots starting to grow and tape breaking several weeks later (F). *Photos:* Jack Kelly Clark.

Figure 8.8. Cleft grafting method for scion and stock of the same size. Make the cleft cut in the center of the stock ¾ to 1¼ inch deep, depending on the stock thickness and length of the scion cuts (A). Be careful not to veer to one side or to split the wood below the blade. Grasping the scion below the cut will stabilize the cut but gloves must be worn. Plump flower buds of a peach whip form on one or both sides of the thinner vegetative (shoot) bud (B). Remove any visible flower buds at two nodes (C). On the scion (top of scion in left hand), make a long, quick sloping cut and another cut on the opposite side (D). After completion, the bottom of the inverted scion comes to a point in the side view (E). Some "carving" can be done, but the cuts should end up straight and smooth. Insert the scion stick into the center cleft cut on stock, matching the cambium layers on both sides (F). Avoid splitting the stock below the cut by making longer sloping cuts on the scion. Wrap the graft union and scion tip with parafilm tape to avoid drying (G). If other tape is used that is nonsealing, daub surfaces with grafting wax (H). Photos were taken in early February. Three months after grating, the two new shoots have grown. Removal of the parafilm shows complete callus formation at the cut surfaces (I). Be sure to remove competing shoots around the grafts to ensure adequate light.

4. Insert the scion into the cut on the stock (see fig. 8.8F) and wrap all cut surfaces, including the scion tip (see fig. 8.8G). Two wraps with parafilm tape will suffice; wraps that are not airtight may need to be coated with grafting wax to make the cut surfaces airtight for several weeks.

5. Remove all shoots that might compete with the scion shoots for sunlight (see fig. 8.8G). Leave the tape or wrap on until significant callus tissue growth has occurred, but not longer than 4 weeks. If necessary, carefully cut the tape (see fig. 8.8H).

Grafting tools

People who have difficulty with or an aversion to using a knife may find a grafting tool to be simpler, more precise, and safer. Several types of grafting tools are available; two of the most common tools are shown in figures 8.9 and 8.10. One of these (with orange handles) has three interchangeable blades: rounded V, omega, and budding (rectangular). If large numbers of grafts are to be made, replacement blades should be purchased along with the grafting tool. Removing and replacing blades require instructions and patience. For best results, blades should be periodically sharpened with sandpaper.

An omega shape differs from a rounded V shape in that the sides of the omega cut are squeezed together somewhat (like a piece of a jigsaw puzzle). The omega blade of some grafting tools has a narrower point than that of other tools, although both are designed to fit snugly and hold together well. But the whip graft discussed previously provides an even stronger connection than these tools do.

Figure 8.9. Grafting tool (Italian) with alternative blade types (A). Grafting tool (Zenport shown here) with a single blade type (exchangeable) and with small trimming blades on top (B). Center the scion branch in the grafting tool such that the bottom of the scion is pointed. Insert scion into stock and be sure the fit is tight. The graft on the left resembles the Greek omega letter and the graft on the left is closer to a V shape (C and D). Both types are satisfactory if wrapped adequately.

Figure 8.10. Grafting tool with budding blade. Stock (peach) branch positioned between buds for cutting rectangular chip out of wood and bark (A). Budding cut made in stock (B). The branch must be thick enough to maintain structural stability; that is, the cut should remove no more than about one-third to one-half the thickness of the stock. Stock and scion branches should be about ½ to ⅝ inches thick (C). Scion branch positioned so the bud is centered in the cut. The scion was turned to show the centered bud, but the bud should be pointed downward toward the tool for making the cut. Bud chip removed and ready for insertion into stock cut (D). Bud chip inserted snugly into stock cut (E). The flowers on either side of the vegetative peach bud were removed (F). The cut edges have been sealed by wrapping with parafilm tape. Do not cover the bud.

The ideal branch diameter for standard grafting tools is about ⅜ to ½ inch thick. If the branch is too thin, the sides of the stock cut may be flimsy and surface contact may be insufficient. A branch that is too thick may also be too difficult for the grafter to easily squeeze the handles together.

Grafting tools are used when branches (whips) are in full dormancy. When the sap starts flowing in late winter or early spring, the bark slips from the wood and is easily damaged, reducing the likelihood of a successful graft. The method for making standard V and omega cuts with a grafting tool is as follows:

1. To make these cuts with a grafting tool (see figs. 8.9 and 8.10), find a 1-year-old whip branch of a compatible species and match it with a stock branch of similar diameter (see fig. 8.7A).

2. On both the stock and scion, position the tool so the branch is sitting in the curved anvil groove (see figs. 8.9A–B). The point created by the cut can be either at the top of the stock or at the bottom of the scion, but the latter is typically used since it is likely more stable. Squeeze the handles so the blade touches the branch, and be sure the blade is positioned in the center of the branch. Examine cuts on both scion and stock to be sure they are centered.

3. Place the scion on the stock (see fig. 8.9C) and wrap all cut surfaces with two layers of parafilm (see fig. 8.8F), or with grafting tape and wax.

Using a tool for budding

The budding blade is about an inch long, and it undercuts the bud in a manner similar to chip budding.

The method provides a snug fit between the bud piece and the stock.

1. Match the stock and scion stem diameter.

2. On the stock, cut a section of the branch between two nodes (see figs. 8.10A–B).

3. On the scion branch, position the desired bud in the center of the blade (see fig. 8.10C). Be sure the bud is positioned perpendicular to the cut. After the cut is made, press open the handles to force the bud out of the blade (see fig. 8.10D).

4. Place the bud upright on the scion branch and remove any obvious flower buds (see fig. 8.10E).

5. Thoroughly seal the cut edges with parafilm tape (see fig. 8.10F), or use grafting tape and grafting wax.

6. In 2 to 3 weeks, or as the buds begin to swell, cut the stock about ½ inch above the uppermost bud cut. Remove all buds on the stock within 1 inch of the new bud. Carefully cut the tape off when buds swell.

Grafting of scion and stock of different sizes

Grafting of scion onto larger stock (topworking)

Topworking, also known as grafting over, is a method of grafting one or more 1-year-old, dormant scion wood sticks onto a large cut branch. Growers use this technique to change the variety of a whole orchard if marketing conditions change. In the home orchard, it can be used to replace an undesirable variety or to add a pollinizer. Topworking connects the scion to a tree's fully developed root and main branch systems, so the new cultivar should begin bearing within 2 years. In this chapter we discuss two methods of topworking: bark and cleft grafting.

To prepare the tree for topworking, cut back the branches to be grafted but leave one or two smaller limbs uncut. These nurse limbs will continue to provide carbohydrates (from photosynthesis in the leaves) to the large root system and pull water through the tree to keep it cool until the new grafts have grown.

Whip grafting with larger stock

A variation of the standard whip graft (stock and scion of the same size) can be used on stocks as large as about 2 to 3 inches in diameter.

1. Cut off the stock and make an upward, slicing cut in the stock. Then make a downward vertical cut, starting about one-third the distance from the top (fig. 8.11A).

2. Make a sloping cut at the base of the scion, then make the vertical cut, starting this time in the middle of the sloping cut (fig. 8.11B).

3. Insert the scion so that it locks tightly into the stock (fig. 8.11C). Make sure the cambium layers match on at least one side. Because the bark of the stock is much thicker than the bark of the scion, the scion will be set in from the edge of the stock cut.

4. Wrap with tape and cover all cut surfaces with grafting compound (8.11D–E).

Cleft grafting with a larger stock

Cleft grafting—using a stock that is larger than the scion—is a challenging method. It requires the use of a heavy, fairly thin knife. You can purchase a cleft grafting tool, but make sure the blade is not too thick or it will cause the bark to split rather than cut cleanly. Inexperienced grafters often have a low success rate with this method, probably because it matches only one side of the scion cambium with the stock cambium and the cambium layers are not easy to align. Cleft grafting must be done in the winter, before the sap begins to flow and the bark begins to slip. The scion wood can be collected and used immediately for grafting—or the wood can be wrapped in a moist paper towel in a plastic bag and stored in a refrigerator until the day of grafting. On a larger stock, you can use two scions—one on either side of the stock—but use only one scion when grafting onto a smaller stock. The method for cleft grafting, using a stock that is larger than the scion (fig. 8.12), is as follows:

1. To use this method, collect scion wood about ⅜ to ⅝ inch in diameter. Select wood that is stiffened and does not bend easily.

2. Saw off a limb or trunk of the stock and pound a cleft grafting knife through the center of the stump.

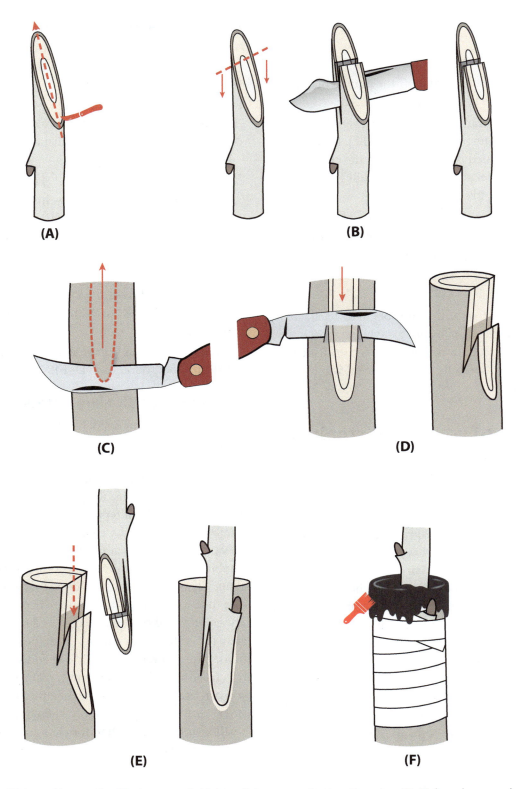

Figure 8.11. Whip grafting method for large stock: Make a slicing upward cut on the scion (A). Make a downward vertical cut, starting one-third the distance from the tip. Notice the highly visible cambium layer (B). Make a long sloping cut on the stock (C) and then make the vertical cut starting halfway between the ends of the sloping cut (D). Lock the scion into place in the stock, matching cambium layers on at least one side (E). Notice that a portion of the thick bark of the stock is visible but the cambium layer of the scion is in contact with that of the stock. Graft covered with a thick coat of grafting wax and wrapped with plastic tape (F).

3. Insert a screwdriver in the center to open the split wood.

4. Prepare the scion stick: Make a sloping cut of 1½ to 2 inches at the base of the scion. Make a second cut on the other side of the stick; the second cut should not be parallel to the first, but at a slight angle to it. This creates a wider bark section, which will be placed to the outside. Make an angled cut through the wood.

5. Insert the scion at the outer edge of the cut in the stock, with the pointed (wider) part to the outside. Make sure that the outer cambium layer of the scion aligns with the cambium layer of the stock. Note that the scion is inset slightly because its bark is thinner than the bark of the stock.

6. Remove the screwdriver, wrap the union tightly with strong tape, and place a thick coating of wax or grafting compound on all cut surfaces and over the tape to seal in moisture.

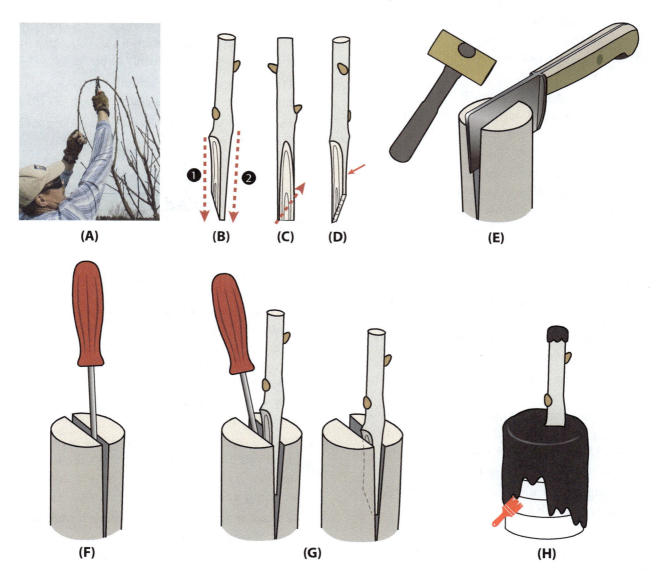

(A)   **(B)**   **(C)**   **(D)**   **(E)**

(F)   **(G)**   **(H)**

Figure 8.12. Cleft grafting method (cherry shown here). Bend a 1-year-old branch and select scion wood below the portion that easily bends; discard the terminal end (A). Make two long, sloping cuts at the base of the scion, with the second cut at a slight angle to the first cut (B, C). Make a sloping cut through the wood so that the wider side is longer (D). Pound a thin cleft-grafting knife through center of cut branch (knife shown here is homemade) (E). Insert a screwdriver to slightly open the split (F). Insert the scion stick into the stock, with the wider side to the outside so that cambium layers align (G). The outer edge of the scion stick will be set in from the outer edge of the stock because their bark thickness differs. Wrap stock tightly with tape and apply grafting compound to all cut surfaces and over the tape (H).

Bark grafting

Bark grafting, like cleft grafting, can be used on relatively large limbs. The technique requires that the bark be slipping (separating readily from the wood), so you can only do it in the spring after the rootstock has started active growth. Bark grafting is also called rind grafting. The method for bark grafting (fig. 8.13) is as follows:

1. Collect 1-year-old scion sticks about ⅜ to ½ inch in diameter in late January or early February, when the tree is fully dormant. Use wood with plump buds on stout branches. Store the scions wrapped in moist paper towel or newsprint in a plastic bag in the refrigerator.

2. In the early spring, when the bark is easy to separate from the wood, saw off the limb or trunk of the rootstock at a right angle to create a stump and scrape off dried outer bark.

3. Make a 1- to 1½-inch sloping cut on the bottom of the scion. If a "tail" was created in the process, place the blade flat against the cut and slice off the tail so the sloping cut is straight. Cut a much shorter diagonal cut on the other side. Cut the scion to 2 buds long.

4. Make two parallel cuts through the bark of the stock to match the diameter of the scion. Make the cuts slightly shorter than the long diagonal cut on the scion. Pull back the cut strip and cut the strip off just below its halfway point.

5. Slide the scion into the remaining cut strip and push it down so it is held firmly. Drive a thin wire nail about 1 inch long through the bark strip and the base of the scion and into the wood of the stock. Drive another nail above the first one, into the scion and the wood of the stock.

6. Thoroughly wax all cut surfaces, including the top of the scion, with a thick layer of grafting compound.

Some grafters prefer an alternative method of bark grafting (fig. 8.14), but it requires two angled scion cuts that can be difficult to make correctly. The method also uses no nails, so there is no danger of splitting the scion—but it requires strong grafting tape. The method for alternative bark grafting is as follows.

7. Make a single cut through the bark of the stock. The cut should be slightly shorter than the scion cuts. Push the knife sideways to scrunch the bark to one side (see fig. 8.14A).

8. Make a long, sloping cut at the bottom of the scion stick. Make a second sloping cut such that the V on one side is larger than the V on the other side (see fig. 8.14B). In doing so, you cause the bottom edge of the scion to slope toward the narrower cut.

9. Slide the bottom edge of the scion into the space created between the bark and the wood of the stock so that the wider V of the scion is facing the bark cut of the stock (see figs 8.14C–D). Push the scion down so it is held firmly in place.

10. Tie strong grafting tape around the stock and pull the final wrap through to cinch it (see fig. 8.14E).

11. Thoroughly wax all cut surfaces, including the top of the scion, with a thick layer of grafting compound (see fig. 8.14F).

Care of budded and grafted plants

Follow-up care is required for all grafts. Following is a checklist to help you ensure good growth of recently grafted plants.

- On older trees that you have topworked, one or two limbs of the old variety that were not selected for grafting should be maintained as nurse limbs for 1 year. Reduce the total leaf surface of the old variety as the graft grows. After 1 year, the new variety should be strong enough for you to remove or graft over the nurse limbs.

- Wax is a sealant that excludes air and prevents drying. If you use wax, check for cracks about 2 days after you graft and then weekly for several weeks, and apply additional wax if necessary.

- With some grafting methods, you will want to paint or whitewash the union to prevent sunburn damage. It is an especially good idea to paint the graft union or stock branch if you used black grafting wax or if you topworked a main limb. Use a commercially prepared tree whitewash or a 50:50 mix of interior white latex paint and water.

- When you cut a branch off for grafting, one result is the growth of many shoots below the cut. Once

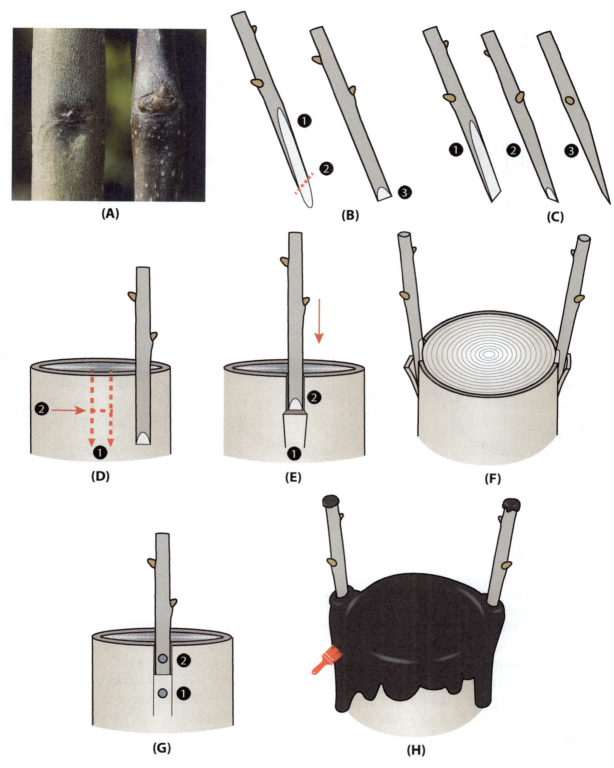

Figure 8.13. Bark grafting method. To prepare scion, choose dormant scion sticks with plump buds (A, right), not sunken buds (A, left); keep sticks moist and cold until the spring. In the spring, cut off a limb of the stock and scrape off the dead bark where grafting is to be done. Make a long, sloping cut on one side of the bottom of the scion wood (B1). Cut off the "tail," if present (B2). View from the opposite side (B3). Scion showing front, back, and side views (C). To prepare stock, make two parallel cuts, slightly shorter than the scion cut, into the bark of the stock (D1). Peel back the bark strip and cut off the top half of the bark strip (D2). Slide the stick between the bark and the wood of the stock (the short cut on the back of the scion is visible) (E). Example of a double scion graft (F). Drive one wire nail through the bark strip and the scion and into the wood of the stock (G1); drive another nail above the first, through the scion and into the stock (G2). Apply grafting compound over all cut surfaces to seal in moisture (H).

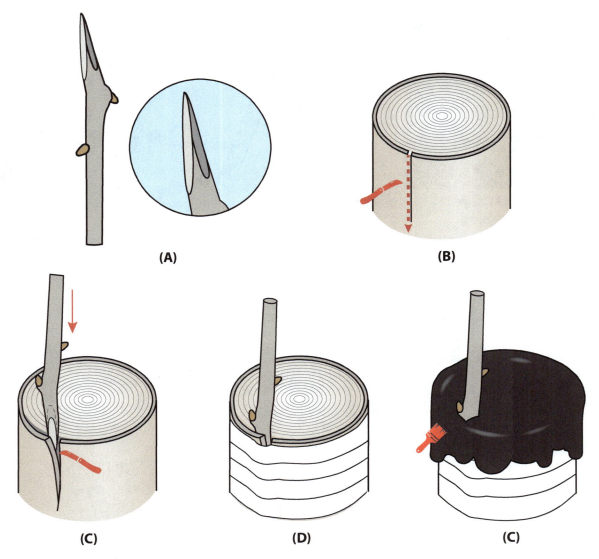

(A)

(B)

(C)

(D)

(C)

Figure 8.14. Alternative bark grafting method: To prepare scion, make two sloping cuts at bottom of scion stick so that the V on one side is narrower than the V of the other side (A). To prepare stock, cut off branch, making a single cut in bark (B). Push knife sideways to separate bark from wood (C). Insert the scion between the bark and the wood so that the wider V faces the cut in the bark. With the scion fully inserted, wrap the stock with strong tape (D). Apply grafting compound to all cut surfaces (E).

you know that the graft is successful, remove these shoots to prevent them from shading out the desired (grafted) variety (fig. 8.15). It is best simply to break the shoots off when they are several inches long rather than cut them off when they are fully grown branches. If the graft is not successful, thin the new growth down to two or three well-placed shoots and try grafting a bud or buds to them.

- When vigorous scion growth begins, cut or remove the tape if necessary so that it will not girdle the branch.

- If necessary, tie new shoots to a stake—or head them back if they grow too long—in order to prevent them from snapping or from growing in the wrong direction.

Reasons for graft failure

Attaining 100 percent success at grafting is very rare. Some people, however, experience frequent failure and may give up. Your chances of success will increase if you use multiple grafts for each desired branch, if possible. Lack of success may result from performing a single step incorrectly or from making

Figure 8.15. When the grafted bud or branch grows, cut or break off undesired shoots when they are young to prevent them from shading out the grafted variety. *Photo:* Jack Kelly Clark.

Further reading

Geisel, P. M. 2015. Plant propagation. In D. Pittenger, ed., California master gardener handbook. 2nd ed. Davis: UC Agriculture and Natural Resources Publication 3382. 109–142.

Hartmann, H. T., and J. A. Beutel. 1994. Propagation of temperate-zone fruit plants. Oakland: UC Agriculture and Natural Resources Publication 21103.

Hartmann, H. T., D. E. Kester, and F. T. Davies, Jr. 1990. Plant propagation: Principles and practices. 5th ed. Englewood Cliffs, NJ: Prentice Hall.

Reames, R., and B. H. Delbol. 1995. How to grow a chair: The art of tree trunk topiary. Williams, OR: Arborsmith Studios.

Toogood, A., ed. 1999. Plant propagation. American Horticultural Society. London: DK Publishing.

errors at several steps during the procedure. Common causes of graft failure include

- improper storage of cut scion wood
- using a particular grafting method at the wrong time of year
- using improper or dull knives or grafting tools
- allowing cut surfaces to dry out or receive excessive sun exposure while grafting
- insufficient contact of cambium layers
- drying of the union due to inadequate sealing
- damage caused by accidental bumping or shifting by birds or weather

Other potential problems could be using incompatible scion and stock species, inserting the scion upside down, and using weak or diseased plant materials.

If a graft fails, you may still be able to graft onto shoots that grow below the stock cut if you use an appropriate method and appropriate timing, later in the season or in winter. Thin out the shoots to ensure that the remaining shoots are well positioned, strong, and well provided with sunlight.

Chapter 9

Fruit thinning

Chuck A. Ingels

Fruit trees often set more fruit than they can physically support or develop to optimal size, especially if the trees were not properly pruned during the previous season. If so much fruit sets that the tree's leaves cannot supply the fruit with energy for growth, the fruit will compete with each other for carbohydrates and remain small. Too much fruit on a tree can also lead to limb breakage or alternate-bearing patterns (see chapter 2, "Growth and development"). By thinning immature fruit at the proper time, you can help correct these problems and allow each remaining fruit to develop to its maximum size. Although fruit thinning reduces the number of fruit and total yield, it is one of the few cultural practices that can improve the taste of fruit. Fruit from properly thinned trees can have sugar concentrations 1 to 2 percent higher than fruit from heavily cropped trees.

Fruit thinning can also reduce the spread of some diseases. Where two fruit are touching on a tree, moisture is trapped between them, providing better conditions for disease development. Also, diseases such as brown rot (see chapter 11, "Integrated management for backyard orchards") can quickly spread from one fruit to another just before harvest. Air moves more freely around separated fruit, which means that the surface of thinned fruit dries more quickly, reducing the chances that disease organisms will multiply and spread. Certain insect pests, such as leafrollers, also prefer to feed in fruit clusters.

Natural fruit drop

Flowers and fruit naturally thin themselves, often at distinct developmental stages (see chapter 2, "Growth and development"). Blossoms that are not pollinated turn yellow and drop off just after flowering. Small, immature fruit often drop naturally during what is known as June drop, which in most parts of California usually occurs in late April or May. Fruit or nuts that are diseased (such as walnuts with walnut blight) or infested with insects (such as apples or pears with codling moth) may also drop prematurely.

In some types of trees, this sort of natural thinning is sufficient; other species need additional thinning to produce high-quality fruit. Cherries, figs, pomegranates, citrus, and nut trees do not usually require thinning.

Species that require thinning

Most stone fruit trees—peach, nectarine, apricot, and plum—require thinning in most years. (Cherry is an exception.) Of pome fruit, all apples and Asian pears, and most European pears, require thinning. Bartlett pears often thin themselves, and if you harvest larger, more mature fruit early, you allow the smaller fruit to increase in size for a second pick 1 to 2 weeks later. Fruit of other species can and should be thinned if the crop is excessive relative to the vigor of the tree

Timing for thinning

Fruit can be thinned any time from right after bloom until a few weeks before harvest. It is a good idea, though, to wait until natural drop has occurred so you can assess the crop load before you thin. The identification and removal of defective fruit is more difficult when fruit are very small, and thinning too early can occasionally result in split pits in stone fruit, especially peaches. If you wait too long to thin, you increase the chances of limb breakage and risk reducing final fruit size. For these reasons, you should usually thin fruit from early April (for early-ripening fruit) to mid-May (for late-ripening fruit). Stone fruit are thinned when they are about ¾ to 1 inch in diameter and pome fruit (apples and pears) are thinned at ½ to 1 inch in diameter, or within about 30 to 45 days after full bloom.

How much fruit to thin

The amount of fruit to thin depends on the species (and sometimes variety) and the overall fruit load on the tree. If a tree is excessively vigorous, less thinning (leaving more fruit) will slow the growth but may still result in broken limbs. Trees that are growing poorly should be thinned far more and the causes of the poor health should be corrected. Many home gardeners are apprehensive about fruit thinning and often leave too much fruit on the tree. In some cases, little to no thinning may result in large fruit and healthy trees. But too often, the trees or fruit will suffer, and the trees may tend toward alternate bearing (see chapter 12, "Failure to bear and physiological disorders").

The recommendations that follow will usually result in healthy trees and adequate amounts of large fruit. When a range is given, use the closer spacing for varieties with smaller fruit and the wider spacing for larger-fruited varieties. You can still use closer spacing, but to do so may mean sacrificing fruit size and quality. If you have had ideal spring conditions for pollination, excessive fruit may have set, and the tree may require even more thinning than the range indicates. If the overall fruit load is light, but one or two branches have a large amount of fruit, the tree may require less thinning.

Peaches and nectarines, which produce fruit on long, 1-year-old branches instead of spurs, should be thinned to about 5 to 7 inches apart along the branch (fig. 9.1). Long lateral fruiting branches—those longer than about 1.5 to 2 feet—should have been shortened by about one-third to one-half their original length during the dormant season in order to reduce the amount of time necessary for thinning (see chapter 7, "Training and pruning"). If a lateral fruiting branch is long and produces fruit along its entire length, thin it more heavily, especially near the terminal end. Remove "doubles" (two fruit fused together) and small, disfigured, or damaged fruit.

Figure 9.1. Peach and nectarine trees form large numbers of fruit along 1-year-old branches. These fruit should be thinned to about 5 to 7 inches apart, which would leave only about three fruit on the branch shown here. *Photo:* Jack Kelly Clark.

Thin apricots and apriums to 3 to 5 inches apart on the branch (fig. 9.2) and thin plums and pluots slightly farther apart, to about 4 to 6 inches apart. On short spurs, thinning may leave only one or two fruit per spur (fig. 9.3).

Unlike stone fruit, which produce one fruit per bud, apples and pears produce a cluster of flowers and fruit from each bud. Thin to one fruit per cluster (fig. 9.4). If the overall crop is light, you can leave two fruit per cluster. Retain the largest fruit whenever possible. If the crop is heavy, fruit should be spaced no less than 6 to 8 inches apart.

Quince do not require thinning. Often, persimmons are not thinned, but thinning increases fruit size. A large fruit load may break branches, so you may want to thin persimmon fruit to 6 inches apart. Any tree with excessive fruit load and poor growth will benefit from fruit thinning (fig. 9.5).

Figure 9.2. Immature apricots before thinning (A) and after thinning (B). Note that about half the fruit were removed and even more fruit could have been thinned. *Photos*: Jack Kelly Clark.

Figure 9.3. Fruit on plum spurs before thinning (A) and after thinning (B). *Photos:* Chuck Ingels.

Figure 9.4. Thin apples and pears to one fruit per cluster. Before thinning (A) and after thinning (B). *Photos:* Jack Kelly Clark.

Figure 9.5. Scaffold branches of young trees, like the persimmon shown here, may bend over or break if the fruit load is heavy. *Photo:* Chuck Ingels.

Figure 9.6. Hand-thin stone fruit by twisting the fruit rather than pulling. This prevents damage to the branch or spur. *Photo:* Jack Kelly Clark.

Methods of thinning

For the home orchardist, there are two main ways to thin fruit—by hand or by pole. Hand thinning is more thorough and accurate than the pole method, but it is also much slower and may not be practical with larger trees. Whichever method you use, thinning is easiest if the trees were adequately pruned the previous winter or summer.

Hand thinning should be done carefully. Do not simply pull the fruit off or you may end up breaking off the entire spur with it. Instead, remove the fruit by twisting (fig. 9.6), cutting the stem with fingernails between the thumb and index finger, or using clippers (fig. 9.7)—especially with apples and pears, which are hard to remove otherwise. When hand-thinning, avoid leaning a ladder against the trunk or branches of a tree because the ladder may become unstable or damage the bark or branches. Also, avoid climbing fruit trees. Branches break easily, and falling can result in serious injuries.

Pole thinning, generally, cannot be used on apples or pears because they are very difficult to remove and the process would excessively damage the remaining fruit. Pole thinning is used mainly on large stone fruit trees, when hand thinning would be cumbersome, impractical, or dangerous. Pole thinning is much faster than hand thinning and, although it is

Figure 9.7. Asian pears and other pome fruit should be thinned using hand clippers. *Photo:* Jack Kelly Clark.

less precise, the results are often acceptable once you have mastered the technique. The pole can be made of a long dowel rod, rigid plastic pipe, bamboo, or other lightweight material. Attach a short length of rubber hose, cloth, or thick tape to the end of the pole to minimize scarring or bruising of fruit left on the tree. Strike individual fruit, clusters of fruit, or the base of the branch to remove some of the fruit (fig. 9.8). With experience, you will be able to strike a cluster or branch once or twice with just enough force to thin the right number of fruit.

Figure 9.8. You can use a pole thinner consisting of a dowel with a short piece of hose attached to its end to thin stone fruit (apricot is shown here) by carefully whacking the cluster or branch. Pole thinning is quicker than hand-thinning, but is harder to do accurately. *Photo:* Jack Kelly Clark.

Further reading

Ingels, C., P. M. Geisel, and C. L. Unruh. 2001. Fruit trees: Thinning young fruit. Oakland: UC Agriculture and Natural Resources Publication 8047. https://anrcatalog.ucanr.edu/Details.aspx?itemNo=8047

Yoshikawa, F. T., and R. S. Johnson. 1989. Fruit thinning. In J. H. LaRue and R. S. Johnson, eds., Peaches, plums, and nectarines: Growing and handling for fresh market. Oakland: UC Agriculture and Natural Resources Publication 3331. 56–59.

Chapter 10

Harvesting fruit and nuts

Pamela M. Geisel

A great deal of effort goes into growing fruit and nut trees so that we can harvest crops of the best possible quality. We prune, thin the fruit, water, fertilize, and manage pests, and yet we often ignore the most critical and timely task of harvest—sometimes, until it is too late to salvage a quality crop. In addition to having a timely harvest, it is important to provide the optimum storage conditions to maintain the fruit quality until the fruit can be either eaten or processed for longer-term storage.

General rules of harvest

Each crop has an optimum period and method for harvest, but the harvest period can vary, depending on the individual tastes of the gardener, physiological characteristics of the fruit, and planned use for the fruit. Fruit and nuts ripen by degrees. They can be harvested when more, or less, mature and ripe.

Some species are harvested when fully ripe and ready to eat; others when simply physiologically "mature," meaning that they will continue to ripen after harvest. For those that do not ripen further after harvest, the sugar they have at harvest is all they ever will have. These species may seem to get sweeter as their acidity decreases, but sugar content itself does not increase. They may also soften after harvest, but this is more a manifestation of decay and breakdown than of ripening. Fruit in this category include blackberries, cherries, grapes, citrus, raspberries, and strawberries.

Other species of mature-harvested fruit may further change in color, texture, and juiciness, but will not improve in sweetness or flavor. These fruit include apricots, blueberries, figs, nectarines, peaches, and plums.

Some fruit, such as apples, European pears, cherimoyas, kiwifruit, mangoes, and papayas, do increase in sugar and sweetness after harvest. These fruit contain starch that can be converted to sugars whether the fruit are on or off the tree.

Nut crops such as almonds, walnuts, and pecans can be harvested late without significant loss of quality to the nut itself. All the same, a timely harvest, when the hulls begin to split, will prevent other creatures, such as squirrels, ants, and navel orange worms, from getting to the crop before it can be harvested.

In all cases, waiting too long to harvest will render fruit overripe and very susceptible to birds, dried fruit beetles, or rot. Overripe fruit does not store well and fruit that is harvested mature-green does not taste the best. Fully tree-ripe fruit flavor cannot be surpassed.

The harvest stage you choose for your fruit also depends on how you plan to use the fruit. For immediate, fresh eating, fully ripe is ideal. For canning, the fruit should be more firm than soft. For drying, fully ripe fruit will yield a full-flavored dried fruit. That is the advantage of growing your own fruit—you get to harvest it when it is at the peak stage for your preference. Notations on your calendar that indicate the ripening period for your individual trees will help remind you to prepare for the harvest. The exact date of harvest will vary from year to year, however, depending upon factors such as weather and water stress.

It is also important to note that most species are harvested over a period of time because ripening usually occurs over 1 or more weeks. You may have to harvest every 3 to 5 days in order to get all the fruit right when it is ready. While more time-consuming than one-time harvesting, this extended harvest period allows you to process a smaller quantity of fruit at one time instead of processing the whole tree all at once. The ripening period also varies with the growing region. Fruit of the same variety tend to have a later harvest period in cooler climates.

Finally, what is considered "optimum ripeness" will vary with your individual preferences. Some people prefer a bit more tang or acidity to their fruit, so they harvest their fruit less ripe. Others prefer a bit more sugar, and so harvest fruit when it is more ripe. Commercial growers follow maturity standards that are based on indices such as the amount of sugar or acid in the fruit, firmness of the fruit, or splitting or browning of nut tissue. In the home garden, however, that determination is up to the individual.

When harvesting fruit by hand, treat it gently. Avoid throwing or dropping the fruit into bags and boxes. Rather, place it gently where it won't get bruised. Also, avoid stacking the fruit too deep in containers because the weight of the fruit on top can contribute to bruising the fruit on bottom.

It is also a good idea to wear cotton gloves in order to reduce bruising and cutting of the fruit. Any opening or wound in the fruit reduces its shelf life. Pay attention to the methods of harvest described for each fruit species. With some species and varieties, improper harvesting can cause damage to the fruiting spurs and destroy the crop in following years.

Storage

A single large tree may produce several hundred pounds of fruit. For a small family, this may be more than the family can use. In situations like this, you can give excess fruit to neighbors or to a local food bank instead of dumping it in the trash. Planning for the harvest and storage is just as important as planning which variety to plant. Do you have a large enough freezer to store the fruit or sufficient time to can or dry it? If not, consider growing "fruit bushes," or small genetic dwarf trees, which produce a smaller quantity of fruit and are easier to manage.

Even if you don't plan on freezing, drying, or canning, you will still need to be able to provide some cold storage for your fruit. The capacity to get fruit cold and keep it that way is the second-most important quality control tool, right after timely harvest. The focus on keeping it cool begins with picking fruit in the morning, when it is cool, and continues when

you get the freshly harvested tree-ripe fruit into a refrigerator as soon after harvest as possible. Most kitchen refrigerators cannot handle the large amount of fruit that may come from a single harvest, in addition to normal household food storage needs. Having a spare "fruit fridge" can be a good idea, but try to get a newer, energy-efficient model and only use it during fruit harvest. Look for one that has wide doors for ease of loading and unloading and that has uniform distribution of cold air. Make sure its temperature controls are functioning accurately.

Temperature is the most crucial factor in determining how fast fruit will degrade in storage. For every 18°F (10°C) above the fruit's optimum temperature, its rate of deterioration increases two to three times (Thompson 2002). Deciduous fruit are not as sensitive to chilling injury as tropical-type fruit. For example, most deciduous tree fruit such as apricots, cherries, figs, nectarines, peaches, and plums are not chilling-sensitive and are best stored at just above freezing, from 32 up to 35°F (0–1.7°C). For optimum ripening, however, temperatures between 68 and 77°F (20–25°C) are best. The more tropical-type fruit, such as olives, citrus, cherimoyas, mangoes, papayas, avocados, and feijoas, which tend to be much more sensitive to chilling injury, are best stored between 50 and 59°F (10–15°C), with optimum ripening temperatures between 68 and 77°F (20–25°C).

It is difficult to maintain lower temperatures in a home-type refrigeration unit. Test your fruit refrigerator with a thermometer at the different settings and on the various shelves to determine what setting is best for your particular harvest. Most of these refrigerators can be maintained at around 45°F (7.2°C), or somewhat lower. If you are dedicating one refrigerator to fruit storage, it would be better to set its temperature at 35°F for all temperate fruit.

When you load the fruit into the refrigerator, try to stack it in a way that allows adequate air circulation around each fruit. Keep fruit away from the walls. Avoid rot by not putting wet fruit into the refrigerator. Layer the fruit in clean newspaper to reduce the amount of fruit-to-fruit infection from decay fungi (fig. 10.1).

Figure 10.1. Storing harvested fruit in layers of newspaper in the refrigerator. *Photo:* Mike Poe.

Figure 10.2. Ripening stone fruit in a fruit-ripening bowl.

Harvesting and storing specific fruit and nuts

Most firm or green-ripe fruit can easily be ripened off the tree. Commercially produced fruit-ripening bowls are available (fig. 10.2), but you can also use a brown paper bag. Place the fruit you would like to ripen more fully into the bag and place a high ethylene–producing fruit, such as an apple, avocado, peach, plum, or passion fruit, in the bag as well. Ethylene is a natural gas given off by ripening fruit, and it has an effect on the aging and ripening of fruit and other horticultural crops that are exposed to it. In some situations, too much ethylene can be a problem, but in this instance it is helpful because it encourages the ripening of green-ripe fruit.

Apples

Harvest. For the best development of fruit's skin color while on the tree, apples require relatively low nighttime temperatures and high light intensity during the ripening period. Low light, high temperatures, or conditions such as summer fog tend to reduce color development. To determine ripeness, taste is the best indicator. If the fruit tastes good to you, it is ready for harvest. In addition, if the fruit has full color both inside and out, as is appropriate for that particular variety, that is a good indication of maturity. Apples that are to be stored into winter should be harvested when "firm-ripe"—physiologically mature, but firm, for cold storage. Winter-stored apples can then be brought out and allowed to ripen at room temperature.

Apples that are ready to harvest should break easily away from the fruit spur. Avoid pulling down on the apple, since that may break the fruit spur. Gently twist the fruit upward, rotating it slightly.

Storage. Apples require relatively high humidity during cold storage to reduce moisture loss from the fruit. You can place a moist towel in the bottom of your fruit fridge to increase the humidity. Apples should not be stored with other produce or where odd odors may exist—they tend to pick up external odors and produce off-flavors. Also, apples give off some ethylene, which can increase the ripening rate of other fruit.

Apples can be eaten fresh or dried or made into apple cider, applesauce, apple butter, or apple leather.

Apricots and apriums

Harvest. Apricots and similar fruit develop the best flavor when allowed to fully ripen on the tree. An individual tree will bear fruit that ripen over a period of 1 to 3 weeks. For canning and drying, the fruit is best harvested when firm-ripe. To harvest, gently pull the fruit from the spur with a slight upward twist.

Storage. Apricots can be stored under refrigeration for about 3 weeks before their quality begins to deteriorate. They are best eaten fresh. You can also dry them, can them, make them into jam, freeze them, or make them into fruit leather.

Cherries

Harvest. Cherries are harvested when fully ripe and usually over a period of 2 weeks or so. They are most often harvested with the stems attached because they

Figure 10.3. Keep stems on cherries at harvest to help them last longer in storage. *Photo:* Chuck Ingels.

Figure 10.4. Dried fruit beetles on figs. *Photos:* Richard Coviello (left) and Jack Kelly Clark (right).

store best that way (fig. 10.3). Grab the stem or stems and twist upward. Be very careful not to break the fruit spur when you harvest. If you are planning to use the fruit for canning or for further processing, you can harvest without the stems, which is much faster.

Storage. Cherries can be eaten fresh or cooked and can be stored by canning, freezing, or drying. It is important that cherries be rapidly cooled after harvesting if processing is to be delayed for some reason. The longer they are exposed after harvest to warm temperatures and pressure in the harvest container, the more rapidly they will begin to break down.

Figs

Harvest. The optimum harvest period for figs is when the neck of the individual fruit begins to bend down over the stem and the fruit begin to crack. The fruit should be soft for fresh eating or firm-ripe if they are to be used for pickling. If beads of milky white sap (latex) ooze from the stem end after picking, the fruit is not yet ready to harvest.

Storage. Figs can be eaten fresh or they can be frozen, pickled, or dried for future use. For optimum flavor of dried figs, allow them to partially dry on the tree and then complete the drying process on drying trays. You can also let them fall naturally to the ground, but be sure to pick them up quickly to avoid insect and disease problems in the fruit (fig. 10.4). For longer storage of fresh fruit, optimum storage temperatures range from 32 to 35°F (0–1.7°C). Storage below 32°F (0°C) may subject the fruit to freeze injury.

Peaches and nectarines

Harvest. Peaches and nectarines for fresh eating are at their most flavorful when they are tree-ripened. Allow the fruit to develop full color on the tree, but harvest when they are still fairly firm to the touch. It is important that you harvest them before they become too soft. Soft-ripe fruit are sweeter, but they tend to break down very quickly and are more predisposed to bruising and injury. Fruit that are to be stored before eating or processing should be harvested when firm-ripe and stored under refrigeration (between 32 and 35°F [0–1.7°C]). Then you can bring them out of refrigeration a few days before you want to eat them, so they can finish ripening.

Clingstone fruit that are to be canned should be harvested when they break away from the stem easily, yet are still firm. Allow them to sit out for a day or two before processing. This will make the skin much easier to peel.

Storage. Peaches can be stored under refrigeration for several weeks when harvested firm-ripe. Optimum storage temperatures range from 32 to 35°F (0–1.7°C). Below 32°F (0°C), they will be susceptible to chilling injury. Peaches and nectarines can be eaten fresh or they can be stored frozen, dried, or canned.

Pears

Harvest. To harvest pears, lift fruit gently upward (fig. 10.5). To avoid breaking the fruit spur, do not twist or pull. If the fruit does not separate easily from the stem, wait a few more days to begin harvesting. European pears are best ripened off the tree. If allowed to ripen on the tree, they will be mealy. Asian

Figure 10.5. Lifting a pear off the spur to harvest it. *Photo: Mike Poe.*

pears, on the other hand, are harvested when firm-ripe and sweet. Harvest European pears when the fruit is still hard and green but has reached the variety's fully developed size. Pears can then be ripened on the shelf at room temperature to full flavor and maturity.

Storage. Store pears under refrigeration between 32 and 40°F (0–4.4°C). They can be stored for many weeks and brought out as needed for ripening at room temperature. Winter pear varieties will store much longer and actually produce a better-flavored pear when exposed to refrigeration for 6 weeks or so before you bring them out to ripen at room temperatures. The winter varieties include Bosc, Winter Nelis, Comice, d'Anjou, and Seckel.

Asian pears can be stored for 2 to 3 weeks at room temperature or longer under refrigeration. Asian pears are best used for fresh eating only.

European pears can be eaten fresh, baked, canned, dried, or made into preserves and fruit leather. The quality of frozen pears is not great, so freezing is not a recommended storage method.

Persimmons

Harvest. Persimmons, both the astringent and non-astringent types, begin to ripen in late September to November. The astringent types (for example, Hachiya) can be allowed to become soft-ripe on the tree but are usually harvested when firm-ripe—and are then allowed to become very soft and ripe at room temperature. The nonastringent types (for example, Fuyu) are harvested when they develop their full orange color for the variety. Fuyu persimmons are eaten when firm (crisp) like an apple. To maintain their

crispness, protect the fruit from exposure to ethylene produced by other fruit.

To harvest the fruit, use hand-pruning shears to cut the stem and allow the calyx (the green collar on the fruit) to remain attached to the fruit (fig. 10.6).

Storage. Fruit will store for a month or more under refrigeration. You can pull the fruit out of refrigeration as required and allow them to ripen more fully at room temperature. You may find, however, that the fruit lose flavor and that their texture deteriorates slightly with cold storage. Persimmons are often frozen for up to a year before being used in persimmon puddings and cakes.

Persimmons can be eaten fresh or they can be frozen or dried for storage. Dried persimmons have an outstanding flavor and sweetness.

Plums, prunes, plumcots, pluots, and cherry-plums

Harvest. To harvest a plum, prune, plumcot, pluot, or cherry-plum, gently lift the fruit off the fruit spur. It should separate easily. For fresh eating, the optimum harvest time is when the fruit are firm-ripe and full-flavored. In many varieties, this period may last for several weeks; for others, the harvest may occur all at one time. Usually the early-maturing varieties are harvested two or three times, with only the ripe fruit picked each time. Later-maturing varieties tend to hang on the tree longer before they become soft-ripe, so they can be picked over a longer period.

Prunes that are to be dried should be allowed to stay on the tree until they are fully ripe and can be easily knocked from the tree. You can wait until a few

Figure 10.6. Use pruning shears to harvest persimmons (shown here) and pomegranates. *Photo: Chuck Ingels.*

of the fruit begin to fall naturally and then pick them all for drying.

Storage. Fresh plums and prunes are best stored under refrigeration between 32 and 40°F (0–4.4°C). You can also store them in a cool, dry place for several weeks–but in that case they should be harvested a little less ripe than if they were going to be used immediately.

Plums and prunes can be processed for long-term storage by canning, drying, or freezing them, or making them into jams and jellies.

Pomegranates

Harvest. Optimum fruit quality is attained when the pomegranate fruit has developed full color but before the fruit starts to split. The splitting significantly reduces its storage life. The best time to eat fresh pomegranates, however, is in the early splitting period. To harvest, cut the fruit from the stem with shears. Avoid pulling the fruit from the tree because you are likely to break fruit spurs that way.

Storage. Pomegranates will shrivel if stored at room temperature for extended periods. The arils (the fruit surrounding each seed) will remain edible after the husk has dried, but the flavor will decline over time without cold storage. Avoid storing split or damaged fruit. You can juice the fruit and freeze the juice in ice cube trays. Remove the frozen cubes from the trays and store the cubes in plastic bags. You can also can the juice.

Quinces

Harvest. Quince fruit are ready in the fall once they begin to lose their green color and develop a full yellow color. The fruit will not soften on the tree and are harvested while still firm. Handle the fruit gently to prevent bruising.

Storage. Quince store well on the tree, but they tend to break down within a few weeks under refrigeration. The woolly outer layer should be retained if the fruit are to be stored. The fruit of most varieties of quince are not edible unless cooked. Quince is most often processed into jams and jellies.

Nut crops

Nut crops have an external hull (or husk), which may be somewhat fleshy prior to harvest. Just under the hull is the shell, which hardens and protects the edible kernel inside. For most nuts, the hull must be removed before the crop is dried or processed.

Almonds

Harvest. Almonds are ready to harvest once the outer hull begins to split, although you can allow almonds to stay on the tree until the hulls are dry and the nuts begin to drop on their own. The kernels, only partially dry when the hull splits, need a few more weeks of drying after harvest in order to cure completely. Once the nuts are ready to harvest, they should be knocked or shaken from the tree rather than allowed to fall naturally. This will avoid problems with insect pests, diseases, and birds that may otherwise get the crop before you do. Once you collect the nuts, remove the hulls and allow them to cure fully for a week or more in a dry, well-ventilated location. Avoid overly hot locations such as driveways because excessively high temperatures can damage the kernels. Make sure to protect the nuts from squirrels, ants, and birds as well. The nuts are dry when the kernel rattles in the shell—and when the dried kernel will snap in two and has a nutty taste, with no bitterness.

Storage. Pest-free, in-shell almonds will store for up to 6 months in a cool, dry, well-ventilated location. Once the almonds have been shelled, though, they should be stored frozen. To kill any pests that may be inside the in-shell almonds, place them in a freezer below 32°F (0°C) for 48 hours. Store them afterwards at room temperature in a sealed container. You can kill insect pests in larger quantities of almonds by exposing the nuts to carbon dioxide in a large, sealed container.

The bucket method for controlling almond pests

If handled properly, solid carbon dioxide (dry ice) can provide safe, economical control for some pests in stored almonds. First, put half a pound of dry ice in the bottom of a 5-gallon bucket (see accompanying figure). Second, fill the rest of the bucket with almond kernels (about 23 lb.). Third, cover the bucket with a sheet of plastic—which can be plastic wrap or part of a plastic trash bag, secured with a large rubber band—and prick a pinhole in the middle of the sheet. The pinhole will allow oxygen to escape as the bucket fills with heavier carbon dioxide gas (which comes from the dry ice). Finally, after 8 hours or so, when all of the dry ice has had time to turn to gas, seal the bucket with a tight-fitting lid—leaving the plastic sheet in place—and further seal the edges of the lid with duct tape.

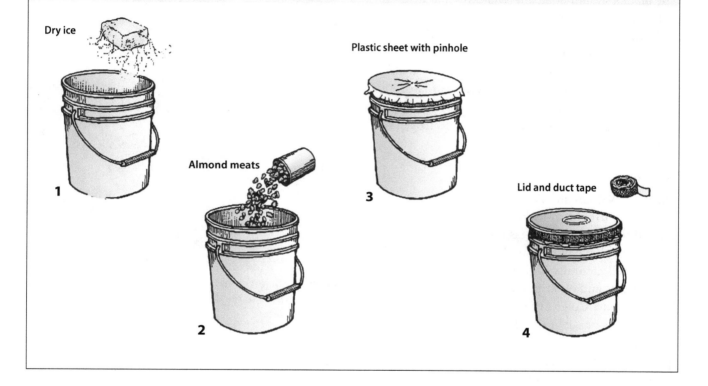

Dry ice

Almond meats

1

2

Plastic sheet with pinhole

3

Lid and duct tape

4

Pecans

Harvest. Pecans should be harvested once the green hull begins to split. It is best to knock the nuts from the tree rather than allow them to fall naturally. That way, birds and other pests will not be able to get to the crop before you do. Collect the nuts and remove the hulls (not the shells) as soon as possible after harvest. It is a good idea to wear gloves to avoid staining your hands during the hulling process. Wash the hulled nuts and then spread them out in the sun for a few days to complete the curing process. Protect the nuts from birds and squirrels while they are drying. The nuts are fully cured when the kernel of a cracked nut will break cleanly rather than bending.

Storage. Pecans in the shell may be stored in a cool, dry, well-ventilated location for many months. Once the nuts are shelled, you can store them frozen (at 32 to 35°F [0–1.7°C]) for up to a year, or under refrigeration for up to about 3 months.

Pistachios

Harvest. Pistachios are ready to harvest when the outside of the hulls begins to change from glossy to dull, indicating that the kernels inside are fully developed. The hull that surrounds the shell will loosen and will be slightly yellow at the stem end. In some cases, the shell will begin to split. To harvest the nuts, shake them from the tree onto a tarp that you have spread underneath. Remove the hulls as soon as possible after harvest. Use a screen made of ½-inch mesh hardware cloth or expanded metal (fig. 10.7) to remove hulls: Lay the nuts on the screen and gently rub the nuts over the screen. The hulls will fall through the screen, away from the nuts in their shells.

Many of the pistachios may be what are called "blanks": They develop a hull and a shell but not a kernel. You can easily cull out the blanks after hulling. Just place the hulled nuts in a bucket of water. The blanks should float, and you can separate them out and discard them.

Storage. You can process pistachios further after hulling by boiling the hulled, unshelled nuts in salted water for a few minutes to "salt them in the shell." The nuts are then dried in a dry, well-ventilated location and then stored. The dried nuts can be stored under refrigeration for 6 weeks or so and frozen to last up to a year or so.

Walnuts

Harvest. Walnuts should be harvested once the green hulls begin to split and when the tissue between and around the kernel halves has just turned brown. It is best to knock the nuts from the tree rather than allow them to fall naturally (fig. 10.8). That way you can keep insects and other pests from getting to the crop before you do. Collect the nuts and remove the hulls as quickly as possible after harvest. You can use a knife to hull small quantities of walnuts. For larger quantities, use a screen made of expanded metal to remove hulls: Lay the nuts on the screen and gently rub the nuts over the screen (see fig. 10.8). The hulls

Figure 10.8. Nut crops (almond shown here) should be harvested by knocking (A) or poling (B) from the tree. *Photos: Maxwell Norton.*

will fall through the screen, away from the nuts in their shells. If hulls stick tightly to the shells, moisten them and cover them with a moist tarp or burlap sheet for several days to loosen them. Hulls may be composted and used in the garden; the composting process degrades any natural toxins present in the hulls.

It is a good idea to wear protective gloves during the hulling process to avoid staining your hands. Wash the hulled nuts and then spread them out in a shaded, well-ventilated location for a few days to complete the curing process. Protect the nuts from birds and squirrels while the nuts are drying. The nuts are fully cured when the kernel of a cracked nut will break cleanly rather than bending and the kernel has developed a nutty taste. If your nuts have had a problem with walnut husk fly, the hulls may stick to

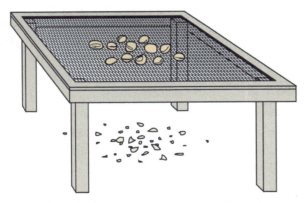

Figure 10.7. A table fitted with an expanded metal top can be used for hulling pistachios, pecans, or walnuts. *Source: Ingels et al. 2007.*

the shells. Place a moist burlap bag over the unhulled nuts overnight to soften the hulls and make removal easier.

Storage. Unshelled walnuts may be stored in a cool, dry, well-ventilated location for many months. Once the nuts are shelled, you can store them frozen for up to a year or up to about 3 or 4 months under refrigeration.

Reference

Ingels, C. A., P. M. Geisel, and M. V. Norton, tech. eds. 2007. The home orchard. Oakland: UC Agriculture and Natural Resources Publication 3485.

Thompson, J. F. 2002. Psychrometrics and perishable commodities. In A. A. Kader, ed., Postharvest technology of horticultural crops. 3rd ed. Oakland: UC Agriculture and Natural Resources Publication 3311. 129–134.

Further reading

Perry, E., and G. S. Sibbett. 1998. Harvesting and storing your home orchard's nut crop: Almonds, walnuts, pecans, pistachios, and chestnuts. Oakland: UC Agriculture and Natural Resources Publication 8005.

Integrated pest management for backyard orchards

Mary Louise Flint, Beth L. Teviotdale, and Niamh Quinn

You will find a wide array of organisms in any backyard orchard. Only a small number of them are pests. Many species are considered beneficial because they decompose organic matter (such as dead leaves or fruit), pollinate crops, prey on pests, provide shelter or food for natural enemies of pests, or perform other useful functions. Still others are just incidental, having little or no impact on the orchard.

The first steps in managing pest problems are to identify pests and to distinguish them from beneficial or nondamaging organisms—and distinguish their damage symptoms from problems such as those caused by inappropriate cultural care. Many pest species are damaging only at certain stages of plant growth, or when their numbers are high, so a good knowledge of pest and plant biology is essential before you choose any pest management practices.

Gardeners can select from a variety of nonchemical and chemical methods to prevent, reduce, or eliminate pest problems. Cultural practices, physical barriers and devices such as traps and nets, biological control organisms, and pesticides are all common tools. Choosing the right tool and applying it properly and at the right time are the keys to success. Integrated pest management (IPM) is a strategy for combining various environmentally sound, effective pest management techniques to protect plants from pests.

What is integrated pest management?

With IPM, you use your knowledge about how the garden ecosystem works to find environmentally sound solutions to pest problems. The goal is long-term prevention of pests or their damage through a combination of techniques such as biological control, habitat manipulation, modification of cultural prac-

tices, and use of resistant crop varieties and rootstocks. Pesticides may be included as part of the program, but only after careful monitoring indicates they are needed. Treatments are made with the goal of removing only the target organisms. Pest-control materials are selected and applied in a manner that minimizes risks to human health, beneficial and nontarget organisms, and the environment.

Pest management methods

The first-choice methods in IPM are those that keep pests from becoming established or abundant in the first place. Although many gardeners look for simple solutions to solve problems easily, a combination of methods is usually more effective over the long term than any single method. Some preferred methods in an IPM program include the following:

- using plant varieties and rootstocks that resist pests—or stock that is certified pest-free and is well adapted to local conditions
- choosing a planting site that is suitable for your trees and has good drainage (and avoiding sites where diseased trees have recently been removed)
- encouraging naturally occurring biological controls, such as insects or mites that prey on or parasitize pests (predators and parasites)
- adopting cultivation, pruning, fertilization, and irrigation practices that reduce pest problems
- changing the habitat to make it incompatible with pest development; for instance, removing mummy nuts or fruit in which insect pests survive over the winter to prevent them from emerging in spring and infesting the new crop; and, likewise, clearing weedy areas and removing brush piles and debris to reduce rodent pests that use these refuges

Figure 11.1. Convergent lady beetle adults and larvae are common predators of aphids. The white specks on these leaves are cast skins of aphids.

Figure 11.2. Green lacewing larvae feed on many types of insect eggs and soft-bodied insects such as the aphid shown here.

Figure 11.3. Assassin bugs are large predators that capture and feed on many pests, including leafhoppers.

- trapping, washing off, pruning, and screening or fencing out pests
- selecting pesticides with lower toxicity to humans, beneficial organisms, and nontarget organisms—and applying them when they will be most effective

Biological controls

Almost every insect and mite pest that occurs in orchard trees may be attacked by one or more biological control agents. Also called natural enemies, these organisms often suppress pest populations and may keep them from reaching levels that would cause serious damage to fruit and nut trees. It is important to recognize and protect these beneficial organisms and encourage their activity. Insect natural enemies can be classified into three groups: predators, parasites, and pathogens.

Arthropod predators hunt down and kill insects and mites, some killing a hundred or more pest individuals during a lifetime. General predators such as those shown in figures 11.1 to 11.6 feed on a variety of prey; others feed on just one or a few species. Large animals can be predators of vertebrate pests such as rodents and birds; however, they do not provide reliable biological control in most circumstances because they do not consume enough prey to bring pest damage to an acceptable level.

In the context of biological control, parasites (often called parasitoids) are tiny wasps and flies that lay their eggs in or on insects; the larvae that hatch from the eggs feed on the insect host, killing it by the time the parasite is ready to pupate. Although parasite larvae kill only one individual, adult females may lay many eggs and can have a significant impact on pest populations.

Pathogens include the many types of fungi, bacteria, viruses, and nematodes that infect and kill insect and mite pests. *Bacillus thuringiensis* is a bacterium that kills caterpillars and is widely used in pest management programs. While a few biological control agents are available for purchase and release (such as *Bacillus thuringiensis*), most biological control involves naturally occurring populations already in the orchard. Antagonistic and competitive microorganisms also play a role in suppressing plant disease, but there are few known ways to manipulate these beneficial microorganisms in the home orchard.

Important biological control agents are discussed in the specific pest sections later in this chapter. See the Natural Enemies Handbook (Flint and Dreistadt 1998) for more information on biological control.

Cultural controls

Cultural controls include any modification of normal management practices that can decrease pest populations by preventing their establishment, reproduction, dispersal, survival, or ability to damage plants. To be successful with cultural controls, you need a good knowledge of plant and pest biology. Changes in irrigation practices, fertilization practices, and planting or harvest time—as well as prompt removal of infested material from the garden and surrounding landscape—are common cultural practices that can reduce pest problems.

Mechanical and physical controls

Mechanical and physical control methods include practices that mechanically destroy pests, trap them, or present a physical barrier to pests by creating conditions unsuitable for their entry or survival. Although some mechanical and physical control methods are labor intensive, many are quite suitable for backyard orchard situations. Common methods include hoeing weeds, mulching, mowing, soil solarization, and setting up barriers and traps. Limited infestations of borers, aphids, leafrollers, or other pests can sometimes be pruned out. Hosing a small tree with a strong stream of water is an effective way to manage aphids, whiteflies, and spider mites. Traps, nets, tree barriers, and fences are key tools for vertebrate pest management in the backyard orchard.

Pesticides

Pesticides can be important tools in an IPM program. For certain pests, they may offer the only realistic method for control. There is a great range of pesticide products, and some of them pose only limited risks for health and the environment. The challenge in an IPM program is to recognize when pesticides are needed and when they are not. Once the decision to use a pesticide is made, choose the safest product that provides effective control with the least impact on the environment. Make sure to time the application for the point in the pest's life cycle that will make it most effective. Use proper application

Figure 11.4. The tiny minute pirate bug feeds on insect eggs, small insects, and mites.

Figure 11.5. Predaceous ground beetles such as this *Calosoma* sp. feed on insects, including larvae and pupae in soil and on the trunks of trees.

Figure 11.6. Spiders such as this *Trachelas pacificus* occur commonly in fruit trees and may be important predators of moth larvae.

equipment and protective clothing. Read the pesticide label carefully, mix the product precisely according to label directions, and be aware of the proper disposal procedures for leftover pesticide and empty containers. Pesticides should be used in combination with other methods. Any application decision should include consideration of the potential for negative impact on the pest's natural enemies.

Certain pesticides are especially compatible with IPM programs because of their low impact on natural enemies and nontarget organisms. Where possible, consider these safer products, such as microbial insecticides and pesticidal soaps and oils:

- Microbial insecticides are derived from naturally occurring diseases of specific insects or insect groups, and most have little negative impact on beneficial insects. *Bacillus thuringiensis* (Bt) is a microbial insecticide that causes disease symptoms in caterpillars (the larvae of moths and butterflies), which are pests of fruit and nut trees. To be effective, Bt must be consumed by the caterpillar. Another microbial, *Codling moth granulosis virus*, controls codling moth.

- Insecticidal soaps provide partial control of soft-bodied insects and mites such as aphids, whiteflies, scale insects, spider mites, and psyllids. They are extremely safe products and in many cases are available in ready-to-use squirt bottles that are convenient for applications to vegetables, annual bedding plants, and small trees; it is more difficult, however, to use them on large trees. Soaps must directly contact the insect's body at the time of application, so good coverage of lower leaf surfaces is essential for good control.

- Pesticidal oils, sometimes called horticultural oils or narrow-range or superior oils, are effective against soft-bodied insects and mites, including aphids, spider mites, whiteflies, scale insects, psyllids, and the overwintering eggs of a number of pests. They can be applied during the dormant season on deciduous trees or during the growing season. They leave no residues and so have limited impact on natural enemies. Most are petroleum based, but several plant-based oils, such as neem oil, are available. Oils are also active against powdery mildews and some other foliar fungal diseases. Oils must directly contact the insect's body at

the time of application to be effective, so good coverage of leaf and bark surfaces is essential for good control.

Virtually all of the petroleum oil products currently available to home orchardists are narrow-range oils (also called superior oils) that are safe to use throughout the growing season except when temperatures exceed 90°F (32.2°C) or when trees are drought stressed. (But don't use these products on walnut trees, which are sensitive to oils, especially in spring.) Prior to the 1980s, many gardeners and growers used heavy oils with high sulfur content, called dormant oils, during the dormant season. These oils damaged plants if they got onto leaves or buds and thus were not safe to use during the growing season. These oils are generally not available anymore. Products currently sold or used as dormant-oil sprays are typically narrow-range oils, containing the same oils as would be applied during the growing season.

Various equipment is available for home orchardists to apply insecticides and fungicides to trees. Compressed-air sprayers are low-pressure sprayers that hold a diluted pesticide mixture in a small tank; a hand pump compresses the air, or a carbon dioxide cartridge propels the spray. Backpack sprayers are similar to compressed-air sprayers except they have straps so you can carry the tank on your back. Hose-end sprayers are also available, but they are generally not recommended because they aren't reliable for delivering a specific rate of pesticide; also, since they are attached to the home water supply via a garden hose, they require a backflow prevention device to protect the water supply. Always follow label directions for application rates and protective clothing and equipment. Lawn and Residential Landscape Pest Control (Cohen et al. 2009) is an excellent source of information for home gardeners on application equipment and the safe use of pesticides.

Common insect and mite pests

This chapter provides information on identification, biology, and management of some key insect, mite, pathogen, and vertebrate pests in backyard orchard trees. Many other insects, vertebrates, and pathogens cause occasional damage in fruit and nut trees. For example, nematodes, which are tiny roundworms, can attack the roots of many fruit and nut trees; the most important management practice is to choose nematode-resistant rootstocks (see chapter 3, "Varieties") if they are available. For more information on nematodes, see Flint 2018 or refer to the UC IPM Pest Notes library at ipm.ucanr.edu/PMG/PEST-NOTES/index.html. Weedy plants are another pest concern for orchardists; most weeds can be managed by a combination of hand removal and mulch, as described in chapter 1, "Climate and soils," and chapter 4, "Orchard design and planting and care of young trees." For more information on nematodes, weeds, and other pests, see the IPM resources listed at the end of this chapter or refer to the UC IPM Pest Notes library at ipm.ucanr.edu/PMG/PESTNOTES/index.html.

Aphids

Aphids are common pests on many orchard trees, especially apple, plum, and walnut trees. They reproduce rapidly, especially in spring. Aphids pierce leaves and young shoots with their sucking mouthparts, removing plant sap and leaving behind sticky honeydew. Some species distort and curl leaves. Different aphid species attack each tree species (table 11.1).

Identification

Aphids are small, soft-bodied, pear-shaped insects with long legs and long antennae. Most species have a pair of tubelike structures called cornicles that project backward out of the rear of their body. The presence of cornicles distinguishes aphids from all other insects.

Adult aphids are frequently wingless (fig. 11.7), but in most species adults also occur in winged forms, especially when populations are high or during the spring or fall. Although aphids may be found singly, they usually are found in dense groups on leaves or stems. Unlike leafhoppers or plant bugs, they do not move rapidly when disturbed.

Aphids can be green, yellow, brown, red, or black, depending on species. Some species have two or more color forms. A few aphids, such as the woolly apple aphid and the mealy plum aphid, have waxy or woolly secretions that cover their body surfaces.

Figure 11.7. This green peach aphid colony contains a wingless adult and several offspring.

Table 11.1. Common aphid species on backyard orchard trees

Tree	Aphid species
Apple	rosy apple aphid, *Dysaphis plantaginea* apple aphid, *Aphis pomi* woolly apple aphid, *Erisoma lanigerum*
Cherry	black cherry aphid, *Myzus cerasi*
Peach, nectarine	green peach aphid, *Myzus persicae*
Pear	green peach aphid, *Myzus persicae* melon, or cotton *aphid, Aphis gossypii* bean aphid, *Aphis fabae*
Plum, prune	mealy plum aphid, *Hyalopterus pruni* leaf curl plum aphid, *Brachycaudus helichrysi*
Walnut	walnut aphid, *Chromaphis juglandicola* dusky-veined aphid, *Callaphis juglandis*

Life cycle

Aphids reproduce rapidly and have many generations a year. Throughout most of the year, the adult aphid population is made up of adult females that give birth to live offspring (as many as twelve per day) without mating. Immature aphids, called nymphs, pass through four instars (growth stages) before becoming adults. Most of the aphids on fruit trees develop into the sexual form in fall. These males and females mate and lay eggs that survive the winter on twigs and branches. Look carefully with a hand lens during the dormant season to find eggs on buds or bark (fig. 11.8). Aphids usually are most abundant on orchard

Figure 11.8. Mealy plum aphid egg. Many aphids overwinter in the egg stage on twigs or on bark.

trees in the spring. Many species migrate to herbaceous plants during the summer and come back in fall to lay their eggs on fruit trees (fig. 11.9).

Damage

Low to moderate numbers of aphids usually are not damaging, but large populations can be a problem. High populations of aphids can produce large quantities of a sticky exudate known as honeydew, which covers leaves and fruit and often turns black with the growth of a sooty mold fungus. Some aphid species inject a toxin into leaves that causes them to curl or distort (fig. 11.10). Very high populations of these leaf-feeding aphids may reduce tree vigor and the sugar content of fruit, but they will not kill trees.

Woolly apple galls at the site of infestation aphid infests roots, trunks, limbs, and shoots, feeding on tender bark and often producing (fig. 11.11). Root colonies can cause galling so severe that it prevents roots from taking up sufficient water and nutrients. High populations can stunt tree growth or kill young trees.

Management

Because aphids have many natural enemies, insecticide treatments usually are not required for backyard fruit trees. Learn to recognize natural enemies and parasitized aphids (fig. 11.12) and avoid treatments

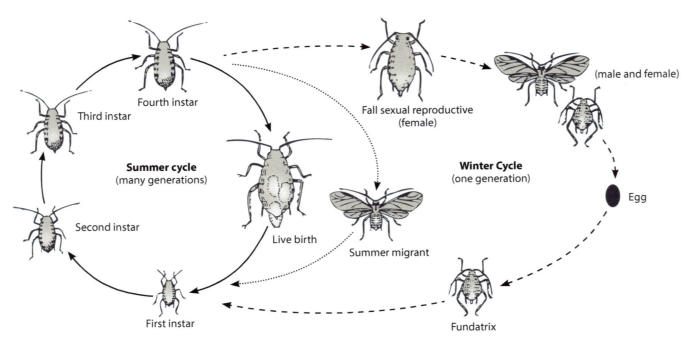

Figure 11.9. General life cycle of aphids. *Source:* Ingels et al. 2007.

with broad-spectrum insecticides (e.g., organophosphates, carbaryl, or pyrethroids) that will kill these beneficials and cause aphid numbers to surge. Common natural enemies include several species of red and black lady beetles (fig. 11.13), syrphid fly larvae (fig. 11.14), lacewing larvae (see fig. 11.2), soldier beetles (fig. 11.15), and many species of parasitic wasps.

Figure 11.10. Some aphids, such as the leaf curl plum aphid, may cause leaves to curl and distort.

Figure 11.11. Woolly apple aphid colony on an apple branch.

Figure 11.12. The bronze color of this walnut aphid mummy indicates that it has been parasitized by the larva of the parasitic wasp *Trioxys pallidus*. The mature wasps emerge through the round exit hole. Healthy walnut aphids are above and below.

Figure 11.13. The multicolored Asian ladybeetle, shown here in adult, larval, and pupal stages, is an introduced predator of aphids and other related insects.

Figure 11.14. A syrphid fly larva feeds within a colony of green apple aphids.

Figure 11.15. Soldier beetles consume large numbers of aphids in many backyards.

Ants frequently climb tree trunks to tend aphids and harvest the honeydew for ant colonies on the ground. At the same time, ants protect aphids from their natural enemies. To enhance the beneficial activities of the natural enemies, keep ants out of trees by applying sticky barriers or baits and pruning branches where they touch buildings, fences, or other plants. When using sticky agents on young or sensitive bark, apply it to a trunk wrap rather than directly, to avoid damaging the bark.

Aphids thrive on vigorously growing and tender terminals and leaves. Avoid applying more nitrogen than recommended.

An application of insecticidal or horticultural oil will kill a significant number of overwintering eggs if applied as a delayed dormant application just as buds swell and eggs are beginning to hatch in early spring. These sprays probably are not justified for aphid control alone, but they also help control scale insects, if these are a problem in the tree. Good coverage of bark and twigs is essential. Delayed dormant sprays of oil will have a minimal negative impact on natural enemies. Sprays later in the season usually are not justified for aphids in backyard fruit trees. A strong spray of water or a water and soap solution can be used to wash off honeydew and sooty mold in some cases. Aphids within curled leaves cannot be washed off.

Woolly apple aphids are more difficult to manage than leaf-feeding aphids. The parasitic wasp *Aphelinus mali* generally provides good control of populations in aboveground portions of the tree where it has not been killed by pesticide applications. Application of oil (or other insecticides) directly to woolly apple aphids on trunks and branches may suppress colonies, but root colonies cannot be treated and are not vulnerable to parasites. Since woolly apple aphids prefer to colonize the soft callus tissue of healing bark wounds, preventing such tree damage can be important in reducing problems.

Scale insects

Scale insects can be serious pests on fruit and nut trees when their populations are high. Scales have many natural enemies, which in most cases provide adequate control, but these biological control agents can be severely disrupted by broad-spectrum insecticide treatments.

Identification

Most scales that cause problems on fruit trees can be divided into two groups: armored scales and soft scales. Armored scales, family Diaspididae, are less than ⅛ inch in diameter and have a flat, plate-like cover. The armored scale cover can usually be removed from the body. Armored scales do not secrete honeydew, but they can cause severe dieback of twigs and limbs and sometimes discoloration of fruit and leaves. The most common armored scale on deciduous fruit and nut trees is the San Jose scale (*Quadraspidiotus perniciosus*) (fig. 11.16).

Mature female soft scales, family Coccidae, are much larger and more rounded and convex than armored scales. Like aphids, they produce large quantities of honeydew when their populations are high. The hard surface of the soft scale is its body wall, which cannot be removed. Soft scales reduce tree vigor but rarely kill trees or branches. The major problem is honeydew and sooty mold. Common soft scales on fruit trees include black scale (*Saissetia oleae*) and European fruit lecanium (*Parthenolecanium corni*) (fig. 11.17). Kuno scale (*Eulecanium kunoense*), which in its adult female stage is brown and more rounded than these other two species, has recently become more common on plum and other stone fruit in Northern California.

Life cycle

San Jose scale, like most armored scales, has several generations a year, while most of the soft scales require a whole year to complete one life cycle. Eggs of both types of scale are usually hidden under the adult

Figure 11.16. San Jose scales are flatter and smaller than soft scales.

Figure 11.17. Adult females of the European fruit lecanium, a soft scale.

female and hatch into tiny, yellow crawlers with legs. Crawlers walk over the plant surface for 1 or more days and then settle. Crawlers of armored scales lose their legs and antennae, whereas immature soft scales retain very tiny legs but rarely move. Once a feeding site has been established, armored scales begin to secrete their hard covers. Soft-scale body walls gradually get harder as they grow. Immature scales molt three or four times before becoming adults. Mature females remain immobile and produce eggs under their cover. Male scales, where they exist, are tiny, winged insects that superficially resemble parasitic

insects. Females of many soft-scale species reproduce without mating.

Most soft scales spend the winter as second-instar nymphs on twigs and branches, grow rapidly in spring, and produce eggs from late May through early July. Eighty percent of San Jose scales spend the winter as first-instar nymphs and the rest as adult, mated females. Usually, the first San Jose scale eggs hatch in April or May and are followed by three or four more generations before the tree drops its leaves in autumn. The life cycle of a typical armored scale is shown in figure 11.18.

Damage

Trees that are heavily infested with San Jose scale often look water stressed. Leaves turn yellow and drop, twigs and limbs may die, and bark may crack and produce gum. This scale may also move onto fruit and cause blemishes that look like halos.

Soft scales may also reduce tree vigor, but the most noticeable damage is associated with their production of sticky honeydew, which may coat leaves and fruit and become colonized by black sooty mold. Although unsightly, sooty mold can generally be tolerated on backyard trees. Most soft scales do not move onto fruit.

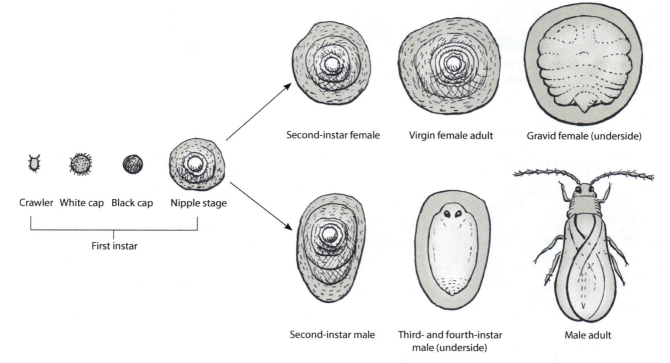

Figure 11.18. Life cycle of a typical armored scale.

Management

Scales have many natural enemies, which often keep scale populations below damaging levels in backyard trees. Look for darkening of scales and holes in scale covers, which indicate parasite activity (fig. 11.19). Parasitic wasps in the genera *Aphytis* (fig. 11.20), *Encarsia,* and *Metaphycus* are important control agents, as are several lady beetle species, including the twicestabbed lady beetle (*Chilocorus orbus*). Lacewings and other general predators may also feed on scales. Learn to recognize these natural enemies of scale. Broad-spectrum insecticides, such as organophosphates, carbaryl, and pyrethroids, will kill beneficials and let scale populations get out of control.

If scale populations are high in spring or summer and little evidence of parasitism is seen, management may be needed the following winter. Also, look for

Figure 11.19. A round exit hole in the immature black scale at left indicates that it has been parasitized. *Source:* Ingels et al. 2007.

Figure 11.20. Parasites, such as this *Aphytis* spp., which is laying its egg in a San Jose scale, often keep scales below damaging levels on unsprayed trees.

evidence of scales when you prune in the winter. Treatment during the growing season in backyard trees is not recommended. A dormant or delayed dormant application of insecticidal oil should provide sufficient control. Never apply oil to water-stressed trees or during fog, rain, or hot or freezing weather.

Codling moth

Codling moth (*Cydia pomonella*) feeds within fruit and nuts and can be a serious pest in apple, pear, quince, and walnut trees. It may also cause occasional damage to plum and other stone fruit. It is one of the most difficult pests to manage in the backyard orchard.

Identification

Adults are small, ½-inch-long, mottled gray moths (fig. 11.21). If you catch them in traps, you can distinguish them from other grayish moths that occur on fruit trees by observing a dark brown and coppery band on their wing tips. Eggs are disk-shaped and flat, about the size of a pinhead, and difficult to see without a magnifier. They are translucent white when first laid and later develop a red ring inside. Just before hatching, the black head of the larva becomes visible. Codling moth caterpillars are white to pink with a mottled brown head and dark shield on the first segment behind the head. Most caterpillars that are found feeding inside pear or apple fruit are codling moth larvae.

Life cycle

Codling moth has complete metamorphosis, with egg, larva, pupa, and adult stages. Depending on temperatures, there may be two to four generations a year in the orchard.

The pest overwinters as a full-grown larva within a thick, silken cocoon under loose scales of bark, or in soil or debris around the base of the tree. In early spring, the larva pupates within the cocoon, emerging as a moth when temperatures warm up from mid-March to April. Moths are most active in the early evening. During the day, they rest on branches and trunks, blending in with the bark. Mating occurs when sunset temperatures exceed 62°F (17°C).

Eggs are deposited singly on fruit, nuts, or nearby leaves. Within hours of hatching, the larvae seek out

Figure 11.21. The codling moth adult has a bronze band at the tip of its wings.

Figure 11.22. Codling moth larvae bore into the center of fruit to feed. Note the excrement, or frass, pushed out of the entry hole.

and bore into fruit or developing nuts. Larvae complete their development within the fruit. When mature, they leave the fruit and drop from the trees to search out pupation sites in the soil, in debris, or in cracks in tree trunks.

Damage

Codling moth larvae bore through the flesh and into the core of apples and pears, leaving brown tunnels in the fruit that are filled with frass (excrement) (fig. 11.22). In walnuts, larvae feed on the kernel, leaving it inedible. When plums are attacked, larvae bore all the way to the pit. If attacked when very small, injured fruit or nuts drop off the trees.

Management

Codling moth is difficult to manage because it spends most of its life deep within the fruit or nut, out of the reach of insecticides or natural enemies. It is essential to use an integrated program that takes advantage of the few vulnerable points in the pest's life cycle. If your trees have low-to-moderate numbers of codling moths, you may be able to keep populations to tolerable levels by using several nonchemical management methods in combination. It is essential, however, that you begin to implement your program early in the season.

Where populations are very high and many infested trees are nearby, it may be necessary to apply insecticides in order to rapidly bring populations down to low levels. Insecticides are very difficult to use effectively, and most materials that are effective are also toxic to natural enemies and honey bees. In some backyard situations, the best course of action may be

to combine nonchemical methods, such as sanitation, fruit thinning, and fruit bagging, and accept a few wormy apples or pears.

Sanitation

You can reduce overwintering populations of codling moth on your trees if you remove debris, loose bark, and other hiding places in winter. As soon as small fruit appear on trees, start to keep an eye on them and remove and destroy any infested fruit you find. Newly infested fruit will have small, frass-filled holes or stings (fig. 11.23). Also, rake up and destroy dropped fruit and nuts as soon as they fall, especially in May and June. Many fallen fruit will contain cod-

Figure 11.23. This small frass-filled hole indicates that a codling moth larva has recently entered. Monitor for these "stings" in spring to determine when to spray or remove fruit with stings as part of a sanitation program.

ling moth larvae, although some will have exited the fruit by the time it falls. These sanitation measures will be most effective in trees that are at least a mile or so away from untreated infested trees.

Bagging

You can reliably protect fruit from attack by covering them with paper bags. Place bags around apple or pear fruit when they are ½ to 1 inch in diameter and again after thinning the clusters to a single fruit. Use standard paper lunch bags (fig. 11.24). Cut a 2-inch slit in the bottom of the bag and slip it over the fruit to form a seal around the stem. Make sure the seal is as tight as possible. Staple the open end shut. You can bag all fruit on a tree or just some of the fruit. Bagging does not affect maturity or quality, but it may result in a loss of color in red varieties. Remove the bag a few days before harvest if you want to allow the fruit to color.

Fruit thinning

Thinning the fruit load can help control codling moth populations. Thin apples or pears to one fruit per cluster or 6 inches apart (see chapter 9, "Fruit Thinning") to reduce preferred egg-laying sites.

1-inch cut on fold equals 2-inch cut

Figure 11.24. Bagging fruit will protect it from codling moth attack. *Illustration:* Valerie Winemiller. *Source:* Ingels et al. 2007.

Pheromone traps

Pheromones are chemicals that insects give off to communicate with other individuals of their species. The pheromone that female codling moths use to attract males for mating has been synthesized and is widely used in pest management to determine when adult moths are flying in the orchard and to time insecticide treatments. Using pheromone traps to lure and trap male moths en masse has not been shown to be effective at reducing codling moth damage. In commercial apple, pear, and walnut orchards, pheromone lures are used effectively to inundate the orchard with the female scent, making males unable to find females for mating. However, this mating-disruption approach is ineffective in single backyard trees or orchards of less than 5 acres.

Insecticides

Codling moth management with insecticides is difficult because they must be applied to kill larvae in the few hours between the time they hatch from eggs and the time they bore into fruit. Once the caterpillar has gone into the fruit or nut, it is protected from pesticides. Unless your insecticide applications are precisely timed to contact caterpillars just before or as they hatch, they are unlikely to give satisfactory control.

In commercial orchards, growers time insecticide applications by keeping track of daily temperatures and calculating heat unit accumulations, measured in degree-days, which, with a computer simulation model, can be used to predict the rate of codling moth development. Home gardeners can use these models as well. To use degree-day calculations to time applications, you will need a pheromone trap, a way to track local daily maximum and minimum temperatures (local weather station data will do), and access to a computer to run the codling moth developmental model. Keeping track of codling moth development may involve more time, effort, and expertise than many gardeners are willing to invest. Details on using degree-days for codling moth management for apple, pear, and walnut are given in the UC IPM Pest Management Guidelines, ipm.ucanr.edu/agriculture/.

An alternative way to time sprays is to check fruit two or more times a week for entry holes or stings that indicate that larvae have begun to bore into fruit (see fig. 11.23). Check places where one fruit touches another: This is the most likely entry point. Spray as soon as you see the first sign of damage. Repeated sprays will be necessary.

See the *UC IPM Pest Note* on codling moth in the Pest Notes library, mentioned above, for insecticides that are suggested for use in the home orchard. Less toxic insecticides are available for home orchards.

Peach twig borer

Peach twig borer (*Anarsia lineatella*) larvae bore into the growing shoots and twigs of stone fruit and almond trees in spring. The tips and leaves of young shoots wilt and turn brown (fig. 11.25). Damage to twigs and shoots is most serious for young trees because it can interfere with the developing shape of the tree. In summer, larvae bore into ripening fruit. Unlike other caterpillars found in fruit, older peach twig borer larvae are chocolate brown, with distinct segments (fig. 11.26). Feeding on fruit is usually superficial, less than ⅜ inch deep, distinguishing it from that of oriental fruit moth. Management is not usually needed in backyard trees.

Peach twig borer overwinters in tiny, protected cells called hibernacula in limb crotches of 2- or 3-year-old wood or in pruning wounds or deep cracks in bark (fig. 11.27). Look for hibernacula on your tree in fall and early spring. At about the time that blossoms open in spring, the larvae emerge from their hibernacula and migrate up the branches to feed on flower buds and shoots. They bore into shoots and then emerge to pupate, and the first generation of adults begin flying between March and May to lay their eggs on shoots, leaves, or fruit. It is the larvae that hatch out of these eggs that are the first generation to damage fruit. There are three or four generations a year.

Low levels of peach twig borer can be tolerated in the home orchard. Various predators, such as lacewing larvae, minute pirate bugs, assassin bugs, and spiders, feed on larvae before the larvae bore into shoots or fruit. The gray ant can be an important natural enemy in some locations. Several wasps parasitize high percentages of peach twig borer in untreated trees in some areas, providing good biological control.

Figure 11.25. Peach twig borers bore into young terminal shoots, causing them to wilt and die.

Figure 11.26. Older peach twig borer larvae have distinct darkened segments. They mostly feed on fruit surfaces as shown here.

Figure 11.27. Peach twig borers overwinter as larvae on trunks in tiny cells called hibernacula. They are difficult to find. Search for them on 2 to 3-year-old wood during the dormant season by looking for the chimneys of frass that often protrude.

If sprays are needed, the best time to apply them is in the dormant season or around bloom time. Dormant treatments of insecticidal oil combined with spinosad (or another insecticide that doesn't disrupt beneficials) are easiest for home gardeners. Oil sprays alone will not be effective. Avoid combining the oil with more toxic insecticides—for example, pyrethroids, or organophosphates such as malathion. These broad-spectrum insecticides can disrupt natural enemies of many pests.

An alternative to the dormant treatment is to make two applications of *Bacillus thuringiensis,* a microbial insecticide that will not disrupt biological control or pollinators, just as trees are beginning to bloom. The first should be applied when larvae start emerging from hibernacula after popcorn bud stage (examine hibernacula to see if about 20 to 40 percent of larvae have left their shelters). The second should be applied 7 to 10 days later. Good coverage of all buds and surfaces is necessary for good control. Since *Bacillus thuringiensis* must be ingested to be effective, it is important to make the application when 2 or 3 days of warm, dry weather are forecast so the larvae will be actively feeding.

Oriental fruit moth

Oriental fruit moth (*Grapholita molesta*) may cause shoot and fruit damage on peach, nectarine, and almond trees. Damage to shoots is similar to that caused by peach twig borer. On fruit, oriental fruit moth caterpillars bore right into the center of green and ripening fruit and feed around the pit (fig. 11.28), causing much deeper fruit damage than the superficial damage caused by peach twig borer.

Oriental fruit moths spend the winter as prepupae inside cocoons that they spin in protected areas on the tree or on the ground. First-generation moths emerge in February or March and lay eggs singly on the undersides of leaves near shoot tips. The larva is white with a black head. First-generation larvae bore into shoots, causing damage similar to that caused by peach twig borer. If you open up damaged shoots and find larvae, you can distinguish the two species: Oriental fruit moth larvae do not have the dark body segments of the peach twig borer larva. When mature, oriental fruit moth larvae leave shoots to pupate under bark or on the ground, from which they later emerge as adults. The next generation of larvae

Figure 11.28. Oriental fruit moth larvae bore into fruit and feed near the pit. They lack the dark segments of the peach twig borer.

hatches in May and attacks fruit. There may be up to five or six generations a year.

You should try to tolerate oriental fruit moth in backyard trees to the extent possible. Management with insecticides can disrupt populations of other pests' natural enemies and are difficult to properly time. Dormant treatments with oils or insecticides do not control this pest. To be effective, an insecticide must be applied in spring just as the eggs hatch and before the larvae bore into shoots or fruit. More details on effective treatment timing for commercial peach or nectarine orchards are available in the UC IPM Pest Management Guidelines, ipm.ucanr.edu/agriculture/.

Many commercial growers are using pheromone dispensers to manage oriental fruit moth. These dispensers, which disperse the female scent to confuse male moths in the orchard so they can't mate, are hung in trees in late February, before the first moths appear. Pheromones have no known negative impact on natural enemies or the environment. Unfortunately, pheromone dispensers are not effective for backyard trees or orchards less than 5 acres.

Leafrollers and other leaf-feeding caterpillars

A number of leaf-feeding caterpillars may be found in backyard fruit trees from time to time (table 11.2). The most serious pests are several leafroller species (fig. 11.29) and green fruitworms (fig. 11.30), which may also feed on the surface of fruit. Caterpillars that limit their feeding to leaves are unlikely to cause sig-

Table 11.2. Some common leaf-feeding caterpillars on fruit and nut trees

Common name	Scientific name	Common hosts	Comments
Fall webworm	*Hyphantria cunea*	plum, prune, walnut, many ornamental and deciduous trees	Hairy. Larvae feed inside silken tents that enlarge to cover them. Prune out tents
Fruittree leafroller	*Archips argyrospila*	apple, almond, pear, stone fruit, walnut	Overwinters in egg masses, so dormant oils may reduce its numbers
Green fruitworm	several species including *Orthosia hibisci* (speckled green fruitworm) and *Amphipyra pyramidoides* (humped green fruitworm)	apple, pear, cherry, apricot, plum, prune	May damage fruit, chewing out small bites on the surface. Bites later scar over
Obliquebanded leafroller	*Choristoneura rosaceana*	apple, pear, stone fruit	Causes surface scars to fruit. Pale green with black or light-colored head
Omnivorous leafroller	*Platynota stultana*	most fruit trees	Light-colored, with brown or black head
Orange tortrix	*Argyrotaenia citrana*	stone fruit, apple	Mostly a coastal pest in California
Redhumped caterpillar	*Schizura concinna*	most fruit trees, especially plum, prune, walnut	When mature, is brightly colored with yellow, black, white, and red markings
Tent caterpillar	*Malacosoma* spp.	stone fruit, apple, pear	Builds large webbed nests or mats but feeds outside. Prune out nests
Western tussock moth	*Orgyia vetusta*	apple, cherry, apricot, walnut, other fruit	Most common on California coast. Colorful with prominent tufts of hair

Figure 11.29. A rolled and webbed leaf has been opened to reveal the fruittree leafroller caterpillar feeding within. Leafroller species are difficult to distinguish.

Figure 11.30. Green fruitworms caused the scarring on this fruit early in the season. The damage later scabbed over and distorted the fruit. The chewed leaf above the fruit has also been damaged by fruitworms.

nificant damage to fruit. For instance, the redhumped caterpillar is a foliage feeder that attacks stone fruit and walnut (fig. 11.31). The colorful larvae of western tussock moth (fig. 11.32) occasionally cause damage to fruit in coastal areas. Treatment is not normally needed.

Because they feed on exposed or semiexposed leaves or within curled leaves, these caterpillars are both much more vulnerable to natural enemies and easier to control with insecticide sprays than caterpillars that feed within fruit. General predators, such as assassin bugs, lacewings, spiders, and minute pirate bugs, may feed on their eggs and larvae. For each species, there usually are several parasitic wasps or flies that can attack and kill them. Preserving these natural enemy populations by avoiding broadly toxic insecticide sprays is an important part of an IPM program.

Sanitation can be important for reducing leafroller populations. Remove webbed leaves and egg masses

Figure 11.31. Older redhumped caterpillars on a walnut leaf. Younger redhumped caterpillars are yellow with a black head.

Figure 11.32. Western tussock moth caterpillars have long hairs and colorful markings.

as soon as you see them in the spring. Remove trash, mummy fruit, and debris around trees in the fall and winter to eliminate the overwintering pupae of some species.

Dormant-oil treatments for scale insects or aphids will kill the eggs of a few of these species, such as fruittree leafroller, which overwinter in the egg stage on branches and twigs. If treatment is needed during the season, *Bacillus thuringiensis* or spinosad sprays are recommended, applied just as eggs hatch. These sprays will have minimal impact on natural enemy species. Young caterpillars must consume treated surfaces within a day of application, so proper timing is essential to success. More-broadly toxic insecticides usually are not warranted in backyard trees and are not recommended because they may cause outbreaks of aphids, scales, and caterpillar pests.

Walnut husk fly

The walnut husk fly (*Rhagoletis completa*) is a common pest wherever walnuts are grown. Its larval stages feed inside the husk, turning it black and gooey and staining the walnut shell. The damage is mostly cosmetic, so treatment is generally not required in the home orchard.

Walnut husk flies spend the winter as pupae in the soil and emerge as adults (fig. 11.33) in early to mid-summer, usually between mid-July and mid-August. Female flies lay eggs in groups below the surface of the developing walnut husks, leaving sting marks. The stings darken and eggs hatch into white maggots within 5 days. The maggots (fig. 11.34) feed inside the husk, enlarging the black area, which remains soft, unsunken, and smooth (fig. 11.35). Although the husk surface stays intact, the fleshy parts below decay and stain the nutshell. The kernel within usually is not affected. Maggots mature after about 3 to 5 weeks and pupate in the soil. There is only one generation per year.

Sprays are not generally suggested for managing walnut husk fly on backyard walnut trees. You can reduce the number of husk flies overwintering near your tree or orchard by removing and disposing of damaged nuts as soon as possible, before the maggots emerge to pupate. Also, a tarp placed under the tree from July through August may prevent maggots from entering the soil to pupate.

Figure 11.33. The adult walnut husk fly has striped wings and is about the size of a house fly.

Figure 11.34. Walnut husk fly larvae are maggots that feed under the husk surface.

Figure 11.35. Walnut husk fly maggots feed within the husk, causing dark spots that expand over time.

Husk fly damage can make it difficult to remove the husks from nuts. You can remedy this by placing the nuts in a damp burlap bag for a few days before attempting to remove the husks. Be sure to dispose of infested husks in a tightly sealed bag.

Commercial walnut growers apply insecticide-laden baits to control high husk fly populations. Timing of application is critical and difficult. Proper timing requires that you trap and dissect female flies. For details on this method, see the UC IPM Pest Management Guidelines for walnut, ipm.ucanr.edu/agriculture/, or the *UC IPM Pest Note* on walnut husk fly, in the Pest Notes library, ipm.ucanr.edu/PMG/PEST-NOTES/index.html.

Spotted wing drosophila

The spotted wing drosophila, *Drosophila suzukii,* can cause serious damage on ripening cherries. It also attacks strawberry, raspberry, and blueberry, and occasionally stone fruit other than cherry, and is present in most areas where these crops are grown.

Adults are small flies with red eyes and a brown thorax. They look very similar to other *Drosophila,* such as the common vinegar fly; however, unlike vinegar flies, which attack overripe or rotting fruit, they attack healthy ripening fruit. Males of the spotted wing drosophila can be distinguished from vinegar flies by the presence of a dark spot on the tip of each wing (fig. 11.36); females lack this spot and can't be distinguished from other fruit flies without a microscope.

Spotted wing drosophila lays its eggs in fruit that is just beginning to ripen. Females use their sawlike ovipositor to place the eggs in a puncture just beneath the fruit skin. Tiny larvae, or maggots, hatch and grow within the fruit, causing the fruit to soften and brown and exude fluids (fig. 11.37). In some cases, almost every cherry on a tree will be infested.

Many larvae may be found within each fruit. Once mature, larvae pupate on the fruit surface or drop to the ground. There are many generations a year. Adult flies are most active at temperatures between 60 and 80°F (15–27°C) and can be found throughout the year in California's mild-weather coastal areas. In areas with hot summers or cold winters, activity may be reduced during those seasons.

Management

Spotted wing drosophila is difficult to manage. Often the pest is not noticed until close to harvest. Once fruit are infested, there is little you can do to protect the crop on the tree. It may be possible to harvest early and sort out clean fruit, but this is very labor intensive and difficult to do.

Removing and destroying all infested fruit as well as fruit that have fallen on the ground may help re-

Figure 11.36. Male spotted wing Drosophila have a black spot on the tip of each wing. Females lack this spot and are difficult to distinguish from other fruit flies. *Photo*: Martin Hauser.

Figure 11.37. A larva of the spotted wing Drosophila on the surface of a damaged cherry. *Photo*: Larry L. Strand.

duce infestation of later-maturing varieties of cherry or other hosts in the garden. Composting or burying fruit is not a reliable way to kill fruit flies. Placing fruit in plastic bags in the trash or solarizing are the best disposal options.

Fine netting (such as 0.98-mm netting made for no-see-ums) may be placed over branches before the fruit begin to ripen and flies are active. Netting must be secured beneath so flies cannot enter from the bottom. Fruit bushes and espalier-trained trees are much easier to cover than large trees (see chapter 7, "Training and pruning").

Traps have not proven effective in suppressing spotted wing drosophila in backyard situations, but they may be useful in detection. You can make your own traps out of yogurt containers baited with pure apple cider vinegar and a drop of unscented liquid dishwashing soap. Hang the trap near your cherry tree or berries in early May or well before fruit begins to soften (about a month before harvest).

Fruit monitoring is important for timing insecticide sprays. When you start catching fruit flies in traps—or, if you are not using traps, once fruit begins to develop any pink color—look for tiny stings on the fruit surface that indicate spotted wing drosophila egg-laying.

Cherry trees that have had spotted wing drosophila infestations will need protection in subsequent years. Sprays on cherry must be applied just as fruit turns from yellow to pink (about 2 to 3 weeks before harvest). A second spray will be needed 7 to 10 days later. Spinosad is an organically acceptable material that can be used against this pest (although some formulations are not organic); other insecticides may be available. See the *UC IPM Pest Note* on spotted wing drosophila in the Pest Notes library, ipm.ucanr.edu/PMG/PESTNOTES/index.html.

Spider mites

Spider mites may become abundant in fruit trees under hot, dusty conditions, especially when their natural enemies have been knocked out by insecticide treatments applied for other pests. Spider mites feed on the undersides of leaves, destroying chlorophyll and causing a pale stippling of leaves. When spider mite numbers are high, their webbing is easily visible on leaves (fig. 11.38).

The two common spider mites in California, twospotted spider mite (*Tetranychus urticae*) (fig. 11.39) and Pacific spider mite (*T. pacificus*), are almost impossible to tell apart; however, biology and management of the two species are the same. They are tiny, about 0.02 inches long when fully grown, and they look like pale moving dots on leaves. Under a hand lens, you can see that they are yellowish, with red eyes, and have a large, dark spot on each side of the body (see fig. 11.39). Spider mites overwinter as mature females, which are reddish orange and lack distinct dark spots, in protected places on the trunk and on the ground. Once the trees leaf out, the female lays spherical, translucent eggs on the leaves. Eggs hatch into tiny mites that rapidly mature and reproduce. There are many generations in a year when the weather is warm.

Spider mites have many natural enemies that regularly limit their numbers. Among the most important are the western predatory mite (*Galendromus occidentalis*) (see fig. 11.39), the sixspotted thrips (*Scolo-*

Figure 11.38. Trees with heavy infestations of spider mites may have yellowing stippling and webbing on their leaves.

Figure 11.39. The twospotted spider mite is at the bottom of this photo. Its clear-bodied predator, the western predatory mite, is at top.

thrips sexmaculatus), the larvae of certain flies such as cecidomyiid species in the *Feltiella* genus, the spider mite destroyer lady beetle (*Stethorus picipes*), and various general predators such as minute pirate bugs, bigeyed bugs, and lacewing larvae. Commercial fruit and nut growers sometimes purchase and release predatory mites to reestablish populations in their orchards, but most backyards already have adequate numbers of natural enemies, if they have not been destroyed by dust or pesticides.

Spider mites are rarely a serious problem in backyard trees that have been kept adequately irrigated, dust-free, and free from broadly toxic insecticides. If problems do occur, reevaluate your irrigation program and pesticide application program to make sure your actions are not the cause of the problems. Sometimes, regular, forceful spraying of plants with water will adequately reduce spider mite numbers on smaller trees. If insecticide treatments are required,

use insecticidal oils or soap sprays. These are less harmful to natural enemies than other types of materials. Don't use oils and soaps on water-stressed trees, or when temperatures are above 90°F (32°C), or within 30 days of a sulfur spray.

Stink bugs and other plant bugs

A number of plant bugs, including stink bugs (figs. 11.40 and 11.41), lygus bugs, calocoris, boxelder bugs, and leaffooted bugs (fig. 11.42), may occur on backyard fruit trees from time to time. Plant bugs have sucking mouthparts, which they use to extract plant juices from under the skin of fruit, from the developing seed of some plants or from the foliage or shoots. Their feeding on fruit may cause dimples, depressions, distortion, or white or dark pithy areas that might not be apparent until well after the bugs have left (fig. 11.43). Early spring feeding by plant bugs like stink bug, calocoris, and lygus bug can cause significant damage and deformity in peaches and nectarines.

Plant bugs are difficult to manage, and damage in backyard trees rarely justifies management beyond good cultural practices. Plant bugs are most common in orchards or gardens next to weedy areas. Keep vegetation mowed under and around fruit trees—or eliminate it, as appropriate. Some plant bugs overwinter in woodpiles, under loose bark, or in outbuildings. Check these refuges for pests and eliminate them where possible.

Check smaller trees for bugs on a regular basis. You can pick off larger bugs, such as stink bugs and leaffooted bugs, and also remove their distinctive egg masses (stink-bug eggs are barrel-like; the eggs of leaffooted bugs are laid in chains).

An invasive species of stink bug, the brown marmorated stink bug, *Halyomorpha halys* (see fig. 11.41), has caused serious problems on fruit trees in the eastern United States and has also been detected in California. Although the damage that individual bugs produce is similar to that of other stink bugs, brown marmorated stink bugs may occur in much denser populations, thus causing much more severe overall damage. See the *UC IPM Pest Note* on brown marmorated stink bug in the Pest Notes library, ipm.ucanr.edu/PMG/PESTNOTES/index.html.

Figure 11.40. The consperse stink bug is a common stink bug in orchard trees.

Figure 11.41. The brown marmorated stink bug recently invaded California and may become a major problem. It can be distinguished from the consperse stink bug by the bands on its antennae.

Figure 11.42. Leaffooted bugs have leafy extensions on their rear legs and may become common on pomegranates and other fruit and nut trees. *Photo:* David R. Haviland.

Figure 11.43. Stink bugs have caused the dimpling in these pears.

Wood and bark borers

Several species of boring insects can cause damage on fruit and nut trees by tunneling into tree bark and wood. Borers cause a greater problem if the tree is newly planted or if it has suffered damage from other pests or poor cultural practices. Sometimes, you can nurse a tree along with improved irrigation and cultural practices, but often the best solution is to remove the damaged limb or tree entirely. Except for the peach tree borer, insecticide applications are not generally recommended for borer control. Soil-applied systemic insecticides are not effective.

Borers are a common problem on young trees that have been sunburned and on mature trees that have received excessive summer pruning. Protect young trees by whitewashing their trunks with white latex paint from 1 inch below ground level to at least 2 feet above (see chapter 4, "Orchard design and Planting and care of young trees"). You can also use tree protectors wrapped around the trunk.

Peach tree borer

The peach tree borer (*Synanthedon exitiosa*), a species of clearwinged moth, attacks the crown or trunk of stone fruit trees and almond trees on peach rootstocks. The adult is a steel blue–black moth with clear wings that emerges in late spring and early summer. Female moths lay their eggs during the summer on bark at the base of tree trunks. Hatching larvae tunnel into the tree just at or above ground level, leaving piles of sawdust-like excrement at their burrow entrances (fig. 11.44). The larvae remain inside the tree, feeding and tunneling until the following spring, when they leave the tree to pupate on the trunk or in the soil beneath. The feeding larvae can girdle and kill healthy young trees. Older trees are sometimes attacked, but they usually tolerate the damage unless borer populations are very high.

It may be possible to control peach tree borer larvae with applications of an insect parasitic nematode, either *Steinernema carpocapsae* or *S. feltia*, if applied

Figure 11.44. The orange sawdust-like excrement and gumming at the base of this trunk indicates damage by a peach tree borer larva.

Figure 11.45. These tiny holes are emergence holes of the shothole borer.

deep into the burrows when larvae are actively feeding in mid-to-late summer. See the UC IPM Pest Note on clearwing moths in the Pest Notes library, ipm.ucanr.edu/PMG/PESTNOTES/index.html, for details on using these beneficial nematodes. Insecticide sprays to the trunk to control peach tree borer adults before they lay eggs in early summer can also be used, but application timing can be difficult, and you need to choose a persistent material such as a pyrethroid, which must be labeled for trunk treatments.

Shothole borer

The shothole borer (*Scolytus rugulosus*) is a pest of many fruit and nut trees, including stone fruit, apple, pear, and almond. It is primarily a pest of trees that have already been weakened by root disease, insufficient irrigation, sunburn, or other maladies. Adults are tiny, black beetles, about 1/10 inch long. Adult females bore small holes in the tree's bark and lay their eggs along a gallery that is 1 to 2 inches long. Hatching larvae feed beneath the bark. Healthy trees exude resin that usually kills shothole borers before they can do much damage, but weakened trees cannot protect themselves. Infested trees are characterized by groups of small shotholes left in branches or trunks after adult beetles emerge (fig. 11.45). Shothole borers can have two to three generations a year.

The key to preventing damage from shothole borers is to keep trees healthy and vigorous. If borers successfully invade, it usually is an indication that the tree has other serious problems. If shothole borers occur in only one limb or scaffold branch, prune it out. If the whole tree is weakened, remove the tree. Burn all infested wood or, at the very least, remove it

from the backyard area. Insecticides are not recommended.

Pacific flatheaded borer

The adult Pacific flatheaded borer (*Chrysobothris mali*) is a large (about 1/2-inch-long) beetle with a bronze cast. Females lay their eggs on injured areas on tree trunks or limbs. Flatheaded borer larvae have a distinctive flat enlargement just behind the head, and the larvae are large—they may grow up to 3/4 inch long (fig. 11.46). Larvae feed under the bark in the rapidly growing outer wood and then bore deeper to pupate.

Prevention is the main way to manage flatheaded borers. Prevent sunburn on young trees with latex paint or trunk wraps. When you prune, leave a few extra twigs to shade the newly exposed limbs beneath. Supply adequate water and fertilizer. Prune out and destroy infested wood. Insecticide sprays are not recommended for this pest.

Figure 11.46. The Pacific flatheaded borer larva is large with an enlarged area behind its head.

Other insects

Figure 11.47. The green fruit beetle, *Cotinis mutabilis*, is a large (1.25 in. long) metallic green beetle that attacks maturing soft fruit. Its larva develops in decaying organic material in the soil or partially decomposed compost or manure. To manage it, remove manure piles and other food sources for larvae and turn the compost regularly.

Figure 11.48. The navel orangeworm, *Amyelois transitella*, damages almond and walnut nuts, leaving copious webbing and excrement—much more than codling moth, which also may damage walnuts. The caterpillar and brown, shiny pupae are shown here. Harvesting as soon as nuts are ready and removing all mummy nuts from trees after harvest will keep navel orangeworm at tolerable levels.

Figure 11.49. Thrips such as this western flower thrips are tiny insects that occasionally scar smooth-skinned fruit such as nectarines, apples, or pears. Some thrips species are beneficial, including the western flower thrips when it is feeding on spider mites. No management is recommended in home orchards.

Common diseases in backyard orchards

Powdery mildew

Powdery mildew infections are characterized by a white powdery growth that may cover leaves, flowers, and fruit. Many fruit trees are attacked by powdery mildew fungi. Several species of fungi are involved. Common fruit-tree hosts, powdery mildew species, and controls are listed in table 11.3.

Identification and damage

The powdery mycelial and spore growth that forms on both sides of leaves (fig. 11.50) and sometimes on flowers, fruit, and shoots makes powdery mildew easy to recognize. Under a hand lens, powdery mildew spores can be seen growing in chains on the tips of fungal strands. Powdery mildew may cause new growth to be dwarfed or distorted. Weblike russet scars may develop on fruit, leaving a rough, corky skin (fig. 11.51).

Life cycle

Powdery mildew fungi survive from one season to the next in infected buds or as fruiting bodies called cleistothecia (fig. 11.52). Once tree growth begins in the spring, the fungus grows as thin layers of mycelia over the plant surface. The fungus produces spores that are blown by wind to new hosts. High humidity, moderate temperatures, and shady conditions are generally most favorable for powdery mildew development. Water is not required for, and may even inhibit, spore germination of some powdery mildew species.

Management

Prevention is the first step in any management program for powdery mildew. Avoid planting the most susceptible fruit-tree varieties and follow good cultural practices. That will be enough to control the disease adequately in many situations. Where possible, choose resistant varieties that meet your growing requirements and personal preferences. Examples of

Table 11.3. Host plants and control measures for powdery mildew species

Hosts	Fungus species	Controls
Apple, nectarine, peach	*Podosphaera leucotricha*	tolerant varieties; pruning out infections in apple trees during dormant season; fungicides if necessary
Cherry	*Podosphaera clandestina*	fungicides if necessary
Apricot, plum, prune	*Podosphaera tridactyla*	tolerant varieties; fungicides if necessary
Apricot, nectarine, peach, plum	*Sphaerotheca pannosa*	fungicides if necessary; removing or treating roses

Figure 11.50. The powdery white spores on the underside of these apple leaves is indicative of a powdery mildew.

Figure 11.51. Fruit which have been damaged by powdery mildew may develop webs of russet scars.

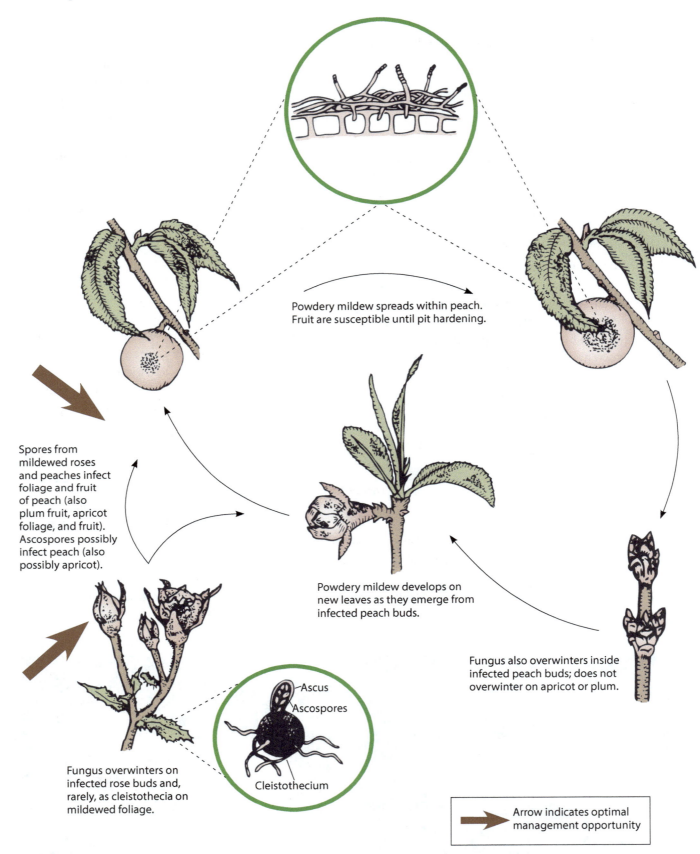

Powdery mildew spreads within peach. Fruit are susceptible until pit hardening.

Spores from mildewed roses and peaches infect foliage and fruit of peach (also plum fruit, apricot foliage, and fruit). Ascospores possibly infect peach (also possibly apricot).

Powdery mildew develops on new leaves as they emerge from infected peach buds.

Fungus also overwinters inside infected peach buds; does not overwinter on apricot or plum.

Ascus

Ascospores

Cleistothecium

Fungus overwinters on infected rose buds and, rarely, as cleistothecia on mildewed foliage.

Arrow indicates optimal management opportunity

Figure 11.52. Life cycle of *Sphaerotheca pannosa*, a powdery mildew fungus. *Source:* Ingels et al. 2007.

the most and least susceptible varieties are listed in table 11.4. Check with your nursery operator about the disease resistance of new varieties when you purchase trees. Fungicide applications may be necessary when you plant varieties that are more susceptible. Susceptible varieties of apple are the fruit trees that most often need fungicide applications.

Cultural practices

High temperatures and low humidity provide the best protection against powdery mildew. Plant trees in sunny locations, provide for good air circulation, and avoid excess fertilization. You can wash spores from trees using a hose or sprinkler—but if you do so, avoid causing any sustained rise in humidity, especially at night. On dormant apple trees, infected terminal shoots are stunted and have a bleached appearance. These infected shoots should be removed during winter.

Sphaerotheca pannosa, one of the common fungi causing powdery mildew in apricot, peach, nectarine, and plum, causes mildew only on the fruit. It overwinters on infected roses. In spring, powdery mildew on apricot or plum fruit and leaves may be reduced by treating garden rosebushes to prevent mildew or by removing rosebushes from the garden since the fungus is not known to overwinter on fruit trees. Powdery mildew spores are, however, known to blow in from infected roses in neighboring gardens, and removing or treating rosebushes won't control other powdery mildew fungi (*Podosphaera* spp.), which don't attack roses.

Fungicide applications

Spraying is not generally necessary in many backyard situations. If you have had serious powdery mildew damage in past years, however, a fungicide application may be advisable. Make applications at 2-week intervals beginning when buds just start to open (green tip stage) in early spring and continue until small, green fruit are present. Various products are available, including wettable sulfurs, horticultural oils, potassium bicarbonate, and synthetic fungicides. Never use sulfur on an apricot tree, and do not apply sulfur within 2 weeks of an oil spray on any fruit tree. Oils and sulfurs should not be applied when temperatures are above 90°F (32°C) or on water-stressed trees. For more information on fungicides, see the UC IPM Pest Note on powdery mildew on fruit and berries in the Pest Notes library, ipm.ucanr.edu/PMG/PESTNOTES/index.html.

Peach leaf curl

The distorted, red foliage typical of a peach leaf curl infection on peach or nectarine trees is a familiar sight for many backyard orchardists (fig. 11.53). The fungus that causes peach leaf curl, *Taphrina deformans,* is especially active during unusually wet springs, but it can generally be satisfactorily managed with a dormant spray of fungicide in winter. Only peach and nectarine are affected by this disease. Aphids are the likely cause of curled leaves on other fruit tree species.

Table 11.4. Susceptibility of fruit varieties to powdery mildew

Fruit	Most susceptible	Moderately susceptible	Least susceptible
Apple	Gravenstein, Jonathan, Rome Beauty, Yellow Newtown	Braeburn, Golden Delicious, Granny Smith, Jonagold, McIntosh	Red Delicious, Stayman Winesap
Cherry	Bing, Black Tartarian, Rainier	—	—
Nectarine	Most varieties are susceptible	—	—
Peach	Elegant Lady, Fairtime, Fay Elberta, Summerset	—	freestone varieties such as Flame Crest, Flavor Crest, O'Henry
Plum	Black Beaut, Gaviota, Kelsey, Wickson	—	—

Note: "—" indicates that cells are intentionally left blank.

Figure 11.53. Puckered and thickened areas on leaves are typical of a peach leaf curl infection.

Identification and damage

Leaf curl symptoms become apparent in spring, about 2 weeks after leaves emerge from buds. Damage first appears as reddish areas on leaves, which rapidly become thick and puckered. Whitish spores develop on affected leaf surfaces. Leaves later turn yellow or brown and may either remain on the tree or fall off. As dry weather sets in, healthy leaves appear on new shoot growth, but the return of wet weather will foster additional infections. The loss of leaves can take a toll on trees, decreasing tree growth and fruit development and size. Leaf loss may also lead to sunburn on branches, opening them up to borer attack.

Twigs and shoots may be infected and become thickened, stunted, and distorted, and die back. Wrinkled, reddish, warty areas occasionally develop on fruit. If a leaf curl infection builds up on a tree and is left uncontrolled for several years, the tree may decline and may have to be removed.

Life cycle

The fungus overwinters as spores on the surfaces of twigs and buds (fig. 11.54). When the buds begin to grow in spring, the spores grow into the developing tissue if frequent rainfall occurs. The fungus grows between cells just under the leaf, fruit, or shoot surface, causing abnormal cell growth in young plant tissue, which results in the characteristic distortion. As the infection progresses, the fungus breaks through the leaf surface, producing a fuzzy gray layer of fruiting bodies called asci, each of which contains asco-spores. The ascospores are released into the air and carried to new tissues, where they can infect right away if moist conditions and young tissue are available—or, if conditions are not favorable, they may remain inactive until the following spring.

Only young leaf, fruit, and shoot tissues are susceptible, so the disease becomes less severe as leaves mature. Also, cooler (below 80–85°F [27–30°C]), wet, or humid weather is required for spores to germinate, so new infections cease in late spring.

Management

The key to preventing leaf curl infections is to make an annual application of fungicide during the dormant season. There is little you can do during spring when the distorted red leaves are obvious on the tree. While some people remove diseased leaves or prune infected shoots, this has not been shown to reduce the disease. Diseased leaves will normally fall off on their own. It is also important to prevent water from sprinkler irrigation from spraying onto the tree. This moisture can enable the disease to continue until temperatures increase in spring.

In most parts of California, it is advisable to make at least two treatments, one in December or early January after leaves have fallen off trees and a second one just before buds begin to swell. Copper fungicides are commonly used for control. Synthetic materials are also effective. Thorough spray coverage is essential to move the fungicide into all the buds. For information about materials available for home orchards, see the UC IPM Pest Note on peach leaf curl in the Pest Notes library, ipm.ucanr.edu/PMG/PEST-NOTES/index.html.

Brown rot

Brown rot is probably the most common cause of fruit rot in stone fruit trees. Flowers also are susceptible, but the damage to flowers and shoots usually is minimal except in a year with a very wet spring. When conditions are favorable to the disease, you can lose an entire crop. Fruit may appear healthy when you harvest it, but then develop brown rot shortly afterward in storage. Susceptibility varies among stone fruit species and varieties. Generally, plum is least susceptible, and the early-ripening varieties of peach and nectarine generally have little trouble with brown rot.

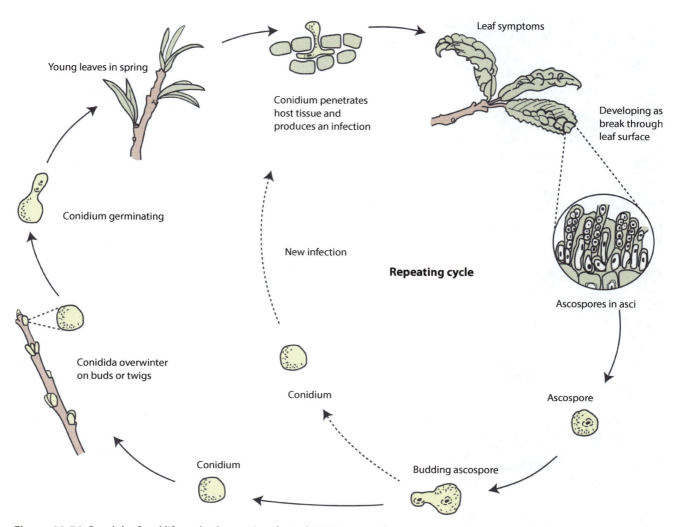

Young leaves in spring

Conidium penetrates
host tissue and
produces an infection

Leaf symptoms

Developing as
break through
leaf surface

Conidium germinating

New infection

Repeating cycle

Ascospores in asci

Conidida overwinter
on buds or twigs

Conidium

Ascospore

Conidium

Budding ascospore

Figure 11.54. Peach leaf curl life cycle. *Source:* Ingels et al. 2007.

Identification and damage

Two fungi, *Monilinia fructicola* and *M. laxa,* cause brown rot. The two cause similar symptoms but differ in their life cycles. *M. fructicola* is most common on peach and nectarine; *M. laxa* is most common on almond; and both are found on apricot, cherry, and prune. Except for a few varieties, plum trees seldom have brown rot.

In spring, the pathogen invades the stigma and stamens of open flowers, causing the flowers to wither, turn brown, and stick to the tree. An amber-colored gum usually is present near the base of the dead flower. If the infection extends into the shoot, the portion of the shoot above the dead flower may die, with wilted dead leaves still attached. In humid or wet weather, the fungus produces visible tan tufts of spores (spore pads) on the dead flowers (fig. 11.55).

As fruit ripen in summer, light brown areas of rot appear on the fruit, followed by more powdery, tan spores over the rotted area (fig. 11.56).

Brown rot and bacterial blast infections are sometimes difficult to distinguish from one another. Shoots and spurs killed by brown rot generally are brown and always have an infected flower present, and spores can be found. Bacterial blast infections are black and do not extend very far into the shoot. Bacterial blast never has spores associated with it.

Life cycle

Both types of brown rot fungus produce spores on dead flowers or twigs in spring that are carried by wind currents to other flowers or, later, to fruit. In summer, especially when there are rains or dews that moisten the fruit surface, the spores germinate and

Figure 11.55. Brown rot–infected flower, showing sporulation.

Figure 11.56. Circular brown rot lesions on ripe fruit.

Figure 11.57. Mummies on the tree provide overwintering spots for brown rot disease.

penetrate the fruit. Some rotten fruit fall from the tree and decay on the ground. Others remain attached to the tree and slowly shrivel into wrinkled, black and tan structures called mummies (fig. 11.57). The mummy is composed of both fungal and plant tissues and is a survival structure for the fungus.

During winter rains, the wet mummies become heavy and fall from the tree.

Mummies on the ground resulting from infection by *M. fructicola* produce small, cup-shaped structures called apothecia. Sexual spores, called ascospores, are produced in the apothecia and released into the air at the same time that trees begin to bloom, beginning the disease cycle again. Both fungi produce vegetative spores on the infected flowers, fruit, and mummies, but only *M. fructicola* is known to produce apothecia and ascospores.

Management

Most backyard trees do not need protection from brown rot. This is especially true of peach and nectarine trees. If you find infected blossoms, remove them to help reduce the inoculum that could infect the fruit. More importantly, remove and destroy all infected fruit from the tree and ground at the end of summer. Although removing infected flowers and infected fruit will not eliminate brown rot, it may help reduce losses from the disease. Avoid overfertilization, since excess nitrogen makes flowers and fruit more susceptible. Any injury to the ripening fruit, such as insects' feeding wounds or fruit split, increases the chances for brown rot infection. Harvesting fruit when they are mature but before they are completely ripe will help reduce the amount of brown rot.

Fire blight

Fire blight is most serious on pears but may also damage apple, quince, and loquat trees—as well as a few ornamentals, especially pyracantha. The disease gets its name from the characteristic blackening and shriveling of affected shoots, flowers, and young fruit, which truly do look like they have been singed by fire (fig. 11.58). The causal agent is the bacterium *Erwinia amylovora*.

Identification and damage

The first evidence of a fire blight infection usually is a watery, tan bacterial ooze that begins to seep out of branch, twig, or trunk cankers as soon as tree growth resumes in spring. The ooze turns dark, leaving dark streaks on bark. Cankers and ooze may be inconspicuous, though, and many people may not notice an infection until several weeks later, when flowers or shoots begin to shrivel and blacken. The disease

Figure 11.58. Blackened fruit and bacterial ooze are typical of a fire blight infection.

Figure 11.59. Fire blight–infected shoots wilt, dry, and look scorched—and often are crooked at the top.

spreads from blossoms into wood, and the newly infected wood may show pink, orange, or red streaks, which are visible upon slicing off the bark. Young branches infected with fire blight quickly develop dry, brown leaves, and their terminals often wilt into a shepherd's crook shape (fig. 11.59). Cankers (dead areas) form on the bark of older branches and trunks and may girdle or disfigure trees—or kill entire branches or even entire trees if the host is highly susceptible. Apple cultivars that are only mildly susceptible may only show dead individual spurs scattered through the tree.

Life cycle

The fire blight bacteria spend the winter in cankers that developed on trunks or branches in previous years' infections. When the tree begins growing in spring and moisture and temperature are adequate, the bacteria begin to multiply and a tan liquid oozes from the canker. Insects (mainly bees and flies) or splashing rain move the bacteria to nearby blossoms or succulent new plant tissue, which they easily penetrate. Daytime temperatures between 75 and 85°F

(24–29°C), coupled with rain or humid weather, are ideal for infection. Dry conditions inhibit further new infections.

Once in the flowers, the bacteria may cause only a localized infection and then eventually die—or, alternatively, they may move into twigs and branches to cause more serious damage in the wood. Insects and rain may also move the bacteria from flower to flower or from flower to succulent shoot. When the bacteria move through the wood, they usually penetrate in a narrow strip about ½ to 1½ inches wide and as far as 3 feet down into the tree. Cankers form where bark has been killed. They ooze bacteria that can then be the source of new infections.

Management

Fire blight management involves choosing less-susceptible fruit-tree varieties, keeping trees healthy but not overfertilized, removing diseased wood as soon as it appears, and in some cases applying copper sprays to prevent new infections. Consider removing susceptible ornamental species growing nearby, such as pyracantha, since bacteria from them can be transferred to apple or pear trees.

Most pear varieties are highly susceptible to fire blight, including Asian pear (with the exception of Shinko). Pear varieties that are resistant include Warren, Blake's Pride, and Hood. Susceptible apple varieties include Fuji, Gala, Golden Delicious, Granny Smith, Gravenstein, Jonathan, Mutsu, Pink Lady, and Yellow Newtown.

Tree vigor has an influence on the extent of fire blight damage. Once within the tree, the pathogen moves at a rate directly related to the rate of tree growth. Vigorously growing new shoots are most severely affected. High soil moisture and high nitrogen levels thus increase the severity of damage. Do not apply more water or fertilizer than recommended.

Diseased wood is best removed when it appears in the spring. The location of the pruning cut is very important. Locate the lowest visible edge of the infection and trace the branch to its point of attachment. Remove the branch at the next juncture down, taking care not to harm the branch collar. Rapidly advancing infections may need to be removed throughout the season in very susceptible varieties of pear, Asian pear, and apple. Never leave a stub. Trunk and major branch infections can sometimes be removed by scraping the bark down to the cambium layer; in this case, all discolored areas of the cambium must be removed. If the infection surrounds the limb (that is, the limb is girdled), it cannot be saved. Disinfect pruning and scraping tools in a 10 percent solution of household bleach in water after each diseased shoot or branch has been pruned. Many pear varieties continue to produce late, or rat-tail, blooms long after the main bloom is over. Remove these flowers before they open to reduce the chances of late-season fire blight infection.

Bactericidal sprays, such as those containing copper, may be necessary for pear and susceptible apple trees if fire blight is an annual occurrence and other infected trees are nearby. Sprays will reduce some new infections but not all of them, and sprays cannot eliminate existing infections. Start sprays as soon as the blossoms begin to open and the average daily temperature (the midpoint between the daily high and daily low) exceeds 60°F (15°C). Reapply at 4- or 5-day intervals during periods of high humidity until late bloom is over. This may mean between five and twelve applications per season. Be aware that copper treatments can cause severe russeting of the fruit surface, especially when applied during a wet spring.

Apple scab

Apple scab, considered the most serious disease of apples in some areas of California, is most severe when conditions are cool and moist. It takes its greatest toll in coastal areas. Symptoms do occur on flowers and leaves, but the scabby lesions on fruit are particularly recognizable (fig. 11.60). Apple scab is caused by the fungus *Venturia inaequalis*. A related fungus, *V. pirina*, causes a similar disease on pear, but pear scab is not usually a major problem in backyard trees. Its symptoms, development, and management are very similar to those discussed below for apple scab.

Identification and damage

The appearance of dark, velvety, or sooty spots on the undersides of leaves in early spring is usually the first noticeable sign of apple or pear scab. The dark growth eventually expands over the entire leaf surface and the leaf puckers or twists (fig. 11.61). Severely affected leaves may yellow and drop. Fruit infections begin as dark green spots that eventually turn black. The center of the infected area becomes cracked and scabby. Affected fruit become misshapen or drops from the tree. Later infections on fruit may cause pinprick surface scars, which usually are tolerable on homegrown fruit.

Figure 11.60. Late in the season, fruit damaged by apple scab have dry, cracked spots and often are distorted.

Figure 11.61. Leaves affected by scab are puckered and twisted and have dark circular spots. On the undersides of leaves, spots are dark and velvety.

Life cycle

The apple and pear scab fungi spend the winter in infected leaves on the ground beneath the tree, where they produce ascospores within fruiting bodies called pseudothecia. When trees begin to grow in spring, the ascospores mature, are forcibly discharged into the air, and can be carried long distances on air currents. If the surface of flowers, leaves, or young fruit of susceptible trees is wet and temperatures are suitable, between 55 and 75°F (13–24°C), the ascospores germinate and penetrate the plant tissue. Once in the plant, the fungus grows and eventually produces secondary spores, which can spread the disease further when moisture and temperature conditions are right. Leaves must be wet for 9 hours or more for infection to occur. If spring weather is dry, from the green-tip stage of bloom through fruit set, scab will not be a problem.

Management

For a single backyard tree, removing leaves from beneath the tree in winter may be sufficient to limit the disease to tolerable levels. In areas where apple scab is a consistent problem, choose apple varieties that are highly resistant to the disease (table 11.5). In plantings of several trees of susceptible varieties in areas with cool, wet spring conditions, you may consider application of fungicides, but careful attention to application timing is critical. See the UC IPM Pest Note on apple and pear scab in the Pest Notes library, ipm.ucanr.edu/PMG/PESTNOTES/index.html.

Table 11.5. Apple varieties susceptible or highly resistant to apple scab

Susceptible	Highly resistant
Bellflower	Easy-Gro
Blushing Gold	Enterprise
Fuji	Florina
Gala	Freedom
Golden Delicious	Gold Rush
Granny Smith	Jon Grimes
Gravestein	Jonafree
Grimes	Liberty
Ida Red	MacFree
Jonathan	Prima
Monroe	Priscilla
Mutsu	Pristine
Paula Red	Redfree
Red Delicious	Sir Prize
Rome Beauty	Spigold
Stayman Winesap	Williams Pride
Winesap	—
Yellow Newtown	—
York Imperial	—

Note: "—" indicates that cells are intentionally left blank.

Shothole disease

Shothole is a disease of apricot, peach, nectarine, and almond trees. The disease is only very rarely seen on cherry and plum trees; the spots and holes seen on plum and cherry leaves usually have other causes. Leaves, twigs, buds, and fruit affected by shothole show small, scabby lesions (fig. 11.62). The disease is caused by the fungus *Wilsonomyces carpophilus* and is most severe following warm, wet winters when wet weather is prolonged into spring.

Identification and damage

Shothole disease first appears in the spring as reddish- or purplish-brown spots about 1/10 inch in diameter on new leaves and occasionally on shoots. As the spots expand, their centers turn brown. If it rains,

Figure 11.62. Small holes in leaves and brownish scabby spots on fruit are typical of shothole infections on apricot.

tiny, dark specks that are best viewed with a hand lens form in the brown centers. These dark specks, which are masses of fungal spores, distinguish shothole lesions from other types of spots. Spots on young leaves have a narrow, light green or yellow margin and a center that often falls out as the leaf expands, leaving a hole something like what you would see if a buckshot pellet had passed through; hence, shothole disease. Leaves may fall from the tree if the infection is severe, especially if the tree is young when it is infected. Blemishes on fruit become rough and corky but rarely show dark specks.

On peach and to some extent on apricot trees, the fungus infects and kills dormant buds in winter. The dead buds are covered with a sticky exudate that dries to look like lacquer (fig. 11.63). If there are several infections on a twig, they may girdle and kill it. The part of the tree that is affected by shothole varies from crop to crop. Shothole on almond and apricot primarily takes the form of leaf and fruit infections. On peach and nectarine, shothole is largely limited to buds and twigs and is thus less noticeable than the conspicuous leaf and fruit spotting on apricot.

Life cycle

The shothole fungus overwinters as spores in infected buds and twig lesions. Twigs and buds can be infected any time between fall and spring when there are 24 hours of wetness. Developing leaves and fruit become infected during spring when the weather is wet. Spores are produced on leaf, bud, and twig lesions, and, rarely, on fruit infections. The disease cycle stops with the onset of warm, dry weather in the spring, but the pathogen survives inside infected buds and twig lesions until wet weather resumes in fall.

Management

Where incidence of shothole is low, it is often possible to manage the disease in backyard trees by means of cultural practices and sanitation. If sprinklers are near your trees, it is important that their angle be low enough to keep the water from getting on leaves. Removal of infected twigs does little good. If you remove them, however, you should do so in winter.

If shothole damage is high, you can apply a protectant fungicide such as copper to protect dormant buds. Such an application should occur after leaf fall and before the first fall rains—but it will not control spring infections of leaves and fruit. This treatment will also help control peach leaf curl, even though it occurs a little earlier than is required for good protection against peach leaf curl. Additional applications should not be necessary for backyard trees. Copper sprays are safe on dormant fruit trees but may burn leaves if the trees are not dormant.

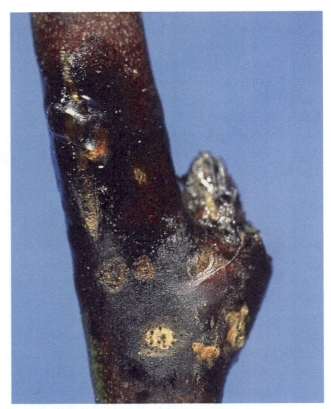

Figure 11.63. This bud was killed by shothole. Note the varnish-like gumming and the shothole lesions with dark spots in the center.

Bacterial canker and blast

Bacterial canker and blast are caused by the bacterium *Pseudomonas syringae.* The canker phase of the disease is most common in stone fruit and is seldom seen in apple or pear. Symptoms appear in late winter and early spring. Cankers begin as irregularly shaped, water- or gum-soaked areas of bark (fig. 11.64), which may grow to girdle and kill entire branches or trunks. Reddish flecking around canker margins distinguishes these cankers from those caused by other pathogens (fig. 11.65). Infected trees have a distinct sour or vinegary odor, and young trees are most severely affected. The disease is active during the winter and ceases when warm weather returns and trees start to grow. Bacterial canker does not affect roots, so if aboveground parts of the tree die in winter or early spring from bacterial canker, there may be suckering at the rootstock in late spring and summer, a typical symptom of the presence of bacterial canker.

The blast phase of the disease, which may occur in pear and apple as well as in stone fruit and almond trees, causes blossoms and shoots to shrivel, turn dark, and die (fig. 11.66). In pear and apple trees, bacterial ooze is never present, distinguishing bacterial blast from fire blight, which also kills flowers and shoots. Gumming may occur, however, on infected stone fruit buds and spurs. Blast can also cause sunken black spots on pear and cherry fruit. Frost injury and cold, rainy weather increase the incidence of blast.

P. syringae bacteria are always present on the surfaces of plants. The bacteria invade trees when the right combination of favorable conditions occurs. It is unclear how the bacteria enter the tree. Infections are not associated with pruning wounds.

Management of bacterial canker must rely on cultural practices. Fungicides and bactericides are not effective. Healthy, vigorous trees suffer less damage from bacterial canker. Choose your planting site carefully, avoiding sites with a history of bacterial canker. Trees grown on sandy, shallow, hardpan, acidic (pH below 5.5), or nitrogen-deficient soils are most susceptible. The presence of ring nematodes in the soil may also predispose trees. Certain stone fruit and pear rootstocks may impart resistance to bacterial canker; see Integrated Pest Management for Stone Fruits (Strand 1999). Provide optimum levels of key nutrients, especially nitrogen, to maintain tree vigor

Figure 11.64. The gumming in this photo indicates the initiation of a new bacterial canker.

Figure 11.65. The reddish flecking around the margins of a bacterial canker distinguishes this disease from cankers caused by other pathogens.

Figure 11.66. Bacterial blossom blast has killed these apple blossoms. Unlike fire blight, damage will not extend below the base of the flower cluster, although fruit spurs can be killed.

Figure 11.67. Gumming from a Eutypa canker. Notice its location adjacent to a pruning wound.

(without overfertilizing). Although acidic conditions favor the disease, there is no apparent benefit from adjusting the pH through addition of soil amendments. These nutritional and cultural practices have no effect on the blast phase of the disease, but apple and pear trees can be protected from frost during bloom by the use of sprinkler irrigation or shelters, which may reduce the incidence of blast. Badly damaged branches may be removed in summer, but this will not prevent future infections.

Eutypa dieback

Eutypa dieback, caused by the fungus *Eutypa lata,* is a special problem on apricot and cherry trees but may also affect apple trees. It is a serious problem in grapevines. Leaves wilt and die early on affected limbs and then remain on the tree through the following winter. Trees usually have a gum-exuding canker located near a pruning wound, or other injury, that was the original site of infection (fig. 11.67). Dieback symptoms become apparent 1 to 2 years after infection and advance for many years, often eventually killing the limb or tree.

To manage the disease in areas where it is a problem, restrict pruning of apricot and cherry to July and August in California's Central Valley and to August in coastal areas. Prune fruit-bush and espalier trees in spring. This late spring or summer pruning will allow pruning wounds to heal before spores are released during fall and spring rains. Existing infections can be pruned out at least 8 inches below the canker and destroyed. Remove abandoned grape-

vines and apricot trees in the vicinity, as these can be sources of infection.

Walnut blight

Walnut blight is a common disease of walnut that reduces nut production. It causes dark or distorted catkins and leaves, dark spots on husks, and shriveled nutmeats (fig. 11.68). The disease does not damage the tree or cause defoliation. Nuts infected by blight serve as a breeding site for the navel orangeworm and may be more difficult to shake from trees.

Walnut blight is caused by a bacterium, *Xanthomonas campestris* pv. *juglandis,* which survives the winter in dormant buds and catkins and to some extent in old cankers. The pathogen enters new plant tissue

Figure 11.68. The blackened areas on these walnuts are the result of a walnut blight infection. Initial infection sites enlarge, blacken, and often sink. The leaf in the foreground has become distorted around a black lesion that also resulted from a blight infection.

through natural openings when growth begins in spring. Bacteria are spread to other sites with wind-blown rain, sprinkler water, or pollen. The severity of the disease each year is directly related to the presence of free moisture, which is required for infection. Infection rates drop sharply when spring rains cease, unless sprinkler irrigation sends water up into the canopy.

The only management measure suggested for backyard walnut trees is to adjust your irrigation program to keep water from getting into trees and to keep moisture to a minimum. Make sure that any sprinklers are set at an angle low enough to keep young fruit from becoming wet. Remove low limbs that are likely to become wet and train young trees to allow air movement under the trees. Open up older trees during pruning to increase air movement through the tree. Avoid irrigation during bloom. If winter rains were not adequate, schedule a prebloom irrigation. If you are planting a new walnut tree, select a variety that blooms late so that most spring rains will be over by the time young fruit are present.

Armillaria root rot (oak root fungus)

Most fruit and nut trees and many ornamentals are susceptible to Armillaria root rot. The fungus that causes the disease, *Armillaria mellea,* is often called oak root fungus because it is frequently associated with oak trees. The disease is common in floodplains and along rivers. Trees suffering from Armillaria show the same general symptoms of decline as trees suffering from other root diseases. These include wilting of leaves and a general decline in growth and vigor, often on one side of the tree at first. Trees usually die within 1 to a few years.

Armillaria-infected trees can be readily distinguished from trees damaged by other root diseases if you search for the distinctive features of the fungus. Thin, white or yellowish mats of mycelium grow beneath the outer layer of infected bark (fig. 11.69), and they have a strong mushroom smell. Also, dark brown to black rootlike structures called rhizomorphs spread over the surface of infected roots and beneath the bark of severely decayed roots or crowns. Finally, clusters of light brown or honey-colored mushrooms (fig. 11.70) sometimes appear around the base of infected trees during wet weather in fall or winter.

Figure 11.69. Mycelial mats produced by *Armillaria mellea* grow between bark and wood.

Figure 11.70. Honey-colored mushrooms at the base of the tree may be a sign of an Armillaria root rot infection.

When a susceptible plant is affected by Armillaria root rot, little can be done except to remove the plant, including as much of the infected root system as possible, and allow the soil to dry out. Replant with a tolerant species.

Trees that are somewhat tolerant to Armillaria, such as varieties of pear and apple grown on certain rootstocks, may be saved if less than half of the crown's circumference is affected: Cut away and destroy all infected material and remove soil at the base of the tree to expose the crown and the top of the root system for several months. Avoid overirrigation.

Phytophthora root and crown rot

Almost all fruit and nut trees may develop Phytophthora root and crown rot, caused by various *Phytophthora* species, if soil around the base of the tree remains wet for prolonged periods. Trees infected in the crown may decline rapidly and die within a year.

Any time a tree suddenly collapses with the onset of warm weather, you should suspect that something is debilitating the root system or crown. The first noticeable symptom is usually on leaves, which wilt and turn dull green or yellow. Often trees leaf out normally in spring and then collapse and die suddenly with the first hot weather, retaining dead leaves. If only smaller roots are infected, the trees grow slowly, do not respond to irrigation or fertilization, and may die after several years. Cankers on roots and crowns appear as dark patches of bark that exude copious quantities of gum that can be amber (on stone fruit) or black (on walnut). Wood underneath the gum is dark reddish brown on stone fruit and almond trees (fig. 11.71) and mustard brown to black on walnut trees. There is no fungus mycelium as with Armillaria root rot. Positive confirmation of a Phytophthora root and crown rot infection requires laboratory analysis.

A number of *Phytophthora* species are capable of causing Phytophthora root and crown rot. They survive in soil, in plant material, or as resistant spores. They are carried to new locations on infected plants, in contaminated soil, or in water. Within the orchard, *Phytophthora* species spread as zoospores that require water to move, germinate, and infect bark at new sites. Under saturated soil conditions, more zoospores are produced and new infections escalate. Although *Phytophthora* can form other types of spores that can survive when conditions are dry, populations decline with prolonged exposure to dry soil.

The most important factor in reducing the threat of Phytophthora root and crown rot (and other root and crown rots) is avoiding prolonged saturation of soil and any standing water around the base of trees. Irrigate only as much and as often as necessary. Choose an appropriate planting site and provide good soil drainage. In some cases, planting trees on mounds or berms will improve drainage. Don't plant trees deeper than they were planted at the nursery, and never cover the graft union with soil. Don't grow irrigated turf or other plants around the base of trees and do not irrigate crown areas directly. Some rootstocks are more susceptible to Phytophthora root and crown rot than others; consult your local nursery or the materials listed at the end of this chapter to help you choose more-resistant rootstocks before you plant.

At the first sign of aboveground symptoms, check the tree at the soil line for crown rot. Carefully cut away bark that looks affected. If crown rot is present, a tree can sometimes be saved by removing the soil and vegetation from the base of the tree down to the tops of the main roots and allowing the crown tissue to dry out over the summer. Make sure to keep ground cover and sprinklers away from crowns and do not allow saturated conditions in the future.

Crown gall

Crown galls are rough, warty tumors caused by the soil-inhabiting bacterium *Agrobacterium tumefaciens* (fig. 11.72). Galls first appear as smooth swellings but

Figure 11.71. Gumming and reddening of wood beneath the crown area of this trunk indicates a Phytophthora infection.

Figure 11.72. Rough galls grow at the base of a plum tree affected by crown gall. Younger trees are the most seriously damaged.

develop rapidly into larger, woody tumors with a cracked appearance. Galls disrupt the flow of water and nutrients in the tree's conducting tissue and can quickly girdle and kill young trees. Older trees can usually tolerate galls, but if the galls are invaded by secondary wood decay organisms, even older trees may be injured.

Most infections start in the nursery. Reduce potential problems by obtaining planting material from a reputable nursery. Examine trees for signs of galls before purchase. Established plants are infected only through fresh wounds to the crown or roots, such as those caused by planting, pruning, cultivation equipment, or growth cracks, so take care not to injure the crowns or roots. In severely infested sites, nearly all new trees may become infected. If crown gall has been a problem in your planting area, excavate several wheelbarrows of soil and replace it with clean soil from somewhere else on the property.

Common vertebrate pests

Vertebrate pests often cause damage in home orchards. The most serious are generally birds and rodents. However, wildlife such as rabbits and deer can also injure trees. It is important to use an integrated approach when dealing with vertebrate pests. Often habitat modification and exclusion are sufficient to reduce vertebrate pest damage. When these do not work, lethal management tools such as trapping or toxicants may be considered. More information on vertebrate pests can be found in Wildlife Pest Control around Gardens and Homes (Salmon et al. 2006) and the UC IPM Pest Notes on specific vertebrate pests in the Pest Notes library, ipm.ucanr.edu/pmg/pestnotes/index.html.

Birds

Many species of birds cause damage in home orchards. Trees that bear soft fruit are particularly vulnerable (fig. 11.73). In addition to injury to ripening fruit, some bird species, such as crown sparrows or house finches, feed on dormant flower buds. It is often difficult to identify the bird species responsible by looking at the damage on fruit and nuts. Identifying the birds while they are causing the damage is the best way to know which species are pests in your orchard.

Figure 11.73. Bird damage on stone fruit.

The most common pests of fruiting trees and vines in California include the crowned sparrow (*Zonotrichia* species), house finch (*Carpodacus mexicanus*), American robin (*Turdus migratorius*), scrub jay (*Aphelocoma coerulescens*), crow (*Corvus brachyrhynchos*), European starling (*Sturnus vulgaris*), and yellow-billed magpie (*Pica nuttalli*). Some bird species found in home orchards are classified as migratory nongame birds and can be removed only after obtaining a depredation permit from US Fish and Wildlife Service or while under the supervision of the local agricultural commissioner. These bird species include crowned sparrows, house finches, American robins, and scrub jays.

Management

Although the initial cost is expensive, bird netting is often the most effective management option available for small orchards and individual trees. Attach ¼ to ½-inch plastic mesh netting to a large frame that covers the tree (fig. 11.74). The frame holds the netting away from the tree and prevents birds' access to the fruit. Monitor and maintain netting to ensure there are no holes in it; birds that find their way through the netting can get tangled and not find their way out. The netting can be pinned using clips at the tree trunk, below the canopy, to eliminate gaps. If covering the whole tree is not possible, individual fruit or branches can be enclosed in net bags.

Frightening devices can be used to scare birds away. However, devices like bird bombs and shell crackers are not generally practical for urban settings. Birds can also become accustomed to these devices. Mylar streamers and balloons with large eyes on

Figure 11.74. Ideally, netting should be attached to a frame so it is held away from the fruit. This large frame is protecting a cherry tree. *Photo:* Jerry Clark.

Figure 11.75. The circular shape of mole mounds distinguishes them from gopher mounds. *Photo:* Roger Baldwin.

Figure 11.76. Gopher mounds are crescent-shaped, with a plug towards the side. *Photo:* Roger Baldwin.

them can help deter birds, but generally these need to be used in conjunction with other management options to be effective. Red and silver streamers may help if you use many of them and place them in the very top of the trees. Wait until fruit becomes attractive to birds. Remove streamers immediately after harvest so birds do not become accustomed to them. Birds rapidly become tolerant of visual repellents.

Pocket gophers

Pocket gophers (*Thomomys* spp.) are burrowing rodents that spend almost all their time below the soil surface. They get their name from their fur-lined cheek pouches, or pockets: This is where they carry food and nesting materials. They use their large front paws to dig tunnels.

Although gophers can be easily distinguished from other rodents, they are rarely seen above ground. As a result, other evidence must be used to detect them.

Look for gopher mounds, the result of gophers pushing loose soil to the surface after they excavate a tunnel. Gopher mounds can be distinguished from mole mounds by shape: Mole mounds are generally circular (fig. 11.75), whereas gopher mounds are crescent-shaped, with a soil plug (fig. 11.76).

Just below the soil line, pocket gophers cause damage by girdling trees. They can also feed on tree roots. Root or crown damage may allow entry of soilborne pathogens, such as *Phytophthora* species, which can cause decline and death of trees. Gophers also gnaw on drip irrigation.

Management

Several options are available for gopher management in home orchards: exclusion, trapping, baiting with toxic baits, and fumigation.

Exclusion fencing can be installed at planting time to help protect trees from gophers digging upward and causing damage. Bury hardware cloth or poultry wire with a ¾-inch mesh at least 2 feet deep around the tree, with an additional 6 inches bent underground at a right angle away from the tree. Above ground, the fence should extend at least 1 foot above the soil surface. In some cases, persistent gophers will burrow below the fencing. Also keep in mind that exclusionary fencing may restrict root growth.

Trapping is a safe and effective management option for gopher control in home orchards. There are several styles of traps available. Some of the most common traps are pincher traps, like the Gophinator, Macabee, and Cinch traps. Choker-style box traps and modified versions like the Black Hole trap are also popular. Research into gopher trapping techniques has shown that the Gophinator is more effective than the Macabee. No attractants or baits are needed for traps. While it is not necessary to cover set traps, a covering may help keep traps away pets and children. Human scent does not affect trap success, so wearing gloves is not necessary, but gloves may help protect your hands if a trap is accidentally triggered.

Place traps in pairs underground in the burrows; face them in opposite directions (fig. 11.77) so that gophers coming from either end of the burrow are intercepted. Choose burrows that have fresh mounds, indicating recent gopher activity. Check traps daily. If a gopher hasn't been caught within a few days, move the traps to a location with a fresh mound.

Various baits are available for gopher management. Registrations for these products change over time; for current information on materials and application, see the UC IPM Pest Note on pocket gophers, in the Pest Notes library at ipm.ucanr.edu/PMG/PESTNOTES/index.html. Gopher baits are applied below ground, and proper placement is extremely important for success. It is vital that bait be placed in active tunnels and not in backfilled tunnels where gophers no longer travel.

Some fumigants are also effective management tools. However, these products are often restricted-use materials and can be used only by or under the direct supervision of a certified applicator. They often cannot be applied if application sites are within 100 feet of a structure. If pocket gophers are causing high levels of damage, consider hiring a pest management professional to manage the outbreak.

Squirrels

Two types of squirrels can be very destructive in home orchards: tree squirrels and ground squirrels. It is easy to distinguish ground squirrels from tree squirrels. Ground squirrels can climb trees but when frightened will run into their extensive burrow systems on the ground; tree squirrels will run up trees, never retreating into burrows on the ground.

Tree squirrels build their nests in tree hollows or high up in tree crotches and eat fruit and nuts on orchard trees. There are four species of tree squirrels in California; eastern fox squirrel (*Sciurus niger*) is the most likely to cause damage in home orchards (fig. 11.78). It is also the only species that can legally be controlled by trapping or hunting without a hunting license or permit. If you plan to use lethal control methods, be sure to identify squirrels to species and check regulations regarding their management.

The most common pest ground squirrel is the California ground squirrel (*Otospermophilus beecheyi*) (fig. 11.79). California ground squirrels consume fruit and nuts and can damage young trees and vines by girdling the bark (fig. 11.80). California ground squirrels create extensive burrow systems, which can

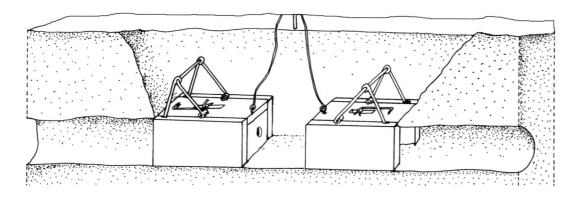

Figure 11.77. Place gopher traps such as these box traps in the burrow facing each other. You do not need to cover the hole.

Figure 11.78. Eastern fox squirrel. *Photo:* Steve E. Lock.

Figure 11.79. California ground squirrel.

Figure 11.80. A California ground squirrel has chewed bark from the crown of this tree. Note also the entry holes to its burrow system.

damage root systems. Fleas that carry bubonic plague are also associated with ground squirrels and their burrows.

Management of tree squirrels

It is extremely difficult to keep tree squirrels out of orchards or backyard fruit and nut trees. Netting an entire tree as you would for birds may keep them out for a while, but persistent tree squirrels will eventually gain access.

Trapping can be used under some circumstances. However, among the tree squirrels, only eastern fox squirrel, when it is causing damage, can be trapped and killed without a license or permit from the California Department of Fish and Wildlife. It is essential that you properly identify the squirrels on your property.

Traps for tree squirrels must be placed along their travel routes—for example, along tree branches or on rooftops (fig. 11.81). Place the traps in a location that nontarget species and pets can't access and carefully secure them with wire, or by other means, so they don't become dislodged. Metal tube or tunnel traps are good choices, but Conibear traps placed inside a cover or box trap can also be used. Prebaiting is recommended for several days before setting the traps. Snap traps are not reliable for squirrel management. Live traps present the problem of having to kill the trapped squirrel because it is illegal to relocate wildlife.

There are no toxic baits that can be legally used to manage tree squirrels. And although shooting is con-

Figure 11.81. A pair of box-type gopher traps have been secured to a tree limb to capture the eastern fox squirrel. Traps cannot be used against other tree squirrel species without a special permit or license.

sidered a good management option, discharging a firearm is illegal in almost all urban municipalities in California. A .22 air rifle can be used if allowed by city ordinances. Remember to consult the California Fish and Game Code for details on squirrel take with a firearm or air rifle. Always consult law enforcement before you consider shooting tree squirrels in a residential area, due to public safety concerns.

Management of California ground squirrels

Tools available for managing California ground squirrels include trapping, baiting, fumigation, and habitat modification. Trapping is the most important tool in backyard situations and can be used effectively any time when California ground squirrels are active (fig. 11.82).

There are several types of traps available for trapping California ground squirrels: Conibear traps,

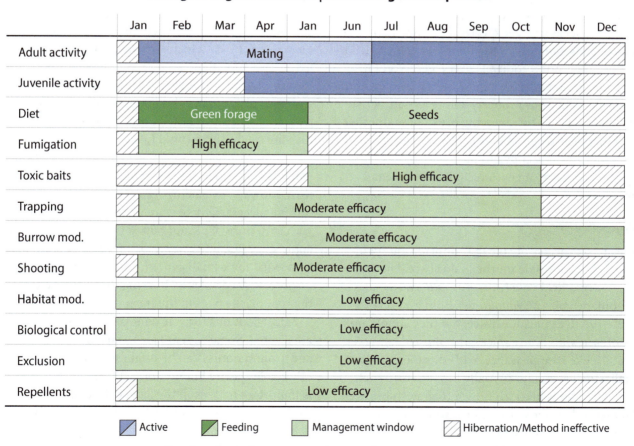

Figure 11.82. Management efforts for ground squirrels can be timed according to this chart. *Source:* Niamh Quinn.

tunnel-type traps, and box traps. Again, be aware that a ground squirrel needs to be euthanized once captured because it is illegal to relocate wildlife. Conibear traps are placed in burrow openings, whereas tunnel and box traps are placed along runways or near the burrows. Traps should be baited with attractive fruit or nuts and not set for a few days to allow the squirrels to become accustomed to the bait. Once set, check the traps daily for catches and properly dispose of killed animals.

Anticoagulant rodenticide options for residential use are no longer available. If you have old products containing anticoagulant ingredients, you should take them to your local household hazardous waste facility to be disposed of safely. Toxic grain baits containing the active ingredient zinc phosphide can only be applied by licensed pest management professionals and are not available for use by residential users for ground squirrel management. Rodenticide products labelled for use against rats and house mice should never be used for the management of ground squirrels unless ground squirrels are specifically listed on the label as a target species. For information on available baits and how to use them, see the UC IPM Pest Note on ground squirrels in the Pest Notes library, ipm.ucanr.edu/PMG/PESTNOTES/index.html.

You can make your property a little less attractive to ground squirrels by removing brush piles or other debris that provide good hiding places. Also, ground squirrels like to reoccupy old burrows, so deep-ripping old burrows to a depth of 20 inches can stall reinvasions.

Voles

There are six species of vole in California, but two species are responsible for the majority of damage: the California field vole (*Microtus californicus*) and the montane vole (*M. montanus*). Sometimes voles are referred to as meadow mice, but they should not be confused with house mice (*Mus musculus*). Voles are mouselike in appearance, with short legs, a short-fur tail, small eyes, and partially hidden ears. Their long, coarse fur is blackish brown to grayish brown.

Well-traveled, aboveground runways are a clear indicator of vole presence in a home orchard. These runways, approximately 1½ to 2 inches in diameter, connect to vole burrow openings. Voles generally build their burrows where there is a good growth of herbaceous plants. Grass or other ground cover usually hides the runways, protecting the voles from predation. If you have difficulty locating runways and burrows, try looking into and pulling back long grass or other ground cover. Voles often leave evidence of feeding in their runways and at the entrances of their burrows, and you may also find their droppings, which are greenish when fresh and brown or gray when old.

Voles gnaw the bark of many fruit and nut trees in home orchards. Damage to tree trunks normally occurs from a few inches above ground to a few inches below ground. Voles are poor climbers; however, if they manage to climb onto low-hanging branches, they may also cause damage higher in the tree.

Management

Unlike gophers and squirrels, voles can be discouraged from establishing large populations in a home orchard by habitat modifications. Voles like dense vegetative cover. Removing weeds, mulch, and other unnecessary vegetation helps protect trees from damage. Wire fences can also help to exclude voles. They must rise at least 12 inches above ground and be buried at least 6 to 10 inches below ground. Keeping areas around the fences weed-free can also help discourage voles. Small cylinder fences placed around tree trunks (trunk guards) protect young trees while they are establishing (fig. 11.83).

Trapping can be an effective management option when vole numbers are low. Voles seldom stray from their runways, so placing traps on the runways is crucial for success. Simple wooden mouse traps, baited with a mixture of peanut butter and oatmeal or with apple slices, are effective. A dozen or more traps may be needed for a small garden. Check traps daily and dispose of dead voles by burying them or placing them in plastic bags in the trash.

Baiting options for vole control in home orchards are limited. Some rodenticides available for use in and around homes can be used for montane voles or other vole species but not for California field voles. It is important to consult the label before purchase because there are many restrictions on the use of rodenticides. More information on baiting is available in the *UC IPM* Pest Note on voles, in the Pest Notes library at ipm.ucanr.edu/PMG/PESTNOTES/index.html.

Figure 11.83. This tree has a trunk guard to protect it from vole injury. Vole burrows can be seen in the foreground.

Fumigation is not generally suitable for the control of field voles because their burrows are too shallow.

Rats

There are several species of rat in California, but the roof rat (*Rattus rattus*) is the most injurious to home orchards. The roof rat causes damage to many fruit and nut trees and is a particular problem on citrus and avocado.

Roof rats, also referred to as black rats or ship rats, have sleek and agile bodies with a pointed muzzle and relatively large ears. The tail is longer than the head and body combined. They can be confused with the larger, more robust Norway rat (*Rattus norvegicus*), but the Norway rat has relatively small ears and a tail that is never longer than the head and body combined.

Although roof rats generally cause damage above ground, taking large bites out of fruit and nuts (fig. 11.84), they have been known to burrow at the base of trees. Multiple burrows can eventually compromise the root system, and the tree can fall over (fig. 11.85).

Figure 11.84. Roof rat damage to macadamia nuts. *Photo: Niamh Quinn.*

Figure 11.85. Roof rat burrows at the base of an almond tree. These burrows can cause the roots to become compromised, at which point the tree could fall over. *Photo: Niamh Quinn.*

Management

Limiting food, water, and shelter is critical for successful roof rat control. Harvest all fruit from the tree when it is ripe, remove fruit that has fallen to the ground, and monitor your property for other food sources for rats, such as poorly sealed garbage containers. Roof rats like to nest in thick bushes near structures or in dense vines around trees or fences. Thinning such vegetation and sealing attics and other off-the-ground nesting areas limit the roof rats' ability to hide and breed. If you make your backyard less hospitable to roof rats, you will have fewer of them. Other management tools, such as trapping and baits, will be less effective if food sources and nesting areas remain.

Trapping can reduce roof rat populations but is often difficult in orchards. The traps must be placed on the top of and also along the bottom edge of walls and fences in secluded areas. They can also be secured in branches of trees. A dozen or more traps placed 10 to 20 feet apart may be necessary for a heavily infested backyard and home. Snap traps are commonly used for roof rats. Glue boards are indiscriminate traps and should not be used outside. As you place traps, it is important to be mindful of nontarget species and pets.

Almost all toxic baits that are registered for roof rat control are available to use only for the control of roof rats associated with structures. Some rodenticides can be used when there is an attractive nuisance, such as a fruit or a nut tree, augmenting populations. All second-generation anticoagulants for roof rat control are restricted-use materials and can be bought and used only by a certified professional for the control of rats that cause damage to structures. All baits used for the control of roof rats must be in a tamper-proof bait station and cannot be placed more than a prescribed distance from a structure. Consult the label before application or contact your local agricultural commissioner's office or UC Cooperative Extension office. Consider hiring a licensed pest control professional if you need to control roof rats; professionals have access to more rodenticides and will be familiar with procedures to protect wildlife and pets.

Deer

Deer can be extremely destructive to young trees in a home orchard. Mule deer, *Odocoileus hemionus,* and black-tailed deer, *O. hemionus columbianus,* are the two most common subspecies in California. Deer consume a wide variety of vegetation, including fruit, nuts, vines, and the tender leaves and shoots of trees (fig. 11.86). They can also trample young trees before the trees establish and can damage older trees by rubbing their antlers on the trunks and larger limbs. Deer browsing generally occurs about 2 feet or more above the ground. Damage caused by rabbits is similar but occurs mostly at ground level. Since deer do not have upper incisors, they must twist and pull branches off. Rabbits remove twigs using their incisors, which results in a clean break at a 45-degree angle.

Deer are often elusive, and since the majority of damage occurs in the early morning or late evening, their presence is often undetected. If you suspect deer damage, examine the orchard for their distinct footprints and feces.

Management

Exclusion is the best management option. A 7- or 8-foot fence is recommended (fig. 11.87). Often deer will not jump a 6-foot fence, but in the Sierra Nevada mountain areas, where deer are often larger, a slightly higher fence may be necessary. On sloping ground, the fence should be 10 to 11 feet high to ensure that deer jumping downslope cannot clear the fence.

Fencing is expensive and often not practical for small orchards. Plant protectors are an alternative for protecting young and establishing trees. Surround each tree with woven wire or strong plastic netting attached to stakes driven into the ground or use

Figure 11.86. Young avocado shoots chewed by mule deer. *Photo:* David Rosen.

Figure 11.87. Small-mesh wire deer fence. *Photo:* W. Paul Gorenzel.

ready-made products. Once branches are 5 to 7 feet off the ground, they are generally out of a deer's reach and protectors can be removed. Keep trees tall and pruned so deer can't reach fruit.

Deer-repellent products applied to leaves or trees are intended to deter deer with their foul taste or smell. They may have some temporary effect, but research has not shown any reliable or long-lasting impact. Some products may be damaging to plants, so test the product on a few leaves before treating a whole tree.

Rabbits

Rabbits can damage fruit and nut trees. They are a particular problem in home orchards adjacent to wilderness areas and uncultivated lands, which provide shelter during daylight hours. Although there are many rabbit species in California, only three are known to be pests of home orchards: the black-tailed jackrabbit (*Lepus californicus*), the desert cottontail (*Sylvilagus audubonii*), and the brush rabbit (*S. bachmani*). Jackrabbits are the largest and, because of their size and abundance, are considered the most damaging.

Young trees with smooth, thin bark are particularly vulnerable to rabbit damage. Gnawing can remove a ring of outer and inner bark, completely girdling a tree. Rabbits may also clip the terminal shoot and lateral branches from very young trees.

Management

Fencing, using chicken wire and light stakes, is a good, economical long-term management option. The fence should be 2 to 4 feet tall, depending on the rabbit species. Cottontails and brush rabbits are not likely to jump a 2-foot fence, but to ensure that they can't enter the orchard, the height can be increased to 3 feet. To exclude all rabbit species, use a 4-foot fence. Bury the chicken wire 6 to 10 inches below ground and bend the edge out at a 90-degree angle to deter rabbits from burrowing underneath. If the whole orchard can't be fenced, individual trees can be protected using trunk guards fashioned from chicken wire.

Occasionally rabbits, and other animals, chew on irrigation lines. To avoid damage, cover the lines or bury them.

References

Cohen, S., M. L. Flint, and N. Hines. 2009. Lawn and residential landscape pest control: A guide for maintenance gardeners. Oakland: UC Agriculture and Natural Resources Publication 3510.

Flint, M. L., and S. H. Dreistadt. 1998. Natural enemies handbook: The illustrated guide to biological control. Oakland: UC Agriculture and Natural Resources Publication 3386.

Salmon, T. P., D. A. Whisson, and R. E. Marsh. 2006. Wildlife pest control around gardens and homes. 2nd ed. Oakland: UC Agriculture and Natural Resources Publication 21385.

Strand, L. L. 1999. Integrated pest management for stone fruits. Oakland: UC Agriculture and Natural Resources Publication 3389.

Further reading

Baldwin, R. A., A. Chapman, C. P. Kofron, R. Meinerz, S. B. Orloff, and N. Quinn. 2015. Refinement of a trapping method increases its utility for pocket gopher management. Crop Protection 77:176–180. https://doi.org/10.1016/j.cropro.2015.08.003

Baldwin, R. A., D. B. Marcum, S. B. Orloff, S. J. Vasquez, C. A. Wilen, and R. M. Engeman. 2013. The influence of trap type and cover status on capture rates of pocket gophers in California. Crop Protection 46:7–12. https://doi.org/10.1016/j.cropro.2012.12.018

Baldwin, R. A., R. Meinerz, and S. B. Orloff. 2014. The impact of attractants on pocket gopher trapping. Current Zoology 60(4):472–478. https://doi.org/10.1093/czoolo/60.4.472

Flint, M. L. 2018. Pests of the garden and small farm: A grower's guide to using less pesticide. 3rd ed. Davis: UC Agriculture and Natural Resources Publication 3332.

Ingels, C. A., P. M. Geisel, and M. V. Norton, tech. eds. 2007. The home orchard. Oakland: UC Agriculture and Natural Resources Publication 3485.

Ohlendorf, B. O. 1999. Integrated pest management for apples and pears. 2nd ed. Oakland: UC Agriculture and Natural Resources Publication 3340.

Strand, L. L. 2003. Integrated pest management for walnuts. 3rd ed. Oakland: UC Agriculture and Natural Resources Publication 3270.

Strand, L. L., and B. O. Ohlendorf. 2002. Integrated pest management for almonds. 2nd ed. Oakland: UC Agriculture and Natural Resources Publication 3308.

Whithaus, S. M., and L. E. Blecker, eds. 2016. The safe and effective use of pesticides. 3rd ed. Davis: UC Agriculture and Natural Resources Publication 3324.

Note: All photos by Jack Kelly Clark unless otherwise indicated.

Chapter 12

Failure to bear and physiological disorders

Chuck Ingels and Maxwell Norton

ruit and nut trees normally begin to bear fruit 2 to 5 years after planting, depending on the species, tree vigor, and the method of training and pruning. Most stone fruit and almond trees begin to bear in 2 or 3 years, although cherries and apricots may not begin bearing for up to 4 years after planting. Apples often begin to bear in 2 to 4 years, while pears can take 1 to 2 years longer. Walnuts and pecans may take up to 5 years to begin bearing.

Fruit set and retention are not only a function of tree age, species vigor, training, and pruning. Fruit set and retention in most species require pollination as well as adequate sunlight, irrigation, drainage, and fertilization. Certain diseases can also affect fruit set and retention (see chapter 11, "Integrated pest management for backyard orchards"). Some rootstocks can also affect when trees begin to bear, mainly because of their effects on vigor (see chapter 3, "Varieties"). For example, Betulafolia rootstock usually imparts more vigorous growth and later bearing than do other pear rootstocks, whereas Gisela rootstock usually imparts less vigor and earlier bearing than do other cherry rootstocks.

If a tree is properly pruned, free of disease, sufficiently irrigated and fertilized, and receives adequate sunlight—and still fails to form flowers or fruit after several years—consider topworking (grafting) a different variety onto the tree (see chapter 8, "Budding and grafting") or replacing the tree entirely.

Normal flower and fruit drop

Over the course of the growing season, it is common for all fruit trees to shed some flowers or fruit. Trees generally produce more flowers than they can maintain. Natural loss of some flowers and fruit is a normal part of tree growth and development and should not be cause for concern unless it results in few fruit or nuts being left on the tree. Some species shed many fruit in what is known as spring or June drop, which in California usually occurs in April and May.

Diagnosing failure to bear

When diagnosing the cause of a tree bearing few or no fruit, note whether the tree does not bloom at all, blooms but does not set fruit, or blooms and sets fruit that fall off before harvest. Listed below are common causes for poor fruit production. For more information on the causes listed below, see the appropriate sections in this chapter or other relevant chapters.

- The tree does not bloom.
  - Tree is too young.
  - Pruning is excessive or done improperly.
  - Excessive nitrogen or other fertilization has led to vegetative growth without bloom.
  - Low carbohydrate reserves provide insufficient energy to bloom.
  - The tree lacks sunlight.
  - Winter chilling was insufficient.
  - The tree variety bears in alternate years.
  - The tree has been damaged by incorrectly or improperly mixed, applied, or timed pesticide applications, such as may occur with dormant oil or lime sulfur spray.
  - Diseases such as shothole disease or bacterial blast have kill dormant buds.
- The tree blooms but does not set fruit.
  - Pollination has not occurred because of a lack of pollinators (there is a lack of bees—or the weather was too cold, wet, or windy for bees).

- No pollinizer variety is planted nearby.
- The tree has suffered frost damage.
- The tree lacks sunlight.
- The tree suffers from nutrient deficiencies.
- Winter chilling was insufficient.
- Heat was excessive during bloom.

• Most or all fruit falls from the tree:
- Pollination was inadequate.
- It's an off year in alternate-bearing cycle.
- Winter chilling was insufficient.
- The tree has suffered frost damage.
- Water is either excessive or insufficient.
- The tree's roots are constricted by hardpan or compacted soil.

Effects of plant environment on fruit retention

Planting site

Fruit trees should be planted where they will receive at least 6 to 8 hours of direct sunlight per day. This amount of sunlight allows the tree to produce enough carbohydrates through photosynthesis to support the growth and development of fruit (see chapter 2, "Growth and development"). If a tree does not receive enough sunlight, it may not produce buds, flowers, or fruit. Over time, if surrounding vegetation casts too much shade on a fruit tree, the vegetation may need to be trimmed or pruned. Poor fruit color, fruit size, or sugar levels may indicate that the tree receives insufficient light.

Adequate sunlight is needed for flower differentiation and fruit yield. Fruit trees do best in full sun, although some species—such as cherries and Asian pears—may benefit from afternoon shade in the hottest climates. Avoid planting trees where shade from a house or other trees will limit light exposure and limit fruit set during the growing season.

Pruning

Excessive or improper pruning can reduce a fruit tree's number of flower buds and encourage vegetative growth that shades the fruiting wood. Most fruit

and nut trees form flowers on spurs, or short branches—although peaches, nectarines, figs, persimmons, and some walnuts bloom on longer branches. When pruning, leave many of the 1-year-old spurs and shoots. Also, provide adequate light to these fruiting shoots by thinning out crowded growth. This process may include summer pruning (see chapter 7, "Training and pruning").

Some fruit trees are late to begin bearing. Species with vigorous, upright growth, such as cherry and pear trees, tend to begin bearing later in life than those with a spreading growth habit, such as peach and apricot. These trees can be encouraged to bear earlier, however, if vertical branches are bent outward during the growing season (before they become too stiff to bend). To hold a bent branch in place, tie it to a stake or to a string attached to a brick or stone on the ground, or to a trellis (espalier). Avoid making excessive heading cuts on these vigorous trees, especially during the dormant season, because heading encourages growth and reduces the development of flowers. Bending unheaded, upright branches outward to about a 45- to 60-degree angle is a proven method for quickly developing spurs and flowers.

Winter chilling

Most fruit trees need a certain amount of cold temperature for their dormancy to end and for spring growth to be promoted. In the desert areas of Southern California, there may be only 250 to 300 chill hours in the winter, so many stone fruit and pome fruit do not perform well. It is crucial in these areas to select low-chill varieties for good fruit production. After a mild winter, flowering and spring growth are delayed and irregular, the flowering period is extended, and fruit set is reduced. The extended bloom period increases the chance that inclement weather will lead to blossom diseases such as brown rot or fire blight. (For detailed information on chilling hours, see chapter 1, "Climate and soils," and chapter 3, "Varieties").

Frost

During or shortly after bloom, frost—in other words, cold injury—can cause young flowers, fruit, or nuts to be injured or killed, and abort. This can occur even if no frost damage is visible. When a heavy frost is expected, covering trees with plastic or bed sheets may prevent or at least reduce injury to the expanding buds or blossoms, as long as temperatures do not fall too low for too long. Adding a heat lamp under the cover, or large old-fashioned Christmas tree lights that produce heat, helps protect flowers and fruit from even the more severe frosts.

Pollination and weather

Pollination is critical for fruit trees. Generally, trees are primarily self-pollinated or cross-pollinated. Pollination, particularly cross-pollination, is either assisted by insects (or other living things) or the wind. Most nuts (walnut, pistachio, chestnut, pecan, and filbert) and olives are wind pollinated. Many temperate fruit are insect pollinated, primarily by bees, whose presence is absolutely necessary for good fruit set. Some fruit and nut trees have separate male and female flowers, but their bloom times do not always overlap; others have perfect flowers, but the pollen is not compatible for self-fertilization. Thus, cross-pollination is essential to good fruit set in these trees. To set a good crop, it may be necessary to grow more than one tree of a particular fruit or nut, and to plant more than one cultivar. On the other hand, a few deciduous fruit trees are self-fertile, eliminating the need for more than one tree. Please see chapter 3, "Varieties"—or, in the second edition of the *California Master Gardener Handbook*, chapter 16, "Temperate tree fruit and nut crops."

Inclement weather is often a significant factor in the fruit production of early-flowering species such as almond and plum. Cold or wet weather conditions prevent the growth of pollen tubes in the female parts of the flower. Also, rain, wind, and cold temperatures can disrupt pollination by limiting the activity of bees and other pollinator insects and by washing pollen off the flowers. Unseasonably warm temperatures may also reduce pollination, especially in cherries.

Diseases

Certain diseases can reduce fruit retention and yield or weaken a tree's health; others directly affect the flowers or fruit. Blossom diseases, such as brown rot and bacterial blast, can be especially damaging on stone fruit during wet springs. Soilborne nematodes, root crown diseases, or crown gall may weaken trees and reduce growth and yields (see chapter 11, "Integrated pest management for backyard orchards").

Irrigation and soil water

Excess or insufficient water can impact flowering, fruit set, and quality. Too much water (from rain or irrigation) and poor drainage can create anaerobic conditions in the soil, reducing root growth and function. A lack of water during the summer also reduces shoot and leaf surface area, along with photosynthesis and resulting root growth and function, leading to reduced fruit numbers, size, and quality. In either of these conditions, leaves usually droop (with drought) or become chlorotic (with poor drainage), and fruit size usually decreases. Root constrictions caused by hardpan, heavy clay soil, or compacted soil can cause trees to have limited root systems and thus become stressed, which can also lead to fruit drop.

Alternate bearing

Fruit trees may bear heavily in 1 year and sparsely the next. This is known as alternate or biennial bearing. The spring-flowering buds of most deciduous fruit trees form during the previous year's spring and summer. Excess fruit load depletes the nutrients needed to form new fruit buds. Some species are more prone to alternate bearing than others. For example, alternate bearing is relatively common in apples and mandarins but less so in plums. Among the nut crops, pistachio is notorious for alternate bearing.

Alternate bearing can usually be reduced by thinning fruit early (shortly after petal fall). Alternate bearing can also be reduced by pruning heavily during a year when the tree has produced a large number of fruit. This encourages the tree to form more flower buds for the next year (see chapter 9, "Fruit thinning"). Trees can also be pruned more heavily in the dormant season prior to an anticipated heavy crop year; selectively removing fruiting wood in this way will reduce alternate bearing. On the other hand, trees can be pruned less heavily before an anticipated light crop.

Figure 12.1. During ripening, cherries may crack if they get wet from rain or irrigation. *Photo:* Jack Kelly Clark.

Figure 12.2. As fruit grow, they may split from an injury or sunburn, but splitting is often caused or exacerbated by improper irrigation. *Photo:* Jack Kelly Clark.

Figure 12.3. Fruit spurring (upper left) and doubling (center) of cherries. *Photo:* Joe Grant.

Physiological disorders

Splitting and cracking of cherries

As cherries ripen, accumulate sugar, and begin to color, they become susceptible to cracking or splitting if they get wet from rain or sprinklers (fig. 12.1). Do not allow sprinklers to wet the foliage. If rain is forecast just before harvest and you have a fairly small or espaliered tree, you can reduce cracking by covering the top of the tree with plastic to keep most of the fruit dry. Remove the plastic as soon as the threat passes.

Splitting and cracking of other fruit

Anything that damages the skin while the fruit is still small will cause the skin to crack or split as the fruit enlarges (fig. 12.2). Sunburn, limb rub, and powdery mildew are a few of the possible causes. Dried plums (prunes and sugar plums) may split on the side or bottom. Side cracking in dried plums occurs approximately during the first 2 weeks in July and is caused by a combination of fruit exposure to direct sunlight and change in fruit size caused by daily fluctuations in moisture. Cool weather at that time will increase the number of side cracks and large fruit will crack more. End cracking in dried plums is caused by moisture stress followed by a heavy irrigation. End cracks can be reduced by making sure trees have uniform, ample moisture in May and June.

Doubling and spurring of cherries

When two fruit are attached at the base or on the side, they are often called doubles (fig. 12.3). A fruit with a partially developed fruit attached to its side is called a spur (see fig. 12.3). Both disorders are caused by high temperatures the previous summer, during the period when the fruit buds began to develop. Doubles and spurs are worse some years than others, and there are differences in severity among varieties. There is nothing you can do about this deformity.

Split pit of peaches and nectarines

Most stone fruit grow in three stages. In stage 1, most of the cell division takes place; in stage 2, the pit begins to harden; and in stage 3, rapid cell enlargement occurs. Excessive soil moisture and rapid fruit growth during stage 2 can cause the pit to split in peaches and nectarines (fig. 12.4). You can determine when this period occurs by cutting a few fruit each week in late spring or early summer and noticing when the pits just begin to harden. Cutting back irrigation at this time may reduce pit splitting. A few cultivars, such as Fairtime peach, are notorious for split pits.

Pit burn of apricot

In California's Central Valley and southern inland valleys, high temperatures during the last month before harvest can cause the flesh next to the apricot pit to become dark and watery due to internal breakdown. This is referred to as pit burn (fig. 12.5). If pit burn occurs early enough, the whole fruit will begin to rot inside. Ensuring that the tree has adequate moisture during this period may reduce pit burn in some cases. Varieties vary in their susceptibility. Blenheim, Wenatchee, Autumn Royal, and Moorpark are most susceptible. Modesto, Patterson, Westley, Castlebright, Katy, Improved Flaming Gold, Helena, Tri Gem, Goldbar, Poppy, Lorna, Robada, Tilton, and Patterson tend to resist pit burning.

Fog spot of apricot

In years when apricot fruit get wet during cool, damp weather, a condition called fog spot may appear as small, reddish spots on the upper surface of the fruit (fig. 12.6). The spots enlarge and darken and may grow together to create a large scab. The center of each spot may turn dark brown while the margins remain reddish. The persistent red color on the edges of the spots and the lack of spots on the leaves distinguish fog spot from shothole disease. As fruit mature, the spots become scablike and may flake off, leaving roughened areas beneath. The cause of fog spot is not known, but a fungal pathogen is suspected.

Bitter pit of apple

Bitter pit is characterized by small, water-soaked spots on the skin of the apple that begin to appear soon after fruit are harvested (fig. 12.7). These spots gradually turn a deeper color than the surrounding fruit surface and later turn brown, while the tissue directly underneath the spots dies. Individual spots are 2 to 10 millimeters in diameter. The dying tissue underneath may look like a tiny bruise. The spots be-

Figure 12.4. Excessive soil moisture during pit hardening can cause peach and nectarine pits to split. *Photo:* Jack Kelly Clark.

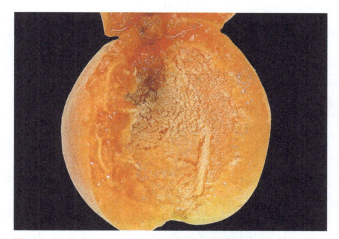

Figure 12.5. Apricot pit burn is caused by excessive heat shortly before harvest. *Photo:* Bill Coates.

Figure 12.6. Fog spot of apricot appears as small, reddish spots (left), which later turn scabby (right). *Photos:* Maxwell Norton.

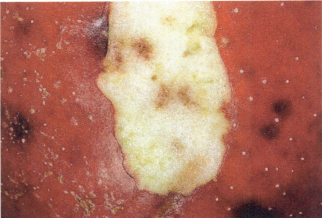

Figure 12.7. Bitter pit of apple is caused by calcium deficiency. *Photos:* Jack Kelly Clark.

come sunken and the tissue below becomes spongy. Vigorously growing trees, trees that were heavily pruned the prior winter, and trees with high nitrogen levels are more prone to bitter pit than others. Fruit that is overripe at harvest may also develop more symptoms. Foliar sprays with calcium applied in June and July may reduce symptoms. Use only calcium that is formulated for foliar sprays. Calcium applied to the soil will not help. Reducing nitrogen applications often helps.

Fruit sunburn

Although fruit trees thrive in full sun, any fruit will sunburn if it is suddenly exposed to hot afternoon sun, as can happen after summer pruning, or if shoot growth is stunted and the fruit are exposed to direct sunlight most of the day (fig. 12.8). Pruning for a rigid framework will stabilize fruit positions in the canopy (see chapter 7, "Training and pruning"). Susceptibility to fruit sunburn is greatest in trees in hot inland and desert climates, those with a sparse canopy, and trees that become water-stressed from root diseases or soil compaction.

Lack of fruit sweetness

Low sugar content in fruit may be caused by several factors, including poorly adapted varieties, warm night temperatures (leading to increased respiration), and excessive crop load, vigor, or nitrogen. Thin the fruit enough to allow the tree to sustain and mature the crop through harvest. This may mean eliminating more than half of the tree's fruit early in the spring while they are still quite small (see chapter 9, "Fruit

thinning"). Trees that were stunted much of the year may have too few leaves to support the fruit load or sweeten the fruit. Make sure the tree is adequately irrigated (but not overirrigated) throughout the spring. Make sure trees have enough sunshine.

Blank and nonsplit nuts in pistachio

Blank nuts occur when there is poor pollination or fertilization. Pollination may induce fruit set but the failed fertilization prevents embryo development and no kernel is produced. There is evidence that boron deficiency contributes to this disorder. Sometimes the kernel will start to develop but never finish enlarging. This may be due to insufficient irrigation in spring and early summer.

Figure 12.8. Fruit are exposed to hot afternoon sun if insufficient foliage is present, as is the case with this peach. Apples are particularly susceptible. *Photo:* Jack Kelly Clark.

Pistachios have a strong tendency for alternate or biennial bearing, and blanks can be more common in the "off" year. This may be related to the low carbohydrate reserves in the tree.

Fall bloom

Occasionally, a tree that became drought-stressed during late summer or early fall may begin to bloom after it is then deeply watered. Under normal circumstances, flower buds for the following year are initiated mainly in the summer through the action of plant hormones (see chapter 2, "Growth and development"). Sometimes, however, some of the buds may be sufficiently developed to have all of their flower parts but are not far enough along to have developed the hormonal inhibition that would have kept them from blooming until they had gone through a winter. Deep late-summer watering after late-summer drought may stimulate a portion of these flower buds to grow. Late-summer applications of nitrogen fertilizer may exacerbate the problem. While this is not harmful to tree health, it will use up many of the flower buds that have developed during the current year, and thereby reduce the crop the following spring. A fall bloom does not result in fruit or nut production.

References

Bradley, L. and M. Maurer. 2002. Deciduous fruit & nuts for the low desert. University of Arizona Cooperative Extension. https://extension.arizona.edu/sites/extension.arizona.edu/files/pubs/az1269.pdf

Costello, L. R., E. J. Perry, N. P. Matheny, J. M. Henry, and P. M. Geisel. 2003. Abiotic disorders of landscape plants. Oakland: UC Agriculture and Natural Resources Publication 3420.

Vossen, P., and D. Silva. 2002. Temperate tree fruit and nut crops. Pages 449–530 in D. Pittenger, ed., California master gardener handbook. Oakland: UC Agriculture and Natural Resources Publication 3382. https://anrcatalog.ucanr.edu/Details.aspx?itemNo=3420

Yao, S. 2010. Why fruit trees fail to bear. Guide H-308. Las Cruces: New Mexico State University Cooperative Extension. https://pubs.nmsu.edu/_h/H308/index.html

Appendix

Appendix A. General schedule of cutural practices for home fruit trees*

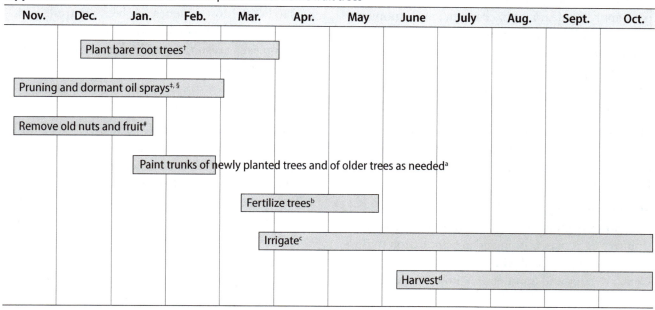

Nov.	Dec.	Jan.	Feb.	Mar.	Apr.	May	June	July	Aug.	Sept.	Oct.

Plant bare root trees[†]

Pruning and dormant oil sprays[‡, §]

Remove old nuts and fruit[#]

Paint trunks of newly planted trees and of older trees as needed[a]

Fertilize trees[b]

Irrigate[c]

Harvest[d]

*Specific timing and additional practices will vary by tree species and location.

[†]Plant bare root trees during the dormant season, which will vary by location in California.

[‡]Prune out any dead, diseased, or broken branches. Pruning cuts, timing, and amounts will vary with tree species.

[§]If scale insects were a problem in the previous season, apply an oil spray in the dormant or delayed dormant period. This spray may also reduce overwintering aphid eggs.

[#]Remove and destroy all old husks, fruit, and nuts on the ground and on tree branches to reduce future pest problems.

[a]In hot regions, paint the trunks and lower branches of young trees that are exposed to afternoon sun with a 1:1 mixture of white latex paint and water to prevent sunburn injury and thus reduce borer infestation.

[b]Fertilize trees with nitrogen around bloom time. The application may be split for sandy soils, with half around bloom time and the other half about a month later. An additional fertilizer application is possible in fall.

[c]Irrigate according to climate and season. See chapter 5, "Irrigation," for details. Provide enough water to wet the soil to a depth of 18–24 in depending upon soil type and environmental conditions. Do not keep tree trunks wet.

[d]See chapter 10, "Harvesting fruit and nuts," for more detail.

Additional notes for various crops

Apricot

Brown rot: Occurrence of brown rot will be affected by weather. Prune out infected blooms if observed. If brown rot is a serious problem on fruit, or if there is excessive rainfall during bloom, spray with a fungi-cide as flowers start to open. If weather is rainy, one to three applications may be required.

Shothole fungus: If shothole fungus has been a prob-lem during the growing season, apply a copper fungi-cide during or just after leaf fall but before the onset of winter rains. This application also helps control peach leaf curl. Avoid the use of sulfur on apricots.

Harvest: Harvest fruit when ripe. Some varieties are harvested over a period of weeks while others ripen at one time. Clean up fallen fruit immediately to minimize brown rot and infestations of dried fruit beetles. Store fully ripe fruit under refrigeration or sun-dry, can, or freeze.

Cherry

Brown rot: If brown rot has been a problem in the past, apply Bordeaux or fixed copper at the popcorn stage of bud development (when the unopened flower buds have matured and the petal color is discernible, so they resemble partially popped corn kernels). Apply again at the full-bloom stage if high moisture conditions exist.

Spotted wing drosophila: If maggots have been a problem, start monitoring and initiate sprays or cover trees when fruit begins to change color from yellow to pink.

Summer pruning: Possibly remove the strong, vigorous shoots from the interior portion of the canopy to improve light penetration and air circulation in the tree's interior. Proceed with caution or omit in the Central Valley and Southern California, since additional pruning may lead to sunburn of wood.

Cover trees with netting in summer: Netting will help protect the fruit from birds.

Harvest: Harvest cherries when fully ripe and avoid damaging the fruit spurs as the fruit are picked. Keep the stems attached to the cherries to keep tearing of the flesh to a minimum. Cherries may be stored for several days under refrigeration. They may be sun-dried, canned, or frozen for longer storage.

Fig

Caprification: On Smyrna type figs, caprification is done during May. Two to four caprifigs are placed in a brown lunch sack with a small hole in the bottom of the bag. The bag is then placed out in the tree and replaced weekly with fresh caprifigs during the pollination period. Caprifigs are not easily located unless there is a tree growing nearby. If grown in the same

yard, overcaprification (or overpollination) may occur and the fruit will be overly seedy.

Pruning: Figs are usually pruned in winter, but they can also be summer-pruned. Remove broken, drooping, crossed, or diseased limbs, and thin out shoots in summer pruning. Once figs have a strong framework, little pruning is necessary on large trees.

Harvest: Figs must be fully tree-ripened before picking. If picked immature, they will not ripen further after harvest. The fruit are ready to harvest when they become somewhat soft and the neck of the fruit begins to bend. Most varieties can be eaten fresh, pickled, or sun-dried. Some varieties may have more than one crop each season, depending upon the degree and time of pruning.

Peach and nectarine

Peach leaf curl and shothole control: In wet spring areas (central and Northern California), spray copper fungicide twice, with the first application in late November or early December (just after the leaves have fallen) and the second about February 1–15. The latter spray should coincide with bud swell but should occur before the flowers open.

Prevent brown rot: Prune out infected blooms if observed. If brown rot is a serious problem on fruit, or if there is excessive rainfall during bloom, spray with a copper fungicide as flowers show pink color but have not yet opened. One to three applications may be required.

Fruit thinning: Thin fruit to about 6 inches apart when they are about an inch in diameter.

Scaffold support: To prevent limb breakage from heavy fruit loads, rope scaffold branches of open-center trees loosely with cotton fiber rope. As the weight of the fruit pulls the scaffold branches down, the rope will tighten and provide adequate support. Alternatively, prop up heavy limbs in summer to prevent breakage.

Summer pruning: Possibly remove the strong, vigorous shoots from the interior portion of the canopy to improve light penetration and air circulation in the tree's interior. Proceed with caution or omit in the Central Valley and Southern California, since additional pruning may lead to sunburn of wood. Generally, two summer prunings will be required for those fruit trees being trained to fruit bushes. See chapter 7, "Training and pruning," for details.

Harvest: Harvest fruit as soon as it is firm-ripe. Clean up fallen fruit immediately to minimize brown rot and infestations of dried fruit beetles. Store fully ripe fruit under refrigeration or sun-dry, can, or freeze them.

Pecan

Dormant pruning: Prune out any dead, diseased, or broken branches. Mature tree pruning is confined to removing broken or dead branches and crossing limbs for modified central-leader trees. For central-leader trees, remove branches originating from the leader that has a narrow crotch angle, preferably when the branch is young; also remove competing leaders.

Remove old nuts: Remove and destroy nuts left on the tree as well as those on the ground following harvest to reduce future pest problems.

Summer training of young trees: Light summer pruning is helpful during the training phase of young pecans. Promote the development of strong central leader and wide-angled scaffold branches.

Fertilization: Pecan trees are often zinc deficient. Apply chelated or liquid zinc to the foliage in April.

Harvest: Harvest begins as soon as the hulls begin to split and the kernels have filled in the shell. The hulls will begin to loosen from the shell and gradually dry over a period of several weeks. Nuts can be shaken or knocked off the tree with a pole. The hulls should be removed from the nuts as soon as possible after harvest. Wear gloves to avoid staining your hands.

Persimmon

Harvest: Harvest astringent varieties when they are hard but fully colored. They will soften on the tree and improve in quality. Nonastringent persimmons are ready to harvest when they are fully colored, but for best flavor, allow them to soften slightly after harvest. Instead of pulling the fruit from the tree to harvest, clip the fruit stem.

Pistachio

Harvest: To minimize insect damage, harvest nuts as early as possible when mature. Harvest when the skin changes from translucent to opaque or from greenish to a yellowish red color. The hulls will begin to loosen from the shell and gradually dry over a period of several weeks. The shells will begin to crack at the same time. Knock fruit down with a pole. It is best for the fruit drop onto a tarp to prevent contamination from soilborne pathogens.

Plum (including cherry-plum, pluot, plumcot, and prune)

Fruit thinning: Thin fruit to about 4 to 6 inches apart when they are ½ to ¾ inches in diameter.

Summer pruning: Remove the strong, vigorous shoots from the interior portion of the canopy to improve light penetration and air circulation in the tree's interior. Proceed with caution or omit in the Central Valley and Southern California, since additional pruning may lead to sunburn of wood. Two or three summer prunings will be required for fruit trees being trained to fruit bushes.

Plum aphid management: Plum aphids often cause curling of the young leaves in spring but will only require control when 50 percent of the leaves are curled and live aphids are present.

Pome fruit (apple, pear, and quince)

Fire blight management: Prune out infected shoots, making pruning cuts into healthy wood to the next juncture below the dead portion of the branch. Remove and destroy all diseased wood. A spray application of fixed copper every 5 to 7 days during the bloom period may help control the disease but may also cause some russeting of fruit.

Fruit thinning: Thin pome fruit when ¾ to 1 inch in diameter. Thin to one fruit per cluster, and no closer than 6 inches apart. Quince do not typically need to be thinned.

Control codling moth: Control should begin in spring, shortly after petal fall. Spray timing should be based on trapping and degree-day calculations or when "stings" are spotted on fruit, and may be required all season. See UC IPM Pest Note on suggested methods of control. One method of control that doesn't involve spraying is to cut a small hole in the bottom of a brown paper lunch sack and slip the hole over a small developing fruit. Staple the mouth of the bag shut to exclude adult moths.

Pomegranate

Remove fruit mummies: Remove and destroy all split and decayed fruit.

Harvest: Harvest fruit when they develop full color and before they crack. Pomegranates have a long storage life when held in cold storage and at high humidity. They improve in juiciness and flavor. Instead of pulling the fruit from the tree to harvest, clip the fruit stem.

Walnut

Scale control: If scale is a problem, monitor the scale population and treat with narrow-range oil when the crawlers appear. Do not apply oil when temperatures go above 90°F and do not use in trees stressed by drought, heavy scale, or other factors. Irrigate the trees well prior to oil applications.

Harvest: Harvest nuts as early as possible. Shake or pole the trees when the green hulls begin to crack and separate from the shells. Remove the hulls as soon as possible after harvesting and discard them. Wear gloves to avoid staining your hands.

Glossary

abiotic disorder: A disorder or disease that is not caused by a living organism such as fungus or bacterium, but instead has an environmental or physiological cause

acaricide: see *miticide*

advective freeze: A phenomenon that occurs when wind moves a subfreezing air mass into an area, displacing warmer air

adventitious bud: A bud that develops where no buds previously existed, usually sending out vigorous growth from a limb that is wounded or headed; compare with *axillary bud*, *dormant bud*, and *latent bud*

alternate (biennial) bearing: A given tree's habit of producing fruit heavily in 1 year and lightly the following year; can be corrected with proper pruning and fruit thinning

anion: A negatively charged ion (e.g., sulfate, nitrate)

anther: The tip of the stamen (male flower part) that contains the pollen grains

anvil lopper: Pruning tool in which one blade cuts down against a flat surface; compare with *bypass lopper*

apical dominance: Hormonal influence, primarily influenced by gravity, through which a terminal bud suppresses the growth of lateral buds

apical meristem: The tissues at the tip of roots and shoots where cells divide, giving rise to new growth; compare with *vascular cambium*

arborsculpture: A horticultural art form in which the shoots of young trees are trained and grafted together to create tree structures

arthropod: Any member of a large group of invertebrate animals with jointed legs and a segmented body, including insects, spiders, and mites

auxin: A generic term for a group of plant hormones that are active at low concentrations and regulate plant growth and development, particularly cell division, cell elongation, adventitious root initiation, and bud dormancy

axil: see *leaf axil*

axillary bud: A typical bud that grows in a leaf axil; bud may develop into a shoot and sometimes one or more flower clusters, or may become latent; compare with *adventitious bud*, *dormant bud*, and *latent bud*

bacteria: One-celled microscopic organisms that lack chlorophyll and may be parasites on plants or animals; examples include the fire blight pathogen and the beneficial *Bacillus thuringiensis*

bactericide: A pesticide used for control of bacteria and the diseases that they cause

banding: The placement of fertilizer in one or more strips near trees or in a circle under the drip line of the tree

bare-root tree: A tree that is dug from a nursery field and sold with no soil around the roots

bark: Tissues outside the vascular cambium that consist of inner bark (phloem) and outer bark

bark grafting: A technique in which the scion is inserted between the bark and the wood of the stock

bark lifter: A part of a budding knife used to separate the bark from the wood so a bud can be inserted; located on the opposite side of the blade from the cutting edge or included as a separate fold-out element of the same knife

bark slipping: In young shoots or branches used for budding or grafting, the propensity of bark to be easily peeled back; greatest when vegetative growth is most active

basal: Lower portion of a shoot or branch near the point of attachment with another shoot or branch

beneficials: Organisms that provide a benefit to crop production; term is applied especially to natural enemies of pests and to pollinators, such as bees

biological control: The action of parasites, predators, pathogens, or competitors in maintaining another organism's density at a lower population than would occur in their absence

bitter pit: A physiological disorder of apple fruit, associated with low levels of calcium in the fruit tissue

blade: The broad, expanded part of a leaf, also called a lamina, which is attached to the petiole

blast: The sudden death of buds, flowers, or young fruit

blight: Any disease causing sudden, severe leaf damage or general killing of stems or flowers

blind wood: Part of a lower or main limb with no shoots, spurs, or other fruiting branches; head pruning these limbs stimulates growth of axillary, latent, and/or adventitious buds; shoots that grow can be selected to develop new limbs

Bordeaux mixture: A mix of copper and hydrated lime, used for dormant-season spraying to control fungal diseases such as peach leaf curl; the addition of lime enhances the steadfastness of copper on the tree

branch: Any woody extension growing from the trunk or limb of a tree

branch (crotch) angle: The angle formed between the trunk and a main limb or between two branches

branch bark ridge: A thin, crescent-shaped area of raised bark in the branch crotch that marks where the branch wood and trunk wood meet; it is usually darker than the surrounding bark

branch collar: The distinct, enlarged portion of woody tissue formed at the base of a branch where it attaches to the trunk

breba crop: The first of two fig crops produced each year; breba figs begin as enlarged lateral buds that develop in the fall and ripen in early to mid-summer

bud: A plant organ at the base of the leaf axil or the tip of a shoot from which a shoot, flower, or flower cluster develops

bud grafting: Grafting by inserting a single bud (scion) onto a branch of the rootstock; also called budding

bud scales: Thin, papery or leathery structures that cover dormant buds

bud swell: The enlargement of buds before growth starts, signaling the beginning of the growing season

budding: see *bud grafting*

budding rubber: A specialized rubber strip used to hold a recently inserted bud in the bark of a stock

budstick: see *budwood*

budwood: Current-season shoots or 1-year-old branches collected for the purpose of bud grafting

bypass lopper: Pruning tool in which two blades pass each other, like scissors; sometimes called eaglebeak loppers; compare with anvil lopper

caliche: A naturally occurring hardpan cemented by lime (calcium carbonate)

callus: Undifferentiated tissue that forms a protective covering around a wounded plant surface

calyx: The usually green outer whorl of sepals of a flower

cambium: see *vascular cambium*

canker: A localized area of diseased tissue on a stem, often sunken or swollen, and surrounded by healthy tissue

canopy: The leaf-bearing portion of the tree

caprification: Pollination of the flowers of certain figs by the blastophaga wasp, using pollen from the caprifig

carbohydrates: Organic compounds, including sugars, starches, and cellulose, which are produced as a result of photosynthesis

caterpillar: Immature form of butterflies and moths; a type of larva

cation: A positively charged ion (e.g., potassium, iron)

catkin: The pollen-bearing male flower of walnuts, pecans, chestnuts, and filberts

central-leader system: A method of tree training in which the trunk is encouraged to form a central axis with branches distributed laterally around it; used primarily for apples and pears, but also persimmons and pecans

chilling hours: The number of hours of temperature below 45°F (7°C) that accumulate during the dormant season

chilling requirement: The cumulative chilling hours required by fruit or nut trees in order to overcome bud dormancy and provide satisfactory growth and fruit or nut production; the requirement may vary considerably between species and varieties

chip budding: A method of budding in which a section of bud and wood is removed from one branch and inserted onto a branch of another plant on which a similar cut was made

chlorophyll: The green pigment of plant cells that absorbs light energy necessary for photosynthesis

chlorosis: Yellowing of foliage that results from a loss of or deficiency in chlorophyll; can be caused by nutritional deficiency, disease, insufficient light, or other factors

clay: 1) A soil particle less than 0.002 mm in diameter; 2) A textural class of soil that is characterized by an ability to hold relatively large amounts of water and nutrients, but may be poorly drained and difficult to cultivate

cleft grafting: A method of grafting in which the scion is inserted into the split-open stub on a branch of the stock

clingstone: A stone fruit in which the flesh (pulp) clings to the pit; compare with *freestone*

cocoon: A sheath, usually mostly of silk, formed by an insect larva as a chamber for pupation

collar: see *branch collar*

compatibility: 1) Of sex cells, the ability of pollen and egg cells to unite and form a viable embryo; 2) Of grafting, the ability to form a successful, long-lived stock/scion union

compound leaf: A leaf divided into two or more parts, or leaflets, all attached to the stem by a single petiole

control valve: The irrigation valve used for supplying water to plants through pipes and/or drip tubing

controller: see *irrigation controller*

cornicles: The pair of tube-like structures that project backward out of the rear of an aphid's body

crawler: The active first instar of a scale insect

crop load: The relative amount of fruit on a tree

cross-pollination: The transfer of pollen from the anther of one plant to the stigma of another plant

crotch: Junction formed between the trunk and a main limb or between two limbs

crown: The area of a tree where the trunk and large roots join (arborists usually use *crown* to refer to the upper portion of a tree [canopy] or the branches and leaves)

crown rot: Disease of the (root) crown, usually caused by the fungus Phytophthora, in which cambium tissues are killed and the tree becomes stunted or dies

cultivar: Cultivated variety (e.g., 'Fuji' apple) a variety that was developed or discovered and is now maintained under cultivation; in common horticultural usage, *cultivar* is synonymous with *variety*

deciduous: Of trees or shrubs, those that typically drop their leaves at the end of each growing season

devigoration: A decline in the overall growth rate of shoots, caused by any of a number of factors

delayed dormant period: The late dormant period when buds are beginning to swell; this timing is important when spraying for peach leaf curl, aphids (eggs), scale, and some spider mites

dichogomous: Of the male and female flower parts of a plant, maturing at different times and thus preventing self-pollination

dioecious: Of plants, species that have male flowers on one plant and female flowers on another, such as kiwifruit and pistachio; compare with *monoecious*

disease: Any disturbance of a plant that interferes with its normal structure or function, usually caused by a microorganism (e.g., fungus or bacteria)

dormancy: A state of inactivity or prolonged rest, such as that of deciduous fruit trees in winter

dormant bud: Of a bud on a 1-year-old branch, inactive during the dormant period, or inactive (latent) for years as the branch ages; compare with *adventitious bud*, *axillary bud*, and *latent bud*

dormant pruning: Pruning during the dormant season that invigorates tree growth the following spring; compare with *summer pruning*

dormant season: The period from late fall, just before leaves fall off, through bud swell

dormant spray: Pesticide treatment applied during the dormant period

drip line: The imaginary vertical line extending downward from the outermost branch tips of a tree to the soil directly below

drip irrigation: A low-volume irrigation system in which drip emitters are connected to or embedded within drip tubing, with discharge rates of ½ to 4 gallons of water per hour

drupe: Botanical name for a one-seeded fruit derived entirely from an ovary with a stony endocarp containing the seed; stone fruit and almonds are drupes

dwarfing rootstock: A rootstock that imparts reduced vigor to a tree and produces a semidwarf tree; compare with *standard rootstock*

embryo: The rudimentary juvenile plant usually contained in the seed

endocarp: The hard, inner ovary wall of a ripened fruit; the stony part of the pit containing the seed of stone fruit and almonds

espalier system: A method of tree training in which the main branches of a tree are trained along a wall or trellis

ethylene: A plant hormone that regulates flowering and ripening; emitted as a gas from ripening fruit and damaged plant tissues

evapotranspiration (ET): The loss of water through evaporation from the soil and transpiration from the leaves; a technical term referring to the amount of water used by a tree

exocarp: The skin or the outermost layer of a fruit

fall budding: Bud grafting performed in late summer or early fall, in which a bud from a current-season shoot is inserted into a current-season shoot on another tree, and that bud is not forced to grow until the following spring; compare with *June budding*

"feel method" for soil: A technique for estimating the amount of sand, silt, and clay in a soil sample that involves squeezing a moist, well-mixed sample of the soil between the thumb and forefinger

fertilization: 1) The process by which a pollen grain germinates and unites with an ovule to form an embryo (see also *pollination*); 2) The application of nutrient fertilizers to the soil or a plant's leaves

fertilizer: A substance added to soil or sprayed onto foliage to provide plants with essential nutrients

fertilizer analysis: A statement, usually appearing on the label of a fertilizer container, of the percentages by weight of nitrogen, phosphoric acid, and potash contained in the material

field capacity: The amount of water a soil can hold against gravity

fine roots/feeder roots: The youngest roots with root hairs, usually less than $1/16$ inches (2 mm) in diameter; important in the absorption of water and minerals

flesh: The soft, pulpy portion of a fruit

flower bud: A bud containing a single flower (e.g., in stone fruit, almond) or a cluster of flowers (e.g., in pome fruit)

foliar fertilizer: A fertilizer mixed with water and sprayed onto the leaves of a plant

forcing: Causing a bud (flower or shoot) to grow at a time when it would normally not be growing; accomplished by cutting the branch off just above the bud (heading cut), girdling or notching above the bud, applying a growth-promoting hormone, or significantly modifying the ambient temperature around the plant

frass: The solid fecal material produced by insect larvae

freestone: A fruit in which the pit does not cling to the flesh of a ripened fruit; compare with *clingstone*

fruit bush: A fruit tree that is kept small through pruning to develop scaffold branches near the ground and through periodic removal, throughout the growing season, of shoots that grow above a certain height

fruit doubling: A phenomenon on stone fruit in which a single ovary produces two fruit, connected near the stem end, instead of one

fruit set: The persistence and development of the ovary (fruit) after flowering

fruit spurring: A phenomenon on stone fruit, particularly cherries, in which a small, spur-like, inedible protrusion forms near the stem end of the fruit, arising from a semi-aborted double

fruit thinning: The removal of a portion of the immature fruit on a tree in order to increase fruit size, reduce insect and disease problems, reduce limb breakage, and reduce alternate bearing

fruiting body: In fungi, a reproductive structure containing spores

fungicide: A pesticide used for control of fungi and the diseases that they cause

fungus: Multicellular organism lacking chlorophyll, such as a mold, mildew, rust, or smut; the fungal body normally consists of filamentous strands called mycelia and reproduces through dispersal of spores

gall: Localized swelling or outgrowth of plant tissue, often formed in response to the action of a pathogen or other pest

genus: The second division of classification, above the species and below the family; the first name of a binomial scientific plant name (e.g., *Prunus* in *Prunus persica*)

genetic dwarf: A scion that produces a small tree (usually due to short internode growth), even if grafted onto a standard rootstock.

girdle: To damage or remove a ring of bark tissue around a stem or root; such damage temporarily interrupts the downward transport of hormones and carbohydrates

grafting: The process of joining a part of one plant to another plant in such a way that the two will unite and continue growth as a single unit

grafting over: see *topworking*

grafting tape: Specialized tape, which might or might not be adhesive, used to hold a scion piece onto the stock

grafting wax: A specialized wax used to prevent a new graft union from drying out

graft union: The point on a trunk or branch where a scion (bud or stick) was grafted onto the stock (trunk or branch)

gummosis: A general disorder, particularly of stone fruit, characterized by the exudation and deposit of sap

hand thinning: Thinning of fruit by hand; compare with *pole thinning*

hanger: Fruiting branch on a peach or nectarine tree that hangs downward from the weight of fruit

hardpan: A subsurface layer of cemented soil that is formed by the chemical bonding of certain ions and soil particles

header, irrigation: A pipe or drip tube used along a landscape edge near the control valve to provide adequate water pressure and flow to individual drip lines; the header must be sized to accommodate the full flow of the entire area it serves

heading cut: A pruning cut that takes a shoot or branch back to a bud, a stub, or a lower lateral branch that is too small to assume apical dominance; this technique is used to produce lateral branches, to stiffen a branch, or to reduce the amount of fruit that a gardener will have to thin from a 1-year-old branch; compare with *thinning cut*

heartwood: The nonliving, darker-colored wood in the center of a trunk, branch, or root; compare with *sapwood*

heavy pruning: Removal of a relatively large number of branches when pruning; compare with *light pruning*

heel in: To temporarily cover the roots of a bare-root tree in preparation for planting

herbicide: A pesticide used to control weeds

honeydew: An excretion from insects such as aphids, mealybugs, and soft scales that consists of modified plant sap

horizon: see *soil horizon*

hormone: see *plant hormone*

horticultural oil: A highly refined petroleum or seed-derived oil that is manufactured specifically to control pests on plants

host: A plant or animal species that provides sustenance for another, often parasitic organism

hull: The dry, external coating common to most nut crops

humus: The decayed residues of organic matter derived from plants and animals

husk: see *hull*

infection: The entry of a pathogen into a host and the establishment of the pathogen as a parasite in the host

infestation: The presence of one or more insects or mites feeding on plant tissues

inoculum: A pathogen, or its parts (spores, mycelium, etc.), which can cause infection

inorganic: Containing no carbon; generally used to indicate materials (e.g., fertilizers, pesticides) that are of mineral or synthetic origin

insecticidal oil: see *horticultural oil*

insecticide: A pesticide that kills insects; many insecticides also function as miticides

instar: The period between molts in young insects

integrated pest management (IPM): A pest management strategy that focuses on long-term prevention or suppression of pest problems through a combination of techniques such as biological control, resistant varieties, alternative cultural practices, modification of pest habitat, or the use of pesticides (as a last resort)

internode: The portion of a stem between two nodes or buds

interveinal: On a leaf, referring to the space between the veins

ion: An atom or group of atoms that carries a negative (anion) or positive (cation) charge; ions can be formed by the breakup of molecules, as when certain molecules or compounds are dissolved in water

irrigation controller: The electronic timer used to schedule and control irrigations

June budding: Bud grafting performed in spring or early summer, in which a bud from a current season's shoot is inserted into the current season's shoot of another tree, and that bud is forced to grow during the same season. In California, June budding is usually practiced in the month of May. Compare with *fall budding*

kernel: The edible portion of a nut within the shell

larva: The worm-like, immature form of an insect that develops through the process of complete metamorphosis including egg, several larval stages, pupa, and adult; examples include the caterpillars of moths, the grubs of beetles, and the maggots of flies

latent bud: A bud, often concealed, that remains dormant for an indefinite period; under certain conditions, such as after severe pruning, it may grow; compare with *adventitious bud*, *axillary bud*, and *dormant bud*

lateral branch: A branch that arises from the side of a larger branch but is not a strong upright branch

lateral bud: A bud on the side of a shoot, spur, or branch

leaching: 1) Removing salts, ions, or other soluble substances from soil through application of abundant irrigation, combined with drainage; 2) The movement of soluble materials downward through the soil with percolating water

leader: A dominant, upright stem that usually becomes the main trunk in a tree trained to a central leader or modified central leader; some branches also have a single leader

leaf axil: The upper angle formed by the petiole (leaf stem) with the shoot, where one or more buds develop

lesion: A well-defined area of diseased tissue, such as a canker or fruit spot, usually sunken and having a different color than the surrounding tissue

light pruning: Removal of a relatively small number of branches when pruning; compare with *heavy pruning*

limb: A large branch of a tree

loam: A soil that contains defined portions of sand, silt, and clay and, as such, has an ideal soil structure for cultivation and plant growth

macronutrients: Plant-essential elements required in relatively large amounts by plants—nitrogen (N), phosphorous (P), potassium (K), magnesium (Mg), sulfur (S), and calcium (Ca); compare with micronutrients

maggot: The legless larva of certain fly species

marginal: Pertaining to the edges of a leaf

mass trapping: Trapping of male moths (e.g., codling moth) in large numbers in an attempt to reduce populations and reproduction and to control fruit damage

meristem: The undifferentiated plant tissue from which new cells and new plant tissues arise; the main meristems in a plant are the apical meristems, which form terminal shoot and root growth, and vascular cambium, which causes thickening of stems

mesocarp: The flesh of a fruit or hull of most nuts

metamorphosis: A change in form during development; some insect families undergo complete metamorphosis, in which the larval, worm-like stage creates a protective cocoon, where it transforms first into a pupa and then into a winged adult form that emerges from the cocoon; other insect families undergo incomplete metamorphosis, in which the young nymphs look like small adults

microclimate: A local variation from the general or regional climate resulting from slight differences in one or more factors, which may include elevation, direction of slope, sun exposure, soil type, density of vegetation, fog pattern, and other conditions

micronutrients: Plant-essential elements that are required by plants in very small amounts [e.g., boron (B), chlorine (Cl), copper (Cu), iron (Fe), manganese (Mn), molybdenum (Mb), and zinc (Zn)]; compare with *macronutrients*

microsprinkler: A low-volume sprinkler, usually connected to drip tubing, that discharges about 6 to 30 gallons of water per hour

mineral oil: see *horticultural oil*

miticide: A pesticide that controls spider mites

mixed bud: Notably in persimmon, a bud toward the end of a branch that will produce a shoot with leaves as well as flowers (and later fruit); the flowers were formed in the bud the year prior to opening

modified central-leader system: A training system in which the central leader is removed or no longer promoted after several lateral branches have been developed along the central leader; can be used for walnut, chestnut, pistachio, persimmon, and pomegranate trees

molt: In insects and other arthropods, the shedding of skin before entering another stage of growth

monoecious: Of a plant, bearing both male and female flowers separately on the same plant, as with walnuts, pecans, filberts, and chestnuts; compare with *dioecious*

mulch: A layer of organic or inorganic material, such as wood chips or landscape fabric, placed on the soil surface to prevent weed growth, conserve moisture, prevent erosion, and moderate soil temperature

mummy: A dried, shriveled fruit or nut that adheres to the tree

mycelium: The vegetative body of a fungus, consisting of a mass of slender filaments called hyphae

natural enemies: Naturally occurring beneficial organisms that attack harmful organisms, and as such can be used to enhance pest or disease control

necrosis: The death of plant tissue, usually at the edges or tip of a leaf

nematode: A microscopic, plant-parasitic worm with a long, cylindrical, unsegmented body

node: The point on a shoot or branch where a leaf is attached and one or more buds arise in the leaf axil

notching: Dragging a small file in a single stroke across a branch above a bud, cutting only through the bark; a technique used to stimulate the growth of the bud below

nurse limb: A limb allowed to remain temporarily on a tree that is being topworked or severely cut back, the function of which is to maintain sufficient leaf area for photosynthesis to provide carbohydrates for roots

nymph: The immature stage of insects, such as aphids, that hatch from eggs and gradually acquire adult form through a series of molts, without passing through a pupal stage; essentially, a smaller version of the full-sized adult

open center (vase) system: A method of training in which three to five primary scaffold branches are developed low in the tree and the center of the tree is kept open

organic: 1) Of, relating to, or derived from living organisms; 2) Of a material (e.g., a fertilizer), made up of molecules that contain carbon and hydrogen atoms; 3) Of crops, those that are grown with organically acceptable rather than synthetic fertilizers or pesticides

ovary: The swollen flower part at the base of the pistil containing the ovule or seed; as a fertilized ovary grows, it becomes the fruit

overcropping: Allowing too many fruit to remain on a tree, to the detriment of the tree's vigor

ovule: The part of the ovary that becomes fertilized and grows to become the seed

parasite: An organism that lives in or on the body of another living organism (its host); in this publication, the term mainly refers to tiny wasps and flies (technically known as parasitoids) that spend their immature stages on or within the body of a single host and also kill the host; compare with *predator*

parthenocarpic fruit: Fruit produced without fertilization and seed development (e.g., in California, the Bartlett pear)

pathogen: Any disease-producing organism

peduncle: The stem of an individual flower or fruit

perfect flower: A flower with both male and female parts

perianth: The outer envelope of the flower, including petals and sepals

pesticide: Any product sprayed onto a plant to control insects (insecticide), mites (miticide), fungal diseases (fungicide), weeds (herbicide), rodents (rodenticide), etc.; pesticides can be chemical-based (synthetic), such as malathion, or natural (organic), such as soaps and oils

petal: A flower part, usually conspicuously colored

petiole: The stalk connecting a leaf to a stem

pheromone: A chemical given off by an insect to attract other insects of the same species; used in trapping of insects or, in commercial orchards, disruption of insect mating

pheromone trap: A sticky trap with a pheromone lure that attracts male insects

phloem: Inner bark tissue that conducts carbohydrates, hormones, and other organic compounds from the site of production to tissues and organs throughout the tree; compare with *xylem*

photosynthesis: The production of carbohydrates from carbon dioxide and water in the presence of chlorophyll, using light energy

phytotoxic: Causing injury to plants; usually refers to sprays that burn the leaves

pinching: see *tipping*

pistil: The female portion of a flower, typically consisting of ovary, style, and stigma

pistillate: Of flowers, having one or more pistils but no stamens; compare with *staminate*

pit: see *endocarp*

pit burn: Softening and darkening of the fruit flesh around the pit, usually as a result of excessive heat; mainly affects apricots

plant hormone: A substance produced in minute amounts in one part of a plant and transported to another part, where it evokes a response

pole thinning: Removal of a portion of the immature fruit on a tree by striking them with a pole; compare with *hand thinning*

pollen (grain): Tiny, grain-like, male sex cells formed in the anther of a flower's stamen

pollen tube: The growth extension of the pollen grain in the style following the pollen grain's germination on the stigma

pollination: The transfer of pollen from the anther to the stigma of the same flower or another flower; see also *fertilization*

pollinizer: The producer of pollen; the variety used as the pollen source for cross-pollination

pollinator: The agent of pollen transfer, usually bees

pome: A fleshy fruit, the outer portion of which is formed by the floral parts that surround the ovary (e.g., apple, pear, quince, or pomegranate)

pomology: The branch of science dealing with fruit and nuts, and with fruit and nut culture; derives from the Latin *pomum*, meaning fruit

popcorn stage: The stage of flowering in stone fruit and pome fruit just before the petals fully open

potash: Potassium oxide (K_2O), containing 83 percent potassium

precocious: Of a tree, bearing fruit early in its life

precut: The first step in a two-step pruning process that prevents damage to the branch collar or tearing of the bark of the trunk or parent stem, when pruning off a large branch

predator: Any animal (including insects and mites) that kills other animals (prey) and feeds on them; compare with *parasite*

primary scaffold branch: A main structural limb arising from the trunk

propagate: To generate or to multiply, whether by sexual or asexual means

pupa: The nonfeeding, inactive stage between larva and adult in insects, such as moths and beetles, with complete metamorphosis

radiation frost: A frost that occurs on calm, clear nights as heat is lost from Earth's surface into the atmosphere, causing cold air to collect near the soil surface and move into low spots

receptacle: The enlarged upper end of the stalk that supports or surrounds the main floral parts; the edible portion of the fruit of some species consists of a fusion of receptacle tissue with the calyx (apples and pears) or the ovaries (figs)

reference evapotranspiration: The maximum evapotranspiration rate as determined from local weather station data; based on how hot, dry, windy, and sunny it is

resistant: Able to tolerate conditions (such as pesticide sprays, temperature extremes, soil moisture, or pest damage) that are harmful to other species or other strains of the same species; plants can be resistant to certain pests and diseases, and pests can be resistant to certain pesticides

resistant variety: A strain of a plant species that is able to resist or tolerate damage from an insect pest or disease that normally would be damaging to plants of that species

respiration: The process by which oxygen and carbohydrates are assimilated by an organism to produce energy, resulting in the release of carbon dioxide and water

rodenticide: A pesticide that kills rodents

root hair: The elongated extension of a single epidermal cell on a plant's root, which serves to absorb water and minerals; compare with *fine roots*

rootstock: The lower portion of most fruit and nut trees, onto which the desired fruiting variety (scion) is grafted; rootstocks are propagated either by seed or vegetatively, through cuttings

rosetting: A cluster of leaves with short internodes

russetting: Brownish, roughened areas on the skin of fruit that results from abnormal production of cork

tissue; may be caused by diseases, insects, certain pesticides, temperature fluctuations, or changes in humidity—or may be a natural characteristic of some varieties or strains

sand: 1) Soil particles that are finer than gravel but coarser than silt, ranging from 2.0 to 0.5 mm in diameter; 2) Any soil class that contains 85 percent or more sand and not more than 10 percent clay

sanitation: Orchard cleanliness practiced in order to prevent the spread of insect or disease pests; can include the removal and destruction of fruit infested with insects or infected with disease

sapwood: The outer wood of a stem or tree trunk, usually light in color and physiologically very active; compare with *heartwood*

scaffold branch: A main structural limb

scion: A branch, shoot, or bud removed from one plant and grafted onto another (the stock or rootstock); also, the aboveground portion of a tree that is asexually produced from a single parent by budding or grafting

secondary scaffold branch: A limb arising from a primary scaffold limb

self-fruitful: Of a fruit or nut tree, able to set fruit with pollen from the same tree; some varieties are only partially self-fruitful

self-unfruitful: Of a fruit or nut tree, unable to produce fruit without a nearby pollinizer tree

semidwarf: A specific tree size that is usually between 40 and 90 percent of the size of a standard large tree as a result of its having a dwarfing rootstock; usually an intermediate-sized tree that reaches about 10 to 15 feet (3.0 to 4.6 m) in height; see also *dwarfing rootstock*

sepal: One of the outermost flower structures; usually encloses the outer flower parts in the bud; part of the calyx

shield budding: see *T-budding*

shoot: A stem with leaves, referred to as "current season's growth" during the growing season; compare with *branch*

silt: 1) Small, mineral soil particles ranging from 0.05 to 0.002 millimeters in diameter; 2) Textural class of soils that contains 80 percent or more silt and less than 12 percent clay

slipping: see *bark slipping*

soaker hose: Low-volume irrigation hose made with numerous small pores along its entire length, through which water can seep out

soil: The upper, arable layer of earth in which plant roots can grow; the soil provides a medium for plant support and the storage and release of water and nutrients

soil aggregate: Clusters of soil particles that vary in shape, size, and degree of association, such as granules or clods, giving a soil its structure

soil amendment: A substance added to soil in order to alter one or more of its physical or chemical properties

soil horizon: A layer of soil with well-defined physical and chemical characteristics produced through the soil-formation processes

soil organic matter: The fraction of the soil consisting of decomposing plant and animal residues

soil pH: A measure of the acidity or alkalinity of the soil

soil profile: A vertical section of the soil through its horizontal layers

soil structure: The arrangement of soil particles (sand, silt, and clay) naturally arranged into soil aggregates; soil structure varies mainly on the basis of the amount of pores within and between the aggregates

soil texture: The relative proportion of the various soil separates (sand, silt, and clay) that make up the soil classes, as described by the textural triangle (fig. 1.2)

soil texture triangle: A triangular graph (fig. 1.2) that is used, after laboratory analysis has determined the percentages of sand, silt, and clay in a soil, to determine the name of the soil texture

sooty mold: Fungus that grows on honeydew

species: The scientific or taxonomic identity of a specific type of fruit or nut tree, written out as a binomial made up of the genus and species names (e.g., *Malus domestica* = domesticated apple; *Juglans regia* = English walnut)

spore: A reproductive body produced by certain fungi and other organisms and capable of growing into a new individual under proper conditions

spring drop: The natural dropping of immature fruit by a tree during the late spring, believed to be caused by embryo abortion or the plant's response to an extremely large crop load; also known as June drop

spur: A short branch that is specialized for flower and fruit production on most fruit species

spur-type tree: A fruit tree (primarily apple and cherry) that has shortened internodes and a greater number of spurs; a spur-type tree grows to about ½ to ⅔ the height of a standard nonspur-type tree

stamen: The male part of the flower that produces pollen, composed of anther and filament (stalk)

staminate: Pertaining to flowers that have stamens but no pistil; staminate flowers of several nut species are called catkins; compare with *pistillate*

standard rootstock: A rootstock that imparts relatively high vigor in a tree; usually originates from a seed (seedling); compare with *dwarfing rootstock*

stigma: The female portion of a flower, located at the tip of the style, that receives pollen

stock: The rootstock or tree onto which the scion (bud or stick) is grafted

stomate: An opening or pore in a leaf through which the plant exchanges gases and loses water vapor

stone fruit: Any of the *Prunus* species; fruit with a hard pit surrounding the seed (e.g., peach or cherry)

strain: Within a variety, a genetic mutation that results in the expression of differences in fruit color, skin smoothness, fruit size, precocity, and other characteristics

stratified soil: A soil consisting of one or more layers of different textures or structures, usually limiting the penetration of water, air, and roots

style: Part of the female portion of the flower; the style connects the ovary and stigma, and the pollen tube grows through it to reach the ovule

subsoil: The layer of soil immediately under the surface soil; the texture or structure of the subsoil often differs from that of the surface soil and the subsoil may contain restrictive or impermeable layers

sucker: A vigorous shoot arising from a tree's base or roots, below the soil line; compare with *water sprout*

summer pruning: Pruning done at any time from early spring through summer in order to train young trees, maintain tree height, and/or improve the availability of light for lower fruiting wood; reduces tree growth to some extent; compare with *dormant pruning*

syconium: A type of multiple fruit in which the flowers are borne on the inside of a balloon-like receptacle (e.g., figs)

T-budding: Bud grafting performed between spring and midsummer, in which a shield-shaped bud patch from a current-season shoot is inserted underneath a T-shaped cut in the bark of a shoot of another tree (the rootstock); also called *shield budding*

taproot: The primary root growing vertically downward from a seedling tree; lateral roots arise from the taproot and the taproot usually becomes insignificant

temperate zone: The part of the Earth between the Tropic of Cancer and the Arctic Circle in the Northern Hemisphere or between the Tropic of Capricorn and the Antarctic Circle in the Southern Hemisphere

terminal bud: A bud that develops at the tip of a shoot or branch when growth stops

thinning: Selective pruning to improve branch spacing, direct growth, eliminate weak and defective branches, and reduce the end weight of branches; for thinning of fruit, see *fruit thinning*

thinning cut: The complete removal of a branch, or cutting back of a branch to a lateral branch that is one-third or more the size of the main branch; used to encourage light penetration or allow access for fruit thinning, harvest, and other cultural operations; compare with *heading cut*

tilth: The physical condition of the soil in relation to its ability to cultivate and/or support plant growth

tipping: Removing the growing tip of a shoot to slow elongation growth or promote lateral branching

tissue: A group of organized plant cells that perform a specific function

tolerant: Able to withstand the effects of an adverse condition (e.g., temperature extremes, high salt concentrations, high humidity, or drought) without suffering serious injury or death

topping: Reducing a tree's size, often through the use of heading cuts to shorten limbs or branches to a predetermined length

topsoil: The fertile upper part of the soil

topworking: Severely cutting back a tree (except for a temporary nurse limb) or main branch and grafting one or more other species or varieties onto the cut limbs

training: Directing the growth of a young plant to a desired shape through pruning, bending, and/or tying

translocation: The movement of water, nutrients, and other dissolved substances through the conducting systems of a plant

transpiration: The loss of water vapor from plant surfaces, mainly through the stomates of leaves; transpiration keeps the plant cool and prevents the leaves from sunburning

tree trunk topiary: see *arborsculpture*

tree water use: The amount of water used by a tree, through both evaporation from the soil and transpiration through the leaves; expressed either in gallons (liters) or inches (centimeters) of water

trunk: The main supporting stem of a tree, connecting the roots to the branches

trunk banding: 1) The placement of a band of corrugated cardboard around a tree's trunk to trap mature larvae as they seek refuges for pupation; 2) Wrapping a tree's trunk with various wrapping materials to protect it from sunburn

variety: A taxonomic group of plants that have unique characteristics within a species; in common horticultural usage, *variety* is synonymous with *cultivar*

vascular: Pertaining to the conducting tissues of a plant (the xylem and phloem)

vascular cambium: An actively dividing layer of cells found between a plant's bark and its wood, which generates new sapwood (xylem) to the inside and new bark (phloem) to the outside; the cambium causes stems and roots to grow in diameter and it forms a tree's annual rings; in grafting, at least a portion of the scion's vascular cambium must match up with that of the stock; compare with *apical meristem*

vegetative bud: A bud that produces only a shoot with leaves

vegetative growth: The growth of shoots, roots, and leaves, as opposed to flowers and fruit

vigorous: Of a plant, healthy and producing fast-growing shoots

water sprout: A vigorous shoot arising from a tree's trunk or a branch, often from an adventitious bud; compare with *sucker*

waterlogged soil: A soil in which the water content is too high (most soil pores are filled with water) to allow normal plant growth, perhaps due to poor drainage

wet feet: Lack of oxygen in a tree's root zone; wet feet may lead to root and crown diseases such as Phytophthora rot

whip: A dormant branch, often used for grafting, that was a vigorous upright shoot the previous summer

whip grafting: A method of grafting in which a 1-year-old branch is attached to the branch of another tree using both a long, angled cut and a vertical cut on the scion and stock

wood: A hard, fibrous substance that makes up most of the stem and branches of a tree, consisting of living and inactive xylem tissues surrounded by the vascular cambium

wound: A mechanical injury that creates an opening in the tree's protective bark, damaging living tissue and allowing the entry of pathogens that can cause wood decay or diseases

xylem: The complex vascular tissue located at the inner edge of the vascular cambium, through which most of the water and nutrients in a tree are conducted in an upward direction; younger xylem tissues are termed sapwood and older, inactive xylem tissues are termed heartwood; compare with *phloem*

Index

Photographs are indicated by italicized page numbers. Tables are indicated by a letter "t" after the page number.